SELF-REGULATION, DBT AND COPING SKILLS
WORKBOOK
for Teens

3 Books in 1
Tools for Mastering Emotions, Improving
Self-Control and Building Emotional Regulation Skills
Using CBT, DBT and Mindfulness

EMILY CARTER

TABLE OF CONTENTS

SELF-REGULATION WORKBOOK FOR TEENS

Part 2: CBT Behavioral Techniques

DBT WORKBOOK FOR TEENS

Part 2: Distress Tolerance

Part 3: Emotional Regulation

Part 4: Interpersonal Effectiveness

COPING SKILLS WORKBOOK FOR TEENS

YOUR FREE GIFT

To really make the most out of your life, and to succeed in it, it's crucial to never stop learning. To further develop your knowledge of important life skills, I've got something for you... something you can really be excited about!

As a way of saying thank you for your purchase, I want to offer you some BONUSES completely FREE of charge:

To get instant access, just go to:

https://lifeskillbooks.com

Here's just a glimpse of what is included:

BONUS 1

Unleashing Your Potential:
*A Teenager's Guide to Developing a Growth Mindset
and Opening Your Path to Success*

Inside the book, you will discover...

✧ The differences between a fixed and growth mindset, how your mindset impacts your personal growth and success, and why a growth mindset is the one you should adopt.

✧ Practical strategies to cultivate a growth mindset, from daily habits to overcoming obstacles.

✧ How to utilize a growth mindset to supercharge your academic and career success.

✧ And much more!

BONUS 2

The Anxiety Handbook:
*Understand the Types, Triggers and Symptoms of Anxiety
to Effectively Cope With It*

Inside this comprehensive guide, you will discover...

✧ Insights into different types of anxiety disorders, so you can understand and identify specific triggers.

✧ Overview of the symptoms of each anxiety type so you can learn to recognize them better.

✧ Proven techniques to manage and reduce anxiety, helping you regain control over your life.

✧ And more!

BONUS 3

Printable Self-Regulation & Coping Skills Worksheets:
Practical Tools for Managing Stress, Anxiety and Emotions

Inside this comprehensive workbook, you will discover...

✧ **Step-by-Step Coping Strategies**: Gain access to structured exercises that help you identify, challenge, and reframe negative thoughts, leading to a more positive mindset.

✧ **Personalized Mood and Habit Tracking**: Utilize detailed trackers to monitor your mood and daily habits, allowing you to identify patterns and make informed changes for better mental health.

✧ **Self-Care and Mindfulness Practices**: Engage in a 30-day self-care challenge and explore various self-soothing techniques to promote relaxation and reduce stress.

✧ **Interactive and Easy-to-Use Worksheets**: Enjoy a user-friendly layout with guided prompts and questions designed to support your journey toward improved mental well-being and personal growth.

✧ **And more!** Everything is in easily printable form.

Now, go to the website below for instant access to these and several other amazing bonuses. Completely free of charge.

https://lifeskillbooks.com

EMILY CARTER

SELF-REGULATION
WORKBOOK
for Teens

Coping Skills and CBT Exercises
for Teens to Improve Self-Control,
Master Emotions, Resist Impulsive
Behavior, and Uplift Yourself
When Feeling Down

INTRODUCTION

"Rule your mind or it will rule you."– Horace

Sounds like a pretty powerful saying, doesn't it? But it seems like lately, all you ever do is let go. You let go of the things that surround you; you let go of every aspect of you; you let go of your thoughts and let them wander around. You notice they're reaching places you don't really want to go, but you go there anyway.

But you've been doing this for a while. In the beginning, it didn't seem like such a scary thing to indulge in. Now, it looks like you've completely changed yourself. When you look in the mirror, you are unrecognizable – and not just physically, but emotionally and mentally too. What happened? When did you decide to hand over control over yourself completely to your mind? In retrospect, was it a good idea?

Go back to the saying, "Rule your mind, or it will rule you." Think about this for a moment. Is it really a good idea to hand everything over to your mind? I mean, it is your most powerful tool, so why not give full control to it?

But you already know the answer to this question. Do you know how I know that? Because you already gave full permission to your mind, and you noticed that it led you astray. It started going to the deepest and darkest corners, ultimately dragging you along. And you were never able to escape from its claws. You succumbed to its power, and now you feel helpless. You are stuck in a vortex of unpredictable behavior and negative thoughts. Of course, you want to step away from that – who wouldn't?

I welcome you to the beginning of the most magnificent and transformative journey you will ever walk on. There is only one project in life you will constantly need to work on – and that is yourself. I am assuming you picked up this book because somewhere deep inside you, you noticed that a change should happen. You notice how incredible you can be and that something is holding you back. That something is yourself and yourself only.

My name is Emily, and I am so glad you allowed me to be a part of your transformative journey. Over the course of these pages, I will try to transfer some of my passion for helping others to you. I have taken most of the examples, exercises, and basically everything in this book from my personal experience. Noticing that there was a gap in my life skills later in life made me realize that I had missed out on plenty. So, while I managed to learn everything I wanted and came out on the other side swinging, I still wanted to help others.

That's how this book came to be. Without giving it much thought, I sat down and started writing. I implemented everything I did and created such a bullet-proof plan that you are hardly ever challenged to make a mistake. What helped me the most during my personal journey was the Cognitive Behavioral Therapy (CBT) approach – which is the book's main topic.

Together, we will explore the CBT method, how it can help you, and how it can be the pillar upon which you will build your self-regulation goals. Whenever you felt like you needed help understanding your thoughts, feelings, and behavior, there was no one to help you – until now! Together, we will cover so much – how to identify and challenge your negative thinking patterns, how to tap within yourself and create balanced and realistic thoughts, and how to focus on building yourself up through the power of positive self-talk.

On top of that, I even touch upon the most well-known CBT behavioral techniques. As you turn the pages, you will discover them, and the best thing about them is that you can try them on your own! How so? I have meticulously added exercises in almost every chapter. While these are small, their impact will be of great benefit to you. They will help you understand better what is written on these pages and help you to understand yourself better. This book is all about being assertive, being smart, developing the best coping skills, and understanding the core of who you are. It is about learning, constantly developing, and working on yourself. For without work, there is no change.

Last but not least, I dedicate the last chapter to you for all of you who are still doubting that this book has the power to change your life. It is all about preventing yourself from entering that swirl of negativity you're so desperately trying to get out of. It is the cherry on top of everything you will learn while reading this book!

I truly hope that what you find between these pages will empower you to develop and grow into the best and brightest version of yourself!

So don't wait any longer – turn the page and allow me to help you reinvent yourself!

PART

01

CBT COGNITIVE TECHNIQUES

INTRODUCTION TO COGNITIVE BEHAVIORAL THERAPY (CBT)

"You have the power over your mind – not outside events. Realize this, and you will find strength." – Marcus Aurelius

Well, you're here, at the beginning of your journey, desperately trying to control everything around you – and yourself. If you have picked this book up, it probably means that you truly are struggling to find your way in this chaotic world.

I am here to tell you that it is okay – it is okay to feel what you're feeling. It is okay to think what you're thinking, and it is even okay to be surprised by everything new that comes your way. Whether you are dealing with some kind of an emotional issue, or you have noticed a behavioral pattern within you that you'd like to change, or maybe even some self-limited thinking, this book can be the answer to everything you're searching for.

In this chapter, together, we are going to start our journey filled with wisdom, and deep insight, and open the magical doors of cognitive behavioral therapy. Here, you will have the ultimate chance to get to know yourself and become a better version of you. Allow me to introduce CBT through a few subchapters.

The Principles of Cognitive Behavioral Therapy

Let's start from the very beginning. Do you know what cognitive behavioral therapy means? CBT is a skill-based psychotherapy treatment that can help people get in control of their feelings, thoughts, and emotions, so they can navigate through life easily. This approach can help you spot the negative influences on your mind and soul and the patterns that result in more harm than good. As a concept, CBT is time-based, goal-orientated, and a very well-structured treatment. Whether you are dealing with depression, anxiety, or any other type of disorder, this approach can help you subsequently change your view of yourself and the world.

By reframing your thoughts, you can improve your overall quality of life. So far, things sound appealing, don't they? Let's explain further. To get into the CBT scheme, you need to know the basic principles. These are considered to be more of "levels" rather than principles. Here they are:

1. **Your core beliefs** – you start from the very beginning – who are you? How do you view yourself? What do you believe in? Do you know that the core beliefs represent the strongest childhood experiences? If you look within yourself, you can discover a whole world filled with beliefs about your future, yourself, your environment, and so on. These beliefs are deeply rooted, and it is your task to uncover them.

2. **Wrong assumptions** – these types of assumptions can be very discouraging about your entire well-being. You are young, filled with energy and hope – but what you're probably not aware of is that people generally hold on to the bad rather than the good. This type of action is classified as a cognitive distortion. Imagine having a lot of irrational thought patterns – seems like, over time, they might take over your perception of reality, right?

3. **A negative way of thinking** – which ultimately leads to overall negative perceptions of reality. After a while of succumbing to the negative patterns and thoughts, they will become your reality. You will start noticing that they have become a habit. The tricky part about them is that they are very short, and they can stir up negative emotions, making them difficult to recognize. However, don't mistake these automatic negative thoughts with the "common" negative thoughts. All of us are human beings after all, and it is only natural to have distorted thoughts* every once in a while. But, when this turns into a habit, that's when you should become alert.

*Distorted thoughts are also known as cognitive distortions. When this happens, you usually believe that one mistake defines your entire being and that the particular mistake makes you a failure. That leads to the belief that you should try to never make mistakes again. Finally, it all results in overgeneralization – thinking that you can never get something right and that things will never get better.

CBT can help you realize that you don't always have to believe in what you think. It will also help you realize that every time you are faced with a challenge, a difficult emotion, or a distortive thought, you have a choice. You can always be kinder, starting by sharing kindness with yourself, and then everything around you.

How CBT Can Benefit Teens

Let's put things into perspective here, shall we? I challenge you to a little thinking game – called action and reaction. You have probably noticed the ever-so-slight changes that happen when you have positive or negative thoughts. What changes did you notice happening (physically) whenever a distorted thought goes through your mind? In contrast, what kind of change do you notice happening when a positive thought overwhelms your mind?

Emotions affect behavior – that is something almost every teen is blissfully unaware of. Your thoughts, emotions, and behaviors are all linked. The first one is the thought – usually caused by a certain situation. The thought is your interpretation of an event. Then comes the emotion. The emotion is the second one in line, and it is triggered by what you thought of earlier on. In most cases, especially with teens, this emotion turns to the negative side. Finally, the behavior enters the scene. The negative emotions you feel influence your behavior, leading to you acting in a way you might regret later.

So, how can CBT help you prevent this negative vortex from further developing into a part of your personality?

CBT is known to have both short and long-term benefits. First, we tap into the short-term ones:

  ✧ This type of therapy shows fast results. Many psychologists and therapists use it to help young people overcome challenges in life. The average time it takes to get deeply familiarized with the CBT skillset is about 15 sessions. The alternative to that is reading carefully selected material with exercises that help you achieve your goal - this book!

  ✧ The activities you may encounter are engaging – meaning you won't have to sit and listen all the time, but rather take matters into your own hands. You get involved, and through a very interesting concept, you change yourself.

  ✧ You are held accountable for your own actions – but don't let this fool you, this is not a negative concept. You are empowered to take control of your life. You constantly apply the new principles you learn.

Together, we slowly approach the long-term benefits of CBT for teens. After a while of working on yourself, you will discover that this is an effective way to increase self-awareness and emotional intelligence – which is ultimately the path to living a healthy and happy life. As time passes, you will notice the following long-term benefits:

✧ You will start to respond to stress in a healthier way. Whenever you are faced with a negative thought or a challenging situation, you shift them toward a realistic or positive attitude and approach them the same way. Not letting anxiety, fears, and phobias take over is an excellent step forward.

✧ Being more compassionate – for some of you, this seems like a state you might never be able to achieve. Well, you couldn't be more wrong about that! You will find that compassion is within you, around you, and a constant part of your life.

✧ Reduce the unhealthy behavior you've indulged in for so long. The negative thoughts you had about yourself, the interactions with other people – all the situations in your life will become something you manage with skill and grace rather than tension and negativity.

With these goals in mind, it is time to look within – and learn the concept of self-regulation.

Setting Goals for Self-Regulation

Being a distressed teen can't be easy – you are constantly thinking that you live in a world where you don't belong anywhere, you allow these negative thoughts to overwhelm your mind, and it seems like you're failing each challenge you face. Keeping the weight of the world on your shoulders is not an easy job to do – and it is also not your job to do too. The sooner you realize that the easier it will be for you to move on and step into a more centered and powerful version of yourself.

What is self-regulation? It is a skill that many teens struggle to obtain at first – mostly because emotions play a big role in their lives. However, self-regulation means being able to manage your thoughts, your emotions, and your behavior, no matter what surrounds you. Having self-regulating skills can help you pull away from the emotional disturbance you've been experiencing, and it can help you navigate the tasks, challenges, and responsibilities more easily.

All of this seems good in theory, but when it comes to practice, how can you implement it?

Now, before you plunge head-first into making some severe changes in your life, you need to understand what kind of difference you want to achieve. Once you've determined who you are, where you are, and where you want to go, you can start utilizing the techniques and skills to complete your goal.

When you clearly know your starting point, setting up some goals can help you outline the path you want to walk to get there. The goals you will start developing will help you achieve the self-regulation act. For example, you can set a goal to react calmly in challenging situations – for instance, you can set a goal that your initial reaction to someone declining your invitation for a cup of coffee would be calm, centered, and respective of the others.

The process of setting goals will not be complete without your willpower, perseverance, and the understanding that those people who have managed to achieve this calm, is because they have made self-regulation their "default setting." Have you ever encountered someone so calm – be that a professor, your parent, or anyone else from your environment, that their calmness made you aware of yourself and your own behavior? Depending on one teen to the next, that kind of calm behavior can either lead to a reaction where you're embarrassed about your way of acting or it may make you want to act out. Needless to say, both situations are far from ideal.

Setting goals is a part of being proactive – and realizing that you want to possess that calmness that you have witnessed in others. You want to be powerful; you want to be in control, and you want to know how to handle yourself in every situation. With this in mind, how do you actually start setting goals? That's where I come into the picture to help.

If you could skip ahead in time where you've obtained all the knowledge and skills necessary to master self-regulation. How would your life be different from the one you're living today? Would anything change? If yes, what? Which are the first specific things that came into your mind – something that changed for the better? Are there some things you can do better than today?

Read through the first exercise below. See what you need to do and start working!

GOAL-SETTING

In this exercise, you are going to set some goals that will allow you to start working on fully stepping into your power.

First step – write down your ultimate goals. While you are writing down your goal, make it well-defined. For example, you can write down "Become more in charge of my emotions." Consider these goals to be the changes you want to see happening to you.

Second step – add a description of each goal, and what it would mean to you to achieve it. Think of this as breaking down your goals into more specific pieces. Use a detailed description to get rid of a certain issue you've been dealing with or use that detailed description to describe your future self. As an addition to the previous example, you can be more specific about it, by saying something like, "Becoming more in charge of my emotions will mean dedicating more time to myself, learning how to be more centered, calm, etc".

Third step – start thinking about the actions you need to take to achieve these goals. These actions need to help you remain consistent and on the right track – something that can show you you're getting closer to reaching your goals. To continue with the same example, you can do the following - "Meditate each day, keep a gratitude journal, channel your energy to positive things, indulge in mindfulness exercises, etc." By making your goal specific you are actually creating a bullet-proof action plan.

Ultimately, each of your goal-setting points should look similar to the example below:

The ultimate goal: Become more in charge of my emotions.

The specific goal: Becoming more in charge of my emotions will mean dedicating more time to myself, learning how to be more centered, calm, etc.

Actions I take to make it happen: Meditate each day, keep a gratitude journal, channel my energy to positive things, indulge in mindfulness exercises, etc.

Now, go ahead and write down at least five goals of yours following the steps above:

_____

_____

_____

_____

_____

_____

_____

_____

_____

_____

By doing this exercise you will be able to tap deep within yourself and uncover the core of your being – and that is the first step toward improvement.

Cognitive behavioral therapy can be fun – as long as there is someone like me who can guide you through the process, break everything down into smaller pieces, and show you that, as long as you keep putting one foot in front of the other (no matter the pace) you can get to your ultimate goal of being better.

What Did You Learn From This Chapter?

As a first chapter, it seemed pretty exciting, right? To sum up, here is what you learned from it:

- ✧ What is cognitive behavioral therapy.
- ✧ What are the three principles of CBT.
- ✧ Distorted thoughts and how they affect your quality of life.
- ✧ Thoughts, emotions, and behaviors are connected – they represent the cycle you are most likely trying to step out of.
- ✧ There are both long-term and short-term benefits of applying CBT in your life.
- ✧ Self-regulation – what it is and how you can use it to improve yourself.
- ✧ How to set goals for self-regulation.

Cognitive behavioral therapy is the key to creating a stronger and more powerful version of yourself. Now, over the course of this book, I will keep focusing on explaining every little detail that you might think we've overlooked. For example, take a look at what the next chapter is about! We discuss what I mentioned earlier – the process of thought, emotion, and behavior – how it affects your life and how it shapes you into an individual. Turn the page and discover all you need to know about it!

CHAPTER 02

UNDERSTANDING THOUGHTS, FEELINGS, AND BEHAVIORS

"The happiness of your life depends upon the quality of your thoughts." –
Marcus Aurelius

Before we continue any further, I need you to realize one thing – no person is immune to life's challenges. No matter what has happened to you and how you experienced certain situations, this is something that will always leave an impact and slightly alter you. After every event that occurs, be that a positive or a negative one, the remains of the experience are what your mind deems important, and that's what's left – long after the event has finished.

But, to truly tap within yourself and uncover "what you're made of," you need to know how to do that first. As a most likely inexperienced young mind, you don't really know where to begin. While in the first chapter, we recognized the essential dots that need connecting, in this chapter, I am helping you delve deep within yourself, dissecting the very core of who you are.

The concepts we will cover together here will help you better understand your thoughts, feelings, and behaviors as well as how to manage them.

Identifying Automatic Thoughts

From the moment you wake up to the moment you fall back asleep, thousands of thoughts pass through your mind. Some are wonderful and happy and fill you with joy, while others are negative and make you feel bad. There are many reasons why this happens, especially when it comes to automatic negative thoughts.

14

Overall, automatic thoughts are what we think of instantly – kind of as a first response to anything that happens around us or to us. These thoughts are mostly triggered by an outside source, but how you manage them in your mind and what you connect them with is what matters. Let's talk about automatic negative thoughts.

These automatic negative thoughts happen for various reasons. For example, teens who are dealing with anxiety or mood swings are more prone to experience negative thinking. Now, don't get me wrong – the automatic negative thoughts are sometimes what helps us survive, but if this is your constant state of mind, then you need to change something. It is a way of "anticipating threats" in a way.

These automatic thoughts connected to a negative thinking pattern are usually a result of your core beliefs and previous experiences. So, your automatic thoughts are actually what you truly believe about yourself, your future, and the world around you.

With that in mind, it is time to start identifying the automatic thoughts (especially the negative ones). Most of the time, people have a difficult time doing this at first, and if that happens to you, remember that it's okay. That is why CBT can help you open doors of your mind you haven't even been aware of until now.

There is a key to identifying automatic thoughts: looking for what first comes to mind when an emotion arises. For example, you open your Instagram account, and you see that your friends got together for a cup of coffee but didn't invite you. How would that make you feel? The immediate response you have is your automatic thought. It can be positive – where you think, "Oh good, it's such a nice day, I hope they're having a good time," or negative – "They didn't invite me, I'm not wanted, nobody likes me."

Both of these responses are extreme, and any profound feeling you get is entirely understandable. But what you do with them later on is what counts the most. Let's face it – whatever comes first to mind is what you truly believe in. However, while we are on the subject of identifying the automatic thoughts, we get a true insight into who we are. It is a type of awareness and understanding of your thinking.

Becoming aware is a process where you can distance yourself from the response you may have and reevaluate yourself. You start looking for the meaning in the situation and ask yourself whether there truly is the worst part about it and what it is. For example, in the example I mentioned earlier, if you have the ability to identify your automatic thought, specifically the negative one, the response would be "What's the worst part of it?" thus tapping into the core reason why you believe you are mistreated.

Recognizing the Connection Between Thoughts, Feelings, and Behaviors

What I personally love about CBT is that it has a unique way of uncovering the connection between thoughts, feelings, and behaviors. If you haven't noticed that by now, allow me to explain – the main goal of cognitive behavior therapy is to connect the three main dots – and allow you to see the full picture about yourself.

Has it ever happened to you that you act in a specific way and keep repeating that behavior? Have you ever concluded that you constantly have the same feelings and don't know why that's so? Shedding a light on your entire mindset is good – it gets you a step closer to change.

So, if the thoughts are ideas, feelings are the emotions you get after a thought occurs, and the behavior is the action you take as a result of the feeling, they seem pretty connected to each other, right? But how?

It is all about discovering whether you keep making the same decision over and over again. Take the example above – if you have noticed your friends going out for a cup of coffee without you often, and your first response was always a negative one, then ask yourself what you're feeling. Give it a moment to identify the emotion. If you are angry, ask yourself why. Slow down with the pace and pay attention to that little voice that's talking. What's it saying? Because this voice is you talking to yourself. Whenever you notice an automatic thought, here are a few questions that can help you make the connection – thoughts, feelings, behaviors.

What are your beliefs?

What is your self-talk?

What are your values?

What do you think about the people in that particular situation?

By recognizing this, you can determine whether the thoughts are realistic or not. Maybe, just maybe, the connection you make is only based on past experiences rather than an objective point of view. The connection between thought, feeling, and behavior will always happen, but it is your job to challenge your thoughts to be objective, and evidence-based rather than relying solely on the emotions, without knowing where that will take you (and let's face it – it's usually a negative direction).

Exploring the Cognitive Triad

The cognitive triad was developed as a framework by the founder of cognitive behavioral therapy, Aaron Beck. He wanted to create this as a scheme that would allow individuals to identify a negative pattern in their behavior easily.

This triad is (as you guessed it) a triangle with three specific points. It suggests that individuals who usually experience emotional distress are often negatively viewing themselves. However, they view the world and the future negatively, too. These are the kinds of negative feelings that arise from a place of anxiety, depression, and low self-esteem. As a teenager, it is your task to identify all of them so you can develop a more positive and realistic approach to life. To make things a little bit more visual for you, here is a figure of the cognitive triad.

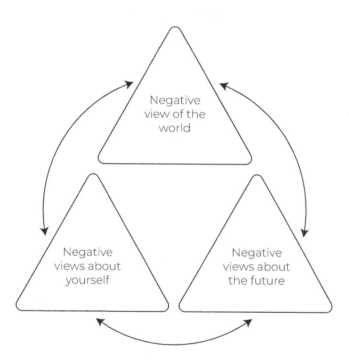

Here is a little example. The cognitive triad always starts with the self. In negative terms, it can represent a saying that you constantly use, such as "I'm never going to be good enough." The second corner of the triad is the views about the future. In negative terms, they can be something like "I will never achieve my goals." Finally, the last bit of the triad includes the views of the world. In negative terms, it goes something like this: "Everybody is out to get me."

While reading this, did one small part of your mind think these thoughts are most likely untrue? Did you find yourself in any of these statements? If that happens, you are on the right path to change. The cognitive triad is an excellent example of providing yourself with the mirror you need. It shows you how you have behaved so far, it shows you what your usual approach is, and it helps you become more aware of yourself and your negative thoughts.

With that in mind, I am giving you a moment to think. Notice your pattern of thoughts and actions, and then, identify the places where you believe you need improvement.

What Did You Learn From This Chapter?

Throughout this chapter, we went deep into the concept of self – once you made this realization that you are more than your thoughts and that there are a lot of dots to be connected, you learned the following:

- ✧ That there is a connection between thoughts, feelings, and behavior.
- ✧ How to identify the automatic negative thoughts.
- ✧ The automatic negative thoughts are normal, but only to a certain extent.
- ✧ Discovering that there is a connection between each part of who you are.
- ✧ Learning to challenge your thoughts whenever you notice it leads to a negative reaction.
- ✧ What is the cognitive triad, and why is it important.

Connecting the dots lifted a veil you didn't even know was there. You learned how everything within you works and that, just like the physical part (our bones are all connected), our thoughts are connected as well. I hope this made you feel a little bit better about yourself, yet you are still questioning how to solve this.

As I mentioned earlier in the chapter, negative thoughts happen all the time. Here, we recognized them and established a connection. In the next chapter, we will challenge them!

CHAPTER 03

CHALLENGING NEGATIVE THINKING PATTERNS

"Change your thoughts and you change your world." – Norman Vincent Peale

No truer words have ever been spoken. But, even with that in mind, people seem to neglect the fact that there is so much more to the act of challenging yourself. It takes great courage, persistence, and knowledge to stand up to probably the one person who gets in your way – yourself.

I have noticed, over my dedicated years of work, that teenagers are not aware of the power they hold within. As with every other adult on the planet, they also have the ability to control their thoughts. Yes, I am talking about you, too. I'm not sure whether the reason why they avoid doing this is because of fear they will fail or just plain laziness, but I am sure of one thing – you, and only you, are in charge of yourself. You are strong and capable, and after reading this chapter, you will know how to challenge negative thinking patterns.

Recognizing Cognitive Distortions

Here is the thing – you probably trust your mind too much. After all, is there anything else you can do? I mean, it is your brain at the end of the day, and it is probably right, right? Generally, it is a good idea to trust your brain. It is designed to look for your own good and find solutions or keep you away from dangers. But there are still situations where you might want to second-guess your trail of thought. Now, keep in mind here that your brain is not trying to trick you, lie to you, or deceive you; instead, it works this way as a result of developing some connections and beliefs that are not healthy.

This happens so often that it may surprise you. As I stated in the previous chapter, your thoughts, feelings, and behaviors are all connected, whether they make up for a good or a bad outcome. When the behavior is biased, that is how you define a cognitive distortion. The cognitive distortions are a representation of the irrational thoughts and beliefs that you constantly reinforce. As time passes, they become a part of who you are.

In the beginning, you may not notice them much – they are simply there – like a feature of your mind and your everyday thoughts. That is the reason why they are thought to be so damaging. You don't recognize them until they have completely taken over your mind. These cognitive distortions come in many forms, but they all result in inaccurate thinking patterns and false beliefs, and they have the potential to do some damage.

Now, it may be scary to admit this is happening to you – and that's perfectly normal. After all, you are human, and it is okay to fall under the spell of your own mind sometimes. We may all stumble occasionally, and some of us struggle with these challenges longer, and some don't. It is all about accepting the fact that some skills and abilities will only improve with practice, and they will help you become the best version of yourself. But let's not get ahead of ourselves.

To know exactly what to work on, you first need to understand how to recognize the cognitive distortions. Here is a list of the most frequent ones:

1. All or nothing – the polarized thinking also known as black-and-white thinking, where you go from one extreme to the next.

2. Overgeneralizing – the distortion where you generalize one example to an overall pattern.

3. Mental filter – focusing on the negative aspects of a situation, completely excluding the positive ones.

4. Removing the positive – a tricky situation where you acknowledge the positive aspects but completely reject them at the same time.

5. Jumping to conclusions – the inaccurate belief about what someone else is thinking, usually based on predictions without any evidence.

6. Catastrophizing – the act of stepping out of your perspective and exaggerating the meaning, likelihood, or importance of things.

7. Emotional reasoning – the realization that all of us have, at some point, experienced any one of these distortions.

8. Should statements – the statements you make about yourself and what you have to do.

9. Labeling – usually mislabeling – the tendency to go to extreme forms of overgeneralization, where you assign judgments of value to yourself and others.

10. Personalization – the situations where you take all things personally and blame yourself for no logical reason.

Recognizing cognitive distortions may seem a little scary at first, but it is all for the greater good. After helping these come to the surface, you can start implementing some techniques that can help you rewire your brain.

Techniques for Challenging and Reframing Negative Thoughts

Reframing negative thoughts may be challenging. Thankfully, there are many successful techniques that can help you achieve that. The techniques I'm about to share with you below can significantly change your overall outlook and mental well-being. Remember, the ultimate goal is not to completely remove the negative thoughts but to find a way to prevent them from overwhelming you.

1. Notice the negative thoughts. Pay attention to everything that pops into your mind. This could be anything – a situation, something about yourself, or something about other people.

2. Reflect and take a break. Identifying negative thoughts means taking a break and questioning whether your thoughts are accurate or not. This will not only lead you to the next step but will also prevent you from spiraling down into an unknown, dark maze of thoughts.

3. Think of the alternatives. When you realize that your thought is probably not true, consider other ways of viewing the situation. You can find both positive and neutral perspectives here and change your mind.

4. Replace the negative thought with a positive one. Once you pinpoint the initial negative thought, replace it with a positive or a neutral thought – and try to stick with it (mostly because it is probably the truth).

5. Stick with it. Any way that works for you is a good enough way to stick with a positive thought. You can be grateful for the work you've done that day, or you can write down your positive thoughts, or you can do any other thing that will help you feel empowered, and in control.

These techniques are amazing. When you start using them, in the beginning, it all may feel a little strange, but stick with it. After some time, you will see how helpful they are in the process of training yourself to be better.

The next exercises go into further detail on how to train your brain.

REFRAMING NEGATIVE THOUGHTS

Let's play this exercise called, "Fact or opinion?" During this exercise, you will have to sit and read through a list of statements that you will write yourself. These statements can be anything. Try to write at least ten of them, but if you have more, feel free to write all of them down. The statements should be your own thoughts - something that constantly pops into your mind. Below are some examples to get you started.

Now, put your thoughts on trial. Next to each of the sentences, write down whether you think they are facts or just your own opinion.

I am a failure. _____

I suck at everything. _____

I am ugly. _____

I rejected a friend when they asked for my help. _____

I'm a bad person. _____

I yelled at my parents. _____

Nobody cares about me. _____

Everything will turn into a disaster. _____

I am overweight. _____

I am selfish. _____

I am not loveable. _____

I failed an exam. _____

_____   _____

_____   _____

_____   _____

_____   _____

_____   _____

_____   _____

_____   _____

_____   _____

_____   _____

_____   _____

_____   _____

_____   _____

_____   _____

_____   _____

_____   _____

After doing so, look at the list again. Has anything changed? Your perception of yourself maybe? Did you notice that when you step back and objectively analyze your thoughts, most of them seem like they are just your opinions, and not reality?

You can take a breath now because, after this exercise, you know everything will be okay.

Creating Balanced and Realistic Thoughts

Balanced thinking seems almost impossible to achieve. You either go for the best or the worst-case scenario, right? Wrong.

Balance is something that should be incorporated into all aspects of your life. I can understand that, as a teenager, you might have difficulty achieving that, but the sooner you start training yourself, the better results you will have. Earlier, I mentioned that a part of the cognitive distortions includes seeing things in only black or white without giving the possibility for all the colors to shine through. Well, creating balanced and realistic thoughts is just that – the ability to see beyond the black and white and enjoy life while looking at things as neutrally and realistically as possible. It is like learning how to appreciate all the colors in the spectrum for the very first time.

It may sound a little less interesting at the moment, but there is a reason behind that, too – extreme thoughts can be exciting – and they usually are, especially for young people. But if you get used to this kind of behavior and abide by the rules of the extreme, it will eventually become a part of who you are.

By thinking in the middle, you get to see all the sides of a situation – sometimes there are two sides, sometimes more, but there is always more than one side. Cognitive behavioral therapy has ensured you can incorporate an approach that is not based on assumptions to get to the bottom of your thought trail.

Think about it – the balanced way of thinking is a calm way of thinking. It will provide you with benefits such as making better decisions, an overall state of calmness, less anxiety, being able to see the bigger picture, and so much more. Oh, and also, cognitive behavioral therapy is so much more than this, but you will have to stick around for the next chapters to find out!

CREATING BALANCED THOUGHTS

To create balanced thoughts is easier said than done – that's why this exercise focuses on just that. It is called "the friend exercise," and here is what you need to do. Whenever you are faced with a challenging situation, something that might make you want to spiral down into that negative pattern you've adopted, first, write down your opinion about the situation and then, think about one of your closest friends. If you share your opinions and thoughts with them, how would they reply? What would they say? Write that down too.

Here is how the exercise would go:

Your opinion	**Your friend's reply**
I am really unhappy.	Is there a particular reason for that?
Everyone's ignoring me.	Have you reached out and noticed they do?
I don't get any attention.	What's the reason you need the extra attention?
I'm a bad person.	No, you're not, you're just having a bad day.
I'm not beautiful.	You are extremely beautiful.
Nothing goes well in my life.	Not true - you have plenty of things to be thankful for.
I am stuck in a loop.	One you can always get out of by making small steps.

I will never get better.

X person doesn't like me anymore.

My terrible past will create a horrible future.

Yes, you will, and I am here for it.

Have you tried talking to them and clarifying?

Not true - you are the creator of your future.

_____

_____

_____

_____

_____

_____

_____

_____

_____

_____

_____

_____

_____

_____

_____

_____

_____

_____

_____

_____

Their feedback will most likely differ from what you think. You don't even have to really share this with your friend – as long as you do the exercise, you practice a different point of view. After a while, you will realize that it is not so difficult to have several points of view about a certain thing – and the freedom to choose the most positive one.

Your thoughts are not always part of reality. Sometimes, the picture they paint in your mind differs from the truth – a lot. That's why this chapter focused on that – showing you how wonderful of a thing it is to have a few different opinions and the best ways to train your brain to look for the more positive in every aspect of life.

What Did You Learn From This Chapter?

✧ All the power you need to change is something you already hold within.

✧ Cognitive distortions are all around you; it is time to learn how to recognize them.

✧ A list of the most common cognitive distortions.

✧ Negative thoughts can be managed with a few well-utilized techniques.

✧ The realization that thoughts can be balanced.

At the end of the day, the sole reason why you picked up this book and decided to make it your ultimate guide toward change is because you want to be better. Once you figure out how to challenge your thoughts, it is time to put that work to some good use, don't you think?

In the following chapter, I will discuss how you can make more out of your trail of thoughts and influence them in a way that will lead to some spectacularly positive thinking – ultimately challenging yourself to improve your entire life.

Shall we? After you.

CHAPTER 04

BUILDING POSITIVE SELF-TALK

"It isn't what you have, or who you are, or where you are, or what you are doing that makes you happy or unhappy. It is what you think about." –
Dale Carnegie

It takes some people a long time after they are born to realize that to be happy, you just need to be. It seems like the most essential things in life are also the most difficult ones to figure out. So, I understand where you are coming from. However difficult it may be to explain it, there is a certain lightness of being when you reach that state of positivity in your life. But to get there, you need to walk the path of building and realization.

In this chapter, we will commence our journey through the magnificence of indulging in positive self-talk together. Bear with me; it's not impossible to achieve, and if you think it is, allow me to change your mind.

Importance of Positive Self-Talk

There is something called "inner voice." This is a voice that only you can hear, and it is a way of talking to yourself. In many cases, you might not even be aware that you're doing it, but you still do it. This is a voice that combines your beliefs and thoughts and creates a sort of "internal monologue" that you "hear" during the day. As a concept, self-talk is a powerful thing because it has a big impact on who you are and how you feel. By underlining this, you realize its importance – ultimately knowing that it will either be a positive thing, something that will lift you, be supportive and beneficial, or turn into a negative thing and completely undermine your confidence.

Self-talk has a great impact on your mental health – the way you see yourself, and the way you view the world (the triad that I mentioned before). But the thing is, this can quickly turn for the worse if you don't know how to focus on the positive.

Negative self-talk can have a significant impact on your health overall – from chronic pain to affecting your confidence and creating a distorted body image; negative self-talk has many consequences. That is why we are solely focusing on the positive. The importance of positive self-talk comes from the fact that the benefits are – you guessed it, plenty. Here is only a handful of them:

- ✦ Improved self-esteem and overall wellbeing.
- ✦ Improved body image and less stress.
- ✦ Motivates you enough to overcome any challenges or obstacles.
- ✦ Reduces the symptoms of personality disorders, anxiety, and depression.
- ✦ Helps you feel in control of your life.
- ✦ Calms you down.
- ✦ Diminishes chronic pain.

Now, it sounds like something you want to try, right? We are headed toward the next exercise; take a look below.

PRACTICING POSITIVE SELF-TALK

Most people (especially the young ones) believe that practicing positive self-talk only limits your exposure to negativity. That is, to a certain extent, correct, but there is a lot more you can do in this situation. In this exercise, I am going to accentuate the power of self-care. I know self-care is something you see everywhere around you these days, especially because it is the talk of the town on social media. But have you ever stopped and wondered why that is so? Social media has a certain power; however, it is still not that great for many people. Nevertheless, the reach you can have with it makes up for a positive stamp you can leave in someone else's life. If you can do that, change the life of even one person for the better, why not try?

Now, let's see the exercise. I mentioned we're going to focus on self-care. The first thing you need to do is give yourself a small amount of time. Yes, start as small as possible – 5 minutes or 10 minutes of your day are enough to create a habit. Within this timeframe, do something for yourself. This is not a selfish act but rather a much-needed one. Engage in something that will lift your spirits and rejuvenate your entire well-being.

I can understand how the options may be plenty in this case, and viewing all of them may make you feel stuck rather than determined, so let's start from the beginning. Here are a few things you can do throughout your day:

- ✧ A little bit of physical activity.
- ✧ Focusing on a hobby of yours (painting, writing, cooking, etc.).
- ✧ Reading a book.
- ✧ Preparing a meal for yourself.
- ✧ Indulging in mindfulness meditation.

After doing any activity, the self-care bit comes later on. Take out a pen and write down three things that you liked about it below. These can be three good things you felt or thought, or whether the activity you engaged in put a smile on your face, made you forget about the time, etc.

The Activity _____

The Three Things I liked About It:

01. _____

02. _____

03. _____

The Activity _____

The Three Things I liked About It:

01. _____

02. _____

03. _____

The Activity _____

The Three Things I liked About It:

01. _____

02. _____

03. _____

The Activity _____

The Three Things I liked About It:

01. _____

02. _____

03. _____

The Activity _____

The Three Things I liked About It:

01. _____

02. _____

03. _____

The Activity _____

The Three Things I liked About It:

01. _____

02. _____

03. _____

The Activity _____

The Three Things I liked About It:

01. _____

02. _____

03. _____

The Activity _____

The Three Things I liked About It:

01. _____

02. _____

03. _____

The Activity _____

The Three Things I liked About It:

01. _____

02. _____

03. _____

The Activity _____

The Three Things I liked About It:

01. _____

02. _____

03. _____

The beauty of this exercise will come only if you are persistent. You won't notice an immediate difference, but after a while of indulging in this exercise, you will start noticing that positive self-talk is your "default setting." It is something your mind immediately jumps to, and it will help you train your brain to think in a healthier and stronger direction.

Identifying and Challenging Negative Self-Talk

I only scraped the surface on the topic of negative self-talk earlier. As a young mind, before we begin, what you need to understand is that negative self-talk is a part of being human. Just like positive self-talk can boost your productivity, improve your mood, and make you happier, negative self-talk has its consequences, too. It can diminish your self-confidence, it can lead to self-blame, and tear down your emotional well-being.

It is your responsibility to find the difference between having negative self-talk every once in a while, and constantly indulging in this pattern. Spotting the difference between the two is the first step toward making a change. It means you have identified the negative self-talk – and the second step is to dismiss it.

CHALLENGE THE NEGATIVE SELF-TALK

That leads us to this next exercise. I know that you want to make a change for the better. I know that you want to challenge yourself, your views, and the core of your beliefs. And in this exercise, that is exactly what you're going to do.

All of us are constantly met with negative thoughts during the day. These thoughts are either about yourself or your environment. But most of these usually pass after a minute or two. This is the correct way to deal with negative self-talk – acknowledge it, let it pass, and do not dwell on it. Once you notice that you are doing the exact opposite, turn to this exercise for help.

Here is what you're going to do.

Every time you notice that your mind is setting on a negative thought, and you find your inner voice saying, "You're not good enough," challenge that negative self-talk with positive self-talk. Keep doing this because persistence is a must for all change to occur.

There are many good things you can tell yourself, contrary to the negative belief that keeps popping up in your mind. Here are just a handful of statements for you to repeat each time you are faced with a negative self-talk pattern:

I will do my best.

I am good at this, and I can do it.

I will be well, and I will do well.

I am good enough.

I am happy, and everything is going well for me.

Below, you can find rows where you can write down your negative self-talk, and the positive self-talk you used to challenge it. Writing them down will significantly boost your progress.

Negative Self-Talk

Positive Self-Talk

_____

_____

_____

_____

_____

_____

_____

_____

_____

_____

_____

_____

_____

_____

_____

_____

_____

_____

_____

_____

_____

_____

_____

_____

_____

_____

_____

_____

_____

_____

_____

_____

Developing Affirmations and Positive Coping Statements

You have probably already noticed this – we are trying to create a positive mindset and cultivate mindfulness and happiness overall. Yes, there will be such things as bad days, but it is your responsibility to prevent them from ruling your life. Affirmations and positive coping statements are more than just a way to help you cope with a stressful situation or improve your mood. It can boost your self-esteem, it can help you look on the bright side of life, and most importantly, decrease negative thinking.

By using these affirmations and statements every day, you can work toward achieving the goals you have set for yourself and work on your overall personal development and growth. All of them are helpful every time you feel insecure or worried or when you need a little push. I know it sounds strange to talk about affirmations at the moment; it may even sound silly to some of you, but that is exactly why you should try them.

Many people undermine the power of affirmations because they seem "too easy." Well, if they are too easy, why not give them a try? Positive thinking has always been effective and beneficial for improving alertness and mindset and effectively coping with every curveball life throws at you.

The idea is – when you constantly repeat these to yourself – whether they are about your body, your mind, your relationship with yourself, your environment, etc, they will become engraved in your mind. After a while, you will truly start believing them and, as a result of that, think more positively.

Not quite sure how to make that happen? I prepared two exercises below so you can differentiate between affirmations and positive coping statements so that you can learn how to implement both of them in your life.

EXERCISE 6

AFFIRMATIONS

This exercise comes in the form of journaling. While you may not be up to the idea at first, hear me out. When you put pen to paper and write down your affirmations, it will seem like they have taken a certain shape, like they make sense, that there is truth to them. That is why this exercise is an extremely powerful one.

Your first step is to take out a pen (and a notebook if you prefer writing to it rather than to the lines below). Then, you are going to choose some affirmations that "make sense" to you or some affirmations you'd like to embed in your mind. You can find some affirmations either in books or online, or you can come up with them yourself. To get you started, here are a few:

I am strong, and I always attract positivity.

———o–◇–o———

I can heal, and I can only attract healthy things into my life.

———o–◇–o———

I am grateful for everything in my life right now.

———o–◇–o———

I am kind, and I am enough.

———o–◇–o———

I see the beauty that lies within me.

———o–◇–o———

I create my own future.

———o–◇–o———

Only good things will happen to me.

———o–◇–o———

_____

_____

_____

_____

_____

_____

_____

_____

_____

_____

_____

_____

_____

_____

_____

_____

_____

_____

_____

_____

_____

_____

_____

_____

_____

_____

_____

_____

Keep writing these affirmations – either one in a day or all of them (depending on how you feel). After some time, you will notice that your self-talk will consist of plenty of affirmations that instantly put a smile on your face.

POSITIVE COPING STATEMENTS

This next exercise is all about focusing on positive coping statements. These are the ones that you can use every time you feel sad or down, something that will help you cope with difficult times. The difference between the previous exercise and this one is in the approach – because basically, you do the same thing – repeat positive things to yourself. But, in the previous exercise, the idea is that you approach affirmations with a neutral mindset. Here, with positive coping statements, you approach the exercise because you have noticed a negative pattern of thoughts in your mind (usually caused by an external event).

So, here is what you need to do. We have all been there – a stressful situation creating a chain of negative self-talk, and whether it is a mild or a severe reaction, it still needs to come to an end. That is when the coping mechanisms come into play. When you are faced with this kind of situation, you can remember and repeat one (or a few) of the following positive coping statements:

This is not final; it will pass.

—o–◇–o—

Stop, give yourself a minute, breathe – because you can do this.

—o–◇–o—

Even if I am feeling angry, I can still deal with this.

—o–◇–o—

Feeling bad is a normal reaction, but I will allow it to wash over me and pass.

———◦–◇–◦———

It is something I have done before, and I will do it again.

———◦–◇–◦———

It will not last forever.

———◦–◇–◦———

I don't need to rush. I can take things slowly.

———◦–◇–◦———

My mind is not always my friend.

———◦–◇–◦———

I feel this way because of past experiences, but I should feel okay now.

———◦–◇–◦———

I am stronger than I think.

———◦–◇–◦———

I learn from experiences, and I see every challenge as an opportunity.

———◦–◇–◦———

Things will be easier next time.

Repeating these statements to yourself each time you are faced with a challenging situation can help you easily move forward and cope with whatever comes your way in a healthier way.

What Did You Learn From This Chapter?

Having to learn a lot about positive self-talk means tapping into the core of who you are and realizing that you have a good side – something light and happy to accentuate. With that in mind, here is an overview of what you learned in this chapter:

- ✦ What is self-talk, and what is the importance of positive self-talk.
- ✦ What is negative self-talk, how to identify it, and what it can do to you long-term.
- ✦ What are affirmations and positive coping statements, and why they are important.

Positive self-talk is the pillar to creating a better and stronger you. This chapter was filled with enlightenment and richness, and it may have even put a smile on your face. However, deep down, you still feel like you can't do this... like you need something more to make this happen and change your life for the better. It seems like the catalyst you're looking for to start this process is still lost.

That's what the next chapter is all about – the catalyst you are looking for is called acceptance, and it is one you need to work on before you continue your journey through the magnificence that cognitive behavioral therapy brings. You have me by your side every step of the way, so don't even try to get discouraged! Instead, turn the page, and let's start working on that together!

CHAPTER  05

MINDFULNESS AND ACCEPTANCE

> *"The curious paradox is that when I accept myself just as I am, then I can change."* – Carl Rogers

When it comes to mindfulness, the beginning is always the most challenging part of it. Somehow, it seems like being present at the moment is both the easiest and the most challenging thing to do. To tell you the truth, almost everything in this book will initially feel that way. But that should not stop you from going after what you want to achieve.

Since this is the chapter where you might have the most questions, I decided to focus it on practice rather than theory – because sometimes, the best way to learn is through exercise. It is time to focus on mindfulness and acceptance.

Introduction to Mindfulness

Allow me to start answering all of your questions in this first bit. Let's start with the easiest thing – do you know what mindfulness is?

Mindfulness is the ability of an individual to be fully present and aware of the moment, where they are going, what they are doing, and refrain from being overly reactive or overwhelmed by the surroundings. Usually, mindfulness is something that everyone possesses naturally, but some people have a better grip on it than others. Do you know why that is so? It's because these people practice it daily. Now comes another question – how do you practice mindfulness daily? What can it do to make your life better?

When you bring mindfulness into your life, you start feeling it through all your senses. Mindfulness is a state of mind through which you can wake up the emotional, mental, and physical processes within you. It is available to you at all given moments; all you need to do is pause, breathe, and allow it to settle in.

There are many mindfulness techniques you can try. By utilizing the techniques below, you can improve your mental clarity and stray as far away from anxiety and negative thought patterns as possible. Some of them may seem a little strange to do at first but trust me on this one – you will find that all of them are successful in the end. But before we go directly into the techniques, let's talk a little bit about acceptance and non-judgemental awareness.

Cultivating Acceptance and Non-Judgemental Awareness

Cultivating acceptance and non-judgemental awareness is not particularly a different subject in itself but rather another aspect of mindfulness. Now, let's take things a step back. We live in a world where jumping to conclusions and judgments happens all around us. The practice of non-judgemental awareness and acceptance seems to fade away slowly. Instead of being the norm, it has become the exception to the rule. That is why it is of utmost importance to explore the significance of being calmer and centered and approach everything in life with less judgment and a more accepting mindset.

To understand non-judgment, you first need to understand the nature of judgment. This is a cognitive process through which you classify, estimate, and then form opinions about yourself, other people, ideas, situations, etc. The way you do that is through your core beliefs and morals. Judgment is a natural part of being a human, but it can easily turn into an issue when you are using too much of it.

Contrary to that, we have non-judgment. Cultivating this can help you view situations and events from multiple perspectives. When you remove judgment from the equation, you provide space for empathy and a deeper understanding. This process promotes effective communication and a healthier way of dealing with everything that happens around you.

But the best part about it by far is enhancing growth and moving in a positive direction. Approaching yourself and the people around you with acceptance and non-judgment means creating a new terrain to walk on – a terrain of growth. This means allowing yourself to move past your vulnerabilities, insecurities, and mistakes and then fostering a mindset that focuses on development and freedom of expression.

All of this may sound like the best thing you can do, but none of it would be possible without using these practical strategies and the exercises below. Let's go over the strategies together before moving on to the exercises.

1. Try to cultivate mindfulness. As I mentioned at the beginning of this chapter, mindfulness is the practice of being completely present in the moment – but you need to achieve that without any judgment. This way, you can reflect and choose a better and calmer response.

2. Challenge your opinion every time – especially if it is a hypothetical one. Judgment is often based on limited information, so every time you find yourself in this situation, challenge your thoughts. Seek out a different perspective, have an open dialogue with different people, and be open to changing your mind and broadening your horizons.

3. Empathy is key. This shows the ability to understand the people around you without immediately turning to judgment. You put yourself in their shoes, and you show genuine compassion.

4. You avoid using stereotypes – about yourself and the people around you. Stereotypes are conceptions (or misconceptions) about a certain individual based on a larger group of people. Stereotypes can limit your understanding and lead to judgment rather than acceptance.

5. Reflecting upon your past self is like challenging your beliefs, impulses, and judgments. See how your behavior history has developed and what you want to change about it. By examining your own impulses, you can work toward creating a less judgmental approach.

6. Indulge in non-comparison. You don't need comparison in your life. Not because it frequently leads to judgments but because it is an arbitrary way of examining yourself. Instead of comparing yourself to others, why not concentrate on your growth? You will get a lot more out of it by doing so.

FIVE SENSES MINDFULNESS

We are starting with the exercises, with the five senses of mindfulness being the first one. As an exercise, it has proven to be incredibly helpful, especially in cases when you want to completely feel like you are present at the moment. This is a practical way to practice mindfulness fast in any situation. All you need to do is follow the instructions. Here they are:

5   Notice five things you can see. Take a good look at your surroundings and bring to your attention five things that you can see. Out of everything that you see, choose something that you normally wouldn't pick.

4   Notice four things you can feel. No matter what your surroundings look like, try to find four things you can feel. This can be anything from the texture of your clothes to the surface of a chair, a table, a sofa, or anything you can find.

3   Notice three things you can hear. Take a moment to shut down all your other senses and notice three things you can hear. These, too, can be anything that surrounds you – from the traffic outside on the street to the birds chirping, to a clock ticking, to someone talking loudly in the background, to the sound of the rain.

2   Notice two things you can smell. This is an important one, as it needs a lot of concentration. No matter what is inside the room, you need to isolate the other senses and focus on the things you can smell – be these pleasant or unpleasant smells. Maybe it's a nice perfume, maybe it's the food from the next room, maybe it's the smell of the rain.

1   Notice one thing you can taste. This is when you can go for the food you've smelled a few minutes earlier. If that is not the case, focus on anything else you can taste – a beverage, a taste in your mouth, a piece of gum – anything.

This is a very easy way to achieve a state of mindfulness. You don't need a lot of time to do it, but you can still be aware of yourself and the current moment.

BODY SCAN MEDITATION

This exercise is like doing an x-ray on your entire body. Get started and sit in a comfortable position. Focus on that, and then shift your focus to your breath. Notice the sensation you have each time your lungs fill with air and each time you exhale. Then, choose one part of the body from which you can start. It can be either the top of your head or the bottom of your body (left or right foot). Be careful, pay attention, and focus on that particular spot. Spend about 20 seconds to a minute focusing on that particular spot before you move on to the next part of your body. Acknowledge the sensation that is happening when you focus on each individual part, and don't forget to breathe in and out through each step in the process. The deep breaths can help you relax and release the tension in your mind and body.

During this exercise, it is okay for your mind to drift a little. Notice that, and when it happens, slowly return your thoughts and focus to the present moment. Remember, if this happens, you haven't failed or anything because you can always bring the thoughts back to your body and move on. If it helps, visualize how you get the thoughts back before continuing.

This awareness exercise can help you maintain your focus on a certain thing, thus helping you be more present in the moment.

BOX BREATHING

This is a very quick and easy way to get yourself into a calmer state. As an exercise, it is something that anyone can practice, especially in cases when you want to bring back your thoughts and keep your concentration. Here are the steps you need to take:

1. First, breathe in through your nose, and count slowly to four while you do. Focus on the present moment and feel how the air fills up your lungs.

2. Then, hold your breath for about 4 seconds. Avoid inhaling or exhaling during this time.

3. Then, slowly exhale through your mouth for a duration of 4 seconds.

4. Wait 4 seconds until you inhale again.

5. Repeat this process 4 times - that's enough to help you to center yourself.

MINDFUL WALKING

There is a certain awareness that happens each time you walk. This awareness can help you observe your impulses, emotions, and thoughts, as well as sensations that run through the body. As an exercise, mindful walking can help you develop positive behavioral change and develop coping skills. Here are the three steps of this exercise:

✧ Prepare yourself to go out for a walk. Before you start walking, try to stand still for a few moments and focus on your breathing. Notice how every part of your body feels.

✧ When you begin your walk, try to notice every movement of each part of your body. Notice how everything feels - your arms, your legs, your head, your skin, every part of you. Notice how you carry your body around.

✧ Once you've done that, start paying attention to everything around you. If you feel like your thoughts are getting distracted, slowly bring them back to the present moment. In the end, how did the walk make you feel?

ACCEPTANCE PRACTICE

The highs and lows in life are unavoidable things, and the sooner you understand that, the better grasp you will have of yourself. I can understand that, as a young person, you don't quite know how to handle situations where you just have to accept yourself, a situation, or a moment. That is why I am proposing this acceptance practice exercise. You'll find this to be especially useful in situations where you're not particularly satisfied with an outcome. Here is what you need to do:

1. Describe the situation you're in right now to yourself. Now answer this - what about that situation makes you unhappy or dissatisfied?

2. Has this situation happened before? If so, how did you react to each time it happened? Did you look for help, did you look for acceptance, or were you angry and hopeless?

3. If you could do something to change the situation, what would that be? What do you think is holding you back to make this change? Or, if you have no other choice but to accept the situation as it is, what do you think is holding you back from surrendering to it?

4. The final question you're going to ask yourself is connected to the future. To remain present, how will you approach this situation from now on?

Take this as an example - you're feeling helpless, like you are in a vortex, and you want to get out of it immediately. Start answering the questions above (honestly and truthfully) and see where they lead you. To help you start thinking in the right direction, here are a few starting points. When you have found yourself in one of the situations below, this is the best exercise to use.

Situation: A grade on a test

Reaction: _____

Can you change the situation? How?: _____

_____

_____

_____

How will you approach this the next time?: _____

_____

_____

_____

Situation: Your favorite sports team lost a game

Reaction: _____

Can you change the situation? How?: _____

_____

_____

_____

How will you approach this the next time?: _____

_____

_____

_____

Situation: A social event where you didn't "deliver" as good as you hoped you would

Reaction: _____

Can you change the situation? How?: _____

_____

_____

_____

How will you approach this the next time?: _____

_____

_____

_____

Situation: A falling out with a friend or at home, maybe with your parents or guardians

Reaction: _____

Can you change the situation? How?: _____

_____

_____

_____

How will you approach this the next time?: _____

_____

_____

_____

Situation: A creative project gone wrong

Reaction: _____

Can you change the situation? How?: _____

_____

_____

_____

How will you approach this the next time?: _____

_____

_____

_____

Situation: _____

Reaction: _____

Can you change the situation? How?: _____

_____

_____

_____

How will you approach this the next time?: _____

_____

_____

_____

Situation: _____

Reaction: _____

Can you change the situation? How?: _____

_____

_____

_____

How will you approach this the next time?: _____

_____

_____

_____

Situation: _____

Reaction: _____

Can you change the situation? How?: _____

_____

_____

_____

How will you approach this the next time?: _____

_____

_____

_____

Situation: _____

Reaction: _____

Can you change the situation? How?: _____

_____

_____

_____

How will you approach this the next time?: _____

_____

_____

_____

Situation: _____

Reaction: _____

Can you change the situation? How?: _____

_____

_____

_____

How will you approach this the next time?: _____

_____

_____

_____

GRATITUDE PRACTICE

Feeling bad is pointless – someone had to say it. I figured, why not me? This last exercise for this chapter focuses on how to do more than accept a situation in your life but rather celebrate it. I know it seems a bit strange to do that, especially if you find yourself in a situation you don't like, but this exercise can help you realize one thing. That even if you are in an unwanted spot at the moment, in the grand scheme of things, you are right where you're supposed to be – and you should be thankful for that.

Let's simplify it – here's what you need to do for this exercise:

✧ Describe yourself as you are at the moment or a situation you're in at the moment that you don't really like.

✧ Think about this for a while – even if you are not in a particularly good situation, how can you benefit from it? There has to be something good about it, but you never gave it much thought. So, in this case, give it a moment and give it the thought.

✧ Before you wrap up this exercise, find one (or a few) different perspectives from the one you have. Remember – feeling pointless about something is normal, but to a certain extent. As a young person, you have the power to appreciate the opportunities and benefits of every thought, feeling, and situation and use them to feel better and act on something.

✧ Finally, what can you do to express gratitude for the situation you're in at the moment? (there has to be something)

Let me give you an example of this. You wake up in the morning, and everything seems okay. You're making yourself a good breakfast and you want to savor it before your day begins. But you burn the breakfast and make a mess out of the kitchen. You start thinking that everything always goes wrong, that you're good for nothing, and that everything is a mess. Once you feel the onset of these thoughts coming, just pause for a while and allow them to pass through you. Among the chaos, find at least one thing you're grateful for - the sun, the cold, the fact that you're standing in the kitchen, still learning how to cook, apparently, the fact that you're alive and well, and these things happen to anyone - it can be anything. Give power to that rather than giving power to the momentary negative feelings you have.

Situation: _____

How can I benefit from it?:

1. _____

2. _____

3. _____

Things I am grateful for:

1. _____

2. _____

3. _____

Situation: _____

How can I benefit from it?:

1. _____

2. _____

3. _____

Things I am grateful for:

1. _____

2. _____

3. _____

Situation: _____

How can I benefit from it?:

1. _____

2. _____

3. _____

Things I am grateful for:

1. _____

2. _____

3. _____

Situation: _____

How can I benefit from it?:

1. _____

2. _____

3. _____

Things I am grateful for:

1. _____

2. _____

3. _____

Situation: _____

How can I benefit from it?:

1. _____

2. _____

3. _____

Things I am grateful for:

1. _____

2. _____

3. _____

Situation: _____

How can I benefit from it?:

1. _____

2. _____

3. _____

Things I am grateful for:

1. _____

2. _____

3. _____

Situation: _____

How can I benefit from it?:

1. _____

2. _____

3. _____

Things I am grateful for:

1. _____

2. _____

3. _____

Situation: _____

How can I benefit from it?:

1. _____

2. _____

3. _____

Things I am grateful for:

1. _____

2. _____

3. _____

Situation: _____

How can I benefit from it?:

1. _____

2. _____

3. _____

Things I am grateful for:

1. _____

2. _____

3. _____

Situation: _____

How can I benefit from it?:

1. _____

2. _____

3. _____

Things I am grateful for:

1. _____

2. _____

3. _____

Situation: _____

How can I benefit from it?:

1. _____

2. _____

3. _____

Things I am grateful for:

1. _____

2. _____

3. _____

Situation: _____

How can I benefit from it?:

1. _____

2. _____

3. _____

Things I am grateful for:

1. _____

2. _____

3. _____

These exercises are more than just a mechanism to help you cope with yourself and your environment – they are the arsenal you need to become better, stronger, and healthier.

What Did You Learn From This Chapter?

This is a chapter where you managed to reach deep within – and uncover a calmer and more centered side of you. Other than realizing that every one of us has it, you learned the following:

- ✧ What is mindfulness and an introduction to a few techniques.
- ✧ What is acceptance and how to cultivate non-judgemental awareness.
- ✧ Learned an exercise about the five senses of mindfulness.

Mindfulness and acceptance should be a core part of who you are. They can help you walk the path of calmness and control of your life. Speaking of control, it still feels like you haven't reached that point where you can have complete control of your behavior patterns, right? Fear not, because, in the next chapter, I am starting the subject of understanding those behavior patterns – taking a step toward grasping the steering wheel of your life. Turn the page, and I hope you're ready because you're in for a wild ride!

PART

02

CBT BEHAVIORAL
TECHNIQUES

CHAPTER 06

UNDERSTANDING BEHAVIOR PATTERNS

> *"Small daily improvements are the key to staggering long-term results."* -
> *Anonymous*

No matter what you do in life – be that personal development, professional development, or any other aspect of your life – it can be improved if you are consistent and work on it daily. Cognitive behavioral therapy is here to show you just that. With me as the vessel, you get to learn new things about yourself with every new chapter.

We all have certain behavior patterns. These affect us in a certain way and are our personal characteristic traits. It is a chain of thoughts and actions that have happened in certain patterns within your life, and they have often repeated themselves over and over. In this chapter, you will notice that I am focusing on two specific aspects – the ABC model and the triggers that lead to impulsive behaviors. Finally, we will wrap up this chapter by learning how to identify behavior patterns.

Exploring the ABC Model – Antecedents, Behaviours and Consequences

The ABC model is a perfect example of how CBT works – focusing on the present rather than the past. This basic CBT technique assumes your beliefs based on how you react to certain events. As a model, it challenges cognitive distortions and irrational thoughts. That, in turn, allows you to reconstruct these thoughts or beliefs into healthier ones.

This model has many benefits for your mental and emotional health. By using the ABC model, you can identify inaccurate thoughts and beliefs and learn how to let go of them. The process itself teaches you how to notice your automatic thoughts. However, instead of immediately acting upon them, you get to give yourself a break and explore different options. Once you see how it works, you will notice that you can use it in many situations – be that with yourself and your private thoughts, in a professional environment, or whenever you come face to face with a challenging situation.

Before I move on to the exercise where you can see the ABC model in motion, remember one thing about it – it can help you develop positive emotions and rational thoughts. So, each time you're faced with anxiety, anger, embarrassment, guilt, fear, or sadness, this is the model to turn to.

THE ABC MODEL IN USE

This model's beauty is that you can pinpoint a negative thought whenever you have it. Things immediately make more sense when you try to shape them in a certain way. In this case, they are shaped into letters. Before you begin this exercise, you should know the components of this model. Here they are:

- ✧ **A** – means the activating event or adversity
- ✧ **B** – means your beliefs about that certain activating event. These beliefs include both obvious and underlying thoughts about yourself, others, or a certain situation
- ✧ **C** – means consequences. These consequences usually include your emotional or behavioral response

Now, when you start the exercise, you work under the assumption that the letters A, B, and C are connected, and B is the most important component. CBT as a concept focuses on B to change the thinking patterns and create new ways of viewing yourself, the people around you, and situations.

Think about it this way - A is the activating situation or moment, B is your beliefs and thoughts about this moment, and C is the consequences of those beliefs.

For example, (A:) your friend agrees to have lunch with you, but they don't follow up on the initial agreement. Your mind immediately jumps to a conclusion (B:), thinking that they don't care about you, and then (C:) you start blowing things out of proportion with the thoughts that nobody cares about you, pick a fight with your friend, and so on.

Your exercise is to think of a situation when something similar to this happened to you and analyze how you reacted to it. When you come up with the situation, start from the very beginning - point A. Only this time, you will try to come to a different outcome. What happened at point A? Sit with that for a while and try to think of exactly what happened.

To come to point B, recognize your thought patterns and all the irrationality around them. Recognize that they make you have negative feelings and are part of a vortex you thought you couldn't get out of – until now. Come up with different approaches and different patterns of thoughts - more positive ones - that will lead you to different conclusions. Abandon the thought you originally had at the moment when the situation occurred and look for alternatives.

When you finally arrive at point C, it means you've done everything to explore other options for your specific situation and have managed to shift your thoughts. They are now neutral or positive, realistic, and don't make you feel angry or sad as a response to them.

Sit with this for a little bit. Learn how you can apply this exercise in various situations. Here are a few examples you can get started with:

1. Instructions given to you by your parents. They do that a lot and you don't really like it.
2. The feeling of peer pressure. It feels like everyone is doing much better than you.
3. Having an exam in the near future. The pressure of the "deadline" before the exam is too much to handle.
4. A reminder that you need to come back home before X o'clock. You don't need a reminder that you're still a teenager.
5. A warning from a teacher. This can lead to the school contacting your parents.
6. Social media. Either too much of it or not enough of it can make you feel anxious.

Antecedent (**A**): _____

_____

_____

Behavior (**B**): _____

_____

_____

Consequences (**C**): _____

_____

_____

Antecedent (**A**): _____

_____

_____

Behavior (**B**): _____

_____

_____

_____

Consequences (**C**): _____

_____

_____

Antecedent (**A**): _____

_____

_____

_____

Behavior (**B**): _____

_____

_____

Consequences (**C**): _____

_____

_____

_____

Antecedent (**A**): _____

_____

_____

Behavior (**B**): _____

_____

_____

Consequences (**C**): _____

_____

_____

Antecedent (**A**): _____

_____

_____

Behavior (**B**): _____

_____

_____

Consequences (**C**): _____

_____

_____

Antecedent (**A**): _____
_____
_____

Behavior (**B**): _____
_____
_____

Consequences (**C**): _____
_____
_____

Antecedent (**A**): _____
_____
_____

Behavior (**B**): _____
_____
_____

Consequences (**C**): _____
_____
_____

Self-Regulation Workbook for Teens

Antecedent (**A**): _____
_____
_____

Behavior (**B**): _____
_____
_____

Consequences (**C**): _____
_____
_____

Antecedent (**A**): _____
_____
_____

Behavior (**B**): _____
_____
_____

Consequences (**C**): _____
_____
_____

Antecedent (**A**): _____

_____

_____

Behavior (**B**): _____

_____

_____

Consequences (**C**): _____

_____

_____

Antecedent (**A**): _____

_____

_____

Behavior (**B**): _____

_____

_____

Consequences (**C**): _____

_____

_____

Antecedent (**A**):
_____
_____
_____

Behavior (**B**):
_____
_____
_____

Consequences (**C**):
_____
_____
_____

Antecedent (**A**):
_____
_____
_____

Behavior (**B**):
_____
_____
_____

Consequences (**C**):
_____
_____
_____

Antecedent (**A**): _____

_____

_____

Behavior (**B**): _____

_____

_____

Consequences (**C**): _____

_____

_____

Antecedent (**A**): _____

_____

_____

Behavior (**B**): _____

_____

_____

Consequences (**C**): _____

_____

_____

With those newfound thoughts and emotions, how would your behavior change? Do you notice it taking a turn for the better?

Recognizing Triggers for Impulsive Behavior

Many people believe that impulsive behavior is a disorder. I am here to tell you that just because you've been stuck in the maze of your mind doesn't mean you are dealing with a disorder. However, you should still know how to manage your impulse control and avoid impulsive behaviors.

An impulsive behavior is every time you act quickly on something without any thought about the consequences. In your mind, only the present moment exists (which is a good starting point), but there is no thought about the future whatsoever. What young minds such as yourself fail to notice here is that we all act on impulses sometimes. It is a part of who we are, and it is an important part of the human experience. But, if you indulge in this behavior for a longer period, instead of only engaging in it from time to time (until you become an adult and learn how to control it), then it means you are walking a thin line.

When you are acting on impulse, it means you are acting spontaneously. You don't consider how it could affect you later on or how it could affect others. You never wonder what might happen because you only think about the here and the now.

Before I move on to the exercise, I am sharing a few examples of impulsive behavior. You may recognize yourself in some, and that's okay because here, I have created a safe space for you to learn and develop at your own pace.

Here are the examples:

- ✧ You have frequent outbursts
- ✧ You overshare details of your personal life with everyone you meet
- ✧ You overindulge in things, showing binge behavior
- ✧ You tend to make all situations a lot scarier and more urgent than they actually are
- ✧ You turn to hurting yourself, physically, mentally, or emotionally, every time you are faced with disappointment.

COMMON TRIGGERS

Every day, you experience a wide range of emotions – be those positive, neutral, or negative. Almost all of them relate to a certain event, something that happens to you that day. However, it is your response to these events that matters. These events are your triggers, and you act on them based on a similar previous experience. It encompasses your state of mind based on past memories, experiences, or events, and it usually results in an intense emotional reaction, no matter what your current mood is at the moment.

This exercise can help you know your common emotional triggers and how to deal with them so you can create and maintain good emotional health.

Take out a pen and dedicate some time to sit with yourself. Think about some situations that made you feel bad. Which part of those situations triggered you? Was it some kind of disapproval, rejection, or exclusion, or maybe you felt ignored, critiqued, unwanted, smothered, insecure, and like you were losing control? These situations are known as common triggers, where you lose your independence and turn to something you're not. Once you pinpoint the feeling, listen to your mind and body. Your mind is probably loud and filled with negative thoughts, and your body also shows symptoms – a pounding heart, shakiness, and sweaty palms.

Some of the most common triggers young people face are fear of rejection, stress, being ignored, negative memories, being ridiculed, conflict, psychological trauma, being vulnerable, helpless, having a lack of socializing, etc.

Now go ahead and write everything down below:

Situation

_____

_____

_____

_____

_____

_____

_____

_____

_____

_____

_____

_____

_____

_____

_____

_____

The Trigger of Bad Feeling

_____

_____

_____

_____

_____

_____

_____

_____

_____

_____

_____

_____

_____

_____

_____

_____

This is when you need to take a step back and acknowledge your current state, but remember, that you know the root and know how to get there and change the reaction. Remind yourself that it is okay to feel whatever you feel, but let it pass through you. Own your feelings, but do so with compassion for yourself, not judgment. Give yourself some space, take a short break to regroup, and return to the situation with a calmer mindset.

Identifying Patterns of Behavior

At the end of the day, you started reading this book so you can not only improve yourself but learn how to accept yourself. For without acceptance, there is no change. It can be difficult to accept that you are dealing with something that is a core part of who you are, but by identifying that part of you, you give yourself the unique chance of improving the situation – improving yourself.

It all comes down to being self-aware and acknowledging a pattern. In this case, whatever happens, I would suggest one thing – that you commit honesty toward yourself. Be honest about every feeling and every thought because you need a certain recognition to strengthen your mind. Identifying your pattern of behavior will do just that – push the subconscious act into the realm of consciousness, where you are fully aware of what is happening to you. Apply logic to this case, and you know that you can shift or tone it down whenever you notice a behavior pattern with a negative frequency. By doing this, you create new opportunities for self-reflection and growth.

What Did You Learn From This Chapter?

It is important to realize that you have so much power within you – and that you can easily take control of yourself. But everything seems so much easier once you find out the perfect steps to make that happen. In this chapter on understanding behavior patterns, you learned precise ways to deal with yourself, among other things, as pointed out below:

✧ What is the ABC model and how it can influence your thinking patterns.

✧ What is impulsive behavior and its triggers.

✧ How the common triggers are connected to your behavior patterns.

When you understand your behavior patterns, that's when all things start to put themselves into perspective. With this, you go through the process of opening up to yourself, right down to your core, to find out what you're truly made out of. When you get that out of the way, only one thing remains: start building yourself up! To do that, you will need to develop a few skills, the first of which is coping skills. I am here to help you achieve that – turn the page because the next chapter is all about it!

CHAPTER 07

DEVELOPING COPING SKILLS

"We cannot solve our problems with the same thinking we used when we created them." – Albert Einstein

What does it mean to cope? It seems like, every day, you are coping with something, and everything feels like it is out of the ordinary. Each experience gives you a different thought, each action creates a reaction within you, and each feeling you have, comes with a set of consequences. The thing is, you noticed that you focus more on the negative rather than the positive. You start feeling like your mind and spirit are both tumbling down. You know, throwing a pebble down the side of the hill will ultimately nudge larger and larger rocks along the way. By the time it all reaches the end, some large rock formations would have fallen.

If you are coping with some emotions and thoughts that cannot be explained any other way than this, it is time for you to learn how to put them aside. In this chapter, I am teaching you all there is to know about effectively managing yourself. The best way to do that is by developing strong coping skills.

Learning Effective Coping Strategies for Managing Stress and Emotions

Negative emotions and stress can sometimes get the better of you. That's understandable to a certain extent, given the lifestyle most of us lead. Even for a young person such as yourself, things can feel a little too much sometimes. But noticing that you have more stressors in life than good feelings is the first step in the right direction. The second is implementing some effective coping strategies.

The main purpose of these strategies is to learn how to tolerate negative events and realities while keeping your positive self-image and emotional control intact.

You implement coping strategies each time you face a life challenge. This challenge is usually a negative situation and requires some sort of adaptation on your end. Other times, some positive changes may make you feel stressed, too. All of them require you to adapt and adjust to a certain new environment or situation, and for a brief moment, until you do that, you might feel like you don't have control over the situation. That may make you feel bad, panicked, anxious, or depressed. In some cases, it can even go to extremes. You are here because of that – so we can push the negative aside and learn how to deal with it. By learning these coping strategies, you will learn how to glide smoothly through life rather than trip and fall every time.

To manage your emotions and stress every time, here are some effective coping strategies for you:

- ✧ When faced with a situation, instead of jumping to conclusions, try to find as much information about it as you can. If necessary, include the people in your support group and find a solution.

- ✧ Any problem can be broken down into small parts. That way, instead of dealing with it as a whole, you deal with smaller, more manageable chunks.

- ✧ Practice breathing and relaxation techniques. They will automatically regulate your nervous system and keep you calm.

- ✧ Don't underestimate the power of a creative outlet. Anything from art, music, or dance can help you healthily process your emotions and be a productive way to spend your time.

- ✧ Get in touch with a friend who makes you feel like you are loved for who you really are.

- ✧ Reach out to a mentor, parent, or teacher – anyone who can guide you further.

- ✧ Work on reframing your negative thoughts and shifting your mindset. Remember, it is all about looking at a situation from a different point of view.

- ✧ The power of journaling is no joke. When you write things down, you put them into perspective, and they start making sense in terms of what you're going through. But they are also easier to handle once you physically see them in front of you.

- ✧ Dedicate your time to helping someone else. When you indulge in such an activity, you can help lower your overall stress levels and connect to others. Ultimately, you work on your well-being and health.

Whenever you feel like you want to react negatively in a given situation, remember that there will be consequences to that. Once you start gathering these consequences, one by one, they will come up to be the core of your personality - since you would be reacting to them, thinking about them, and so on. Since both positive and negative behaviors are repetitive patterns, it is high time you've learned the coping skills for each situation. The next step is building a "toolbox" of the coping skills you've mastered the most.

Building a Toolbox of Coping Skills

Okay, so let me ask you something – what do you do when you're emotionally activated? We all indeed have different ways of coping with stress, but what are your "go-to" tools that you take to deal with an unwanted or stressful situation? If you're reading this book, that means you either want to update your skills or you want to change them completely. As a young adult, trying this on your own may be difficult because you don't have a starting point.

But now, with this book, you can easily focus on building a toolbox of coping skills.

What is a toolbox of skills? These are the skills you have up your sleeve and you use them each time you are faced with a challenging situation. However, before you build your own toolbox, you need to learn something. The key to developing new skills and knowing how to use them is practicing them even when you're not emotionally activated. Once you develop that ability to think clearly in any situation, things will seem a lot easier to cope with. This is something you can rely on each time you move forward and overcome a curveball.

To move on and try to implement those skills in your daily life, you need to decide what you're going to put in your emotional toolbox first. As you are starting from scratch, here are a few suggestions to get you started. You can use these skills every time you feel like you need soothing.

1. **Distract yourself** – there is nothing wrong with distracting yourself every time you feel upset. If you start feeling like you can't keep control over a certain situation, and you don't want to let go of control, then it is most likely best if you step back. Distract yourself with something until the strong emotions pass. This is only the first skill you can implement, so try to combine it with some of the other skills that I mention below. Here, you can watch a movie, listen to music, get into a hobby of yours, do some puzzles, etc.

2. **Mindfulness exercises** – whenever you're feeling emotionally overwhelmed, it is difficult to focus on the present moment. Your mind wanders all over the place, and it is challenging to stay put in the present. That is why mindfulness exercises are a perfect thing. These exercises can help you shift the attention

back to yourself and to where you are right now and how you're feeling right now. The exercises can be anything you want – from a breathing exercise to meditation exercise, journalling, coloring, or maybe even progressive muscle relaxation exercises.

3. **Move your body** – by moving your body, you keep the mind active in the present, so this is another skill you should keep up your sleeve. You don't have to do extreme exercises here; all you need to do is listen to your body and go at your own pace. Sometimes, intense movements are what you need. Other times, you can focus on slow movements. This can be anything – from stepping onto your yoga mat to running, gardening, stretching, or doing some exercise videos.

4. **Calming sensory objects** – using your senses to calm down is a great way to keep yourself grounded and in the present moment. In this case, you can, for example, touch something or engage a few of your senses at the same time. If you are faced with a challenging situation, look around you – that's the first thing that will keep you in the present. Find some sensory objects. These can be a soft blanket, a candle, a lotion, a pen, a toy, a fidget spinner, a warm or cold beverage, a piece of gum, photos of people – it can be anything.

It is such a happy feeling to create a palette of coping skills and keep them up your sleeve just in case a challenging situation arises. This so-called toolbox can help you stay more calm and centered - because you know that, at any given moment, you have something to fall back on rather than falling into a hole of negativity. After this, it is time to learn how to implement these coping skills in day-to-day situations.

Implementing Coping Skills in Daily Life

It is all about dedicating some time out of your day to give something to yourself. Working on yourself is very important, and since you picked up this book, you're already on the right path. But you still need to put in some effort.

For most young people, time management is a challenging concept in itself. Every day has 24 hours, and how you divide your time and attention is what matters the most. Once you subtract the time for rest, time to finish your daily obligations, and time spent with your friends and family, there is rarely some time to focus on yourself, right? Well, the first thing you're going to do is learn how to manage your time and give at least five or ten minutes during the day to yourself. Even in those times when you feel like you are racing with the clock, pause for a second, breathe, and start over.

When you look at it from a different perspective, it is about priority management more than time management. If you want to put in the work and create a better version of yourself, then you need to dedicate minutes, if not hours, to yourself only.

Be careful though, your mind may trick you into believing that self-care is selfishness. That dedicating time to yourself is a bad thing. Don't trust that voice. You are being kind and compassionate to people and yourself. You are working to achieve a certain goal. You are starting a journey to self-care and self-revelation.

So, create a schedule first. You already have the coping skills listed above, and you know you need to work on them every chance you get, not only in a situation where you're emotionally challenged. Now, all you need to do is begin. Implement the coping skills we uncovered in your daily life. Soon enough, you will notice yourself exhibiting a different pattern of behavior. A better one.

What Did You Learn From This Chapter?

The purpose of this chapter was to open your eyes to the world of possibilities. To teach you about all the things you can do and be and how to cope healthily with everything life throws at you. To summarize, here is what you learned from it:

- ✧ Some effective strategies that can help you manage your emotions and stress levels.
- ✧ A set of coping skills you should have in your arsenal.
- ✧ How to implement those coping skills in your everyday life.

Coping skills are easy to master. I know that after the end of each chapter, you are baffled by all the new information you learn, but as you can see, the next chapter always completes the previous one. Using that logic, things will seem a lot easier once you delve into the next chapter – which is all about behavioral activation. Turn the page and learn all about it!

CHAPTER 08

BEHAVIORAL ACTIVATION

"Do not wait, the time will never be 'just right.' Start where you stand, and work with whatever tools you may have at your command, and better tools will be found as you go along." – George Herbert

There is an idea that focuses on enhancing a sort of positive behavior. Behavioral activation is just that – deliberately practicing certain behaviors to activate a positive emotional state. The concept depends on the fact that as long as you engage in good and healthy activities, you will feel good.

How does this seem to you? Is it something you would try? When I was young, I thought this would never work for me. But, despite my doubts, I still gave it a go. After a few failed attempts, I focused on enhancing my behavioral activation. So you see, this is something anyone can do. And I bet that you would be better at it than I was! Do you want to know why I think that? Because you have this book in your hands!

Understanding the Connection Between Behavior and Mood

Remember that I mentioned the relationship between thoughts, emotions, and behavior in the previous chapters. Now, in order to change that, you need to acknowledge and recognize it first.

I want us to begin by distinguishing between emotions and feelings. These are often confused with each other, yet they are pretty different. Now, don't get me wrong; they are still connected, but they come with different time limits and labels. By understanding the difference, you will be able to better control your behavior and make healthier choices in life.

Emotions. They are not conscious. These reactions happen within your body, and they often come as a consequence of thoughts, memories, and experiences. Some of the most common emotions include happiness, anger, sadness, fear, surprise, and disgust. Also, emotions are often associated with facial expressions.

Feelings. On the other hand, feelings happen in the mind. They are conscious. They are a reaction to the emotions you are experiencing. Feelings are based on the reaction to the emotions you are experiencing, as well as the perception of any events and thoughts.

Emotions and feelings are two separate things because emotions happen due to a physical response within the brain, and feelings are a response to the emotional reaction.

So, how can these two impact your behavior?

Because the emotions create a physical response, and the feelings are conscious, they impact your overall behavior. However, in such situations, people tend to believe that their behavior is justified because of their emotions. The thing is, as long as they believe this, they may struggle to understand that behavior is a choice. Behavior does not have to be impacted by your mood. Behavior can be healthy. Once you start noticing this, you can make a change. If your mood often dictates your behavior, you can react in three ways – positively, negatively, or refuse to respond at all. If you allow your emotions to control your behavior, then you live on so-called "autopilot." That kind of behavior may lead to you making choices you will regret later. As long as your behavior is based on your feelings, it can lead you astray.

MOOD AND ACTIVITY DIARY

Let's do an exercise here. Get a pen and locate the worksheet below. Have them handy at all times during the next week or so. Within this timeframe, try to notice your mood every time – when you get up in the morning, before you go to bed, at each time during the day, and every time you come face to face with any type of situation.

Always take a minute to reflect and write down your mood and behavior. As I have already mentioned, when you put anything on paper, it takes a form of its own and becomes more real. Think of you writing down how you felt as a sort of diary. Once the week has passed, you can go back to your notes and see how your mind has gradually shifted for the better, even if it is a little bit.

Activity: _____ Mood: _____

Activity: _____ Mood: _____

Activity: _____ Mood: _____

Activity: _____ Mood: _____

Activity: _____ Mood: _____

Activity: _____ Mood: _____

Activity: _____ Mood: _____

Activity: _____ Mood: _____

Activity: _____ Mood: _____

Setting and Achieving SMART Goals

The reason why I'm adding this as a segment into this book is because it is important to know how to work on your goals, not just to have them. In your case, you are working on creating a better, calmer, and happier self. But, sometimes, everyone needs a little push in the right direction. That's why I am including the SMART goals.

Whatever you put your mind to, you can achieve. Think of the SMART goals as your guide that will help you get to where you want in a specific timeframe. For those of you who are already familiar with this concept, let's revisit it. And for those of you who don't know it, take a look at it below:

SMART is an acronym that can help you determine your goals – make them reachable and clear, as they should be. Here is what every letter stands for:

S – stands for specific, significant, simple, and sensible

M – stands for measurable, motivating, and meaningful

A – stands for achievable, attainable, and agreed

R – stands for relevant, realistic, result-based, and reasonable

T – stands for time-bound, time-based, timely, and time-sensitive

While this sounds simple and straightforward enough, you probably still need some guidance on how to practice it. That's why we are moving on to the next exercise.

SMART GOAL-SETTING

The goal you want to achieve now is to adhere to positive behavior and change a certain aspect of yourself that will affect the quality of your overall lifestyle. With that in mind, here is how to set a SMART goal.

This approach is based on certain criteria. Take a pen and write down your goal. Then, find the SMART letters in a vertical line below it. Add your answers to the following questions next to each letter – see below.

S > be specific. What will you achieve? How will you do that?

M > be measurable. What will you use as a pointer to show you that you've met your goal?

A > be achievable. Do you possess the right skills to achieve this?

R > be relevant. How important will the results be?

T > be time-bound. What is the deadline for you to achieve your goal?

MY GOAL

_____

_____

| S > | _____ |

_____

_____

| M > | _____ |

_____

_____

| A > | _____ |

_____

_____

| R > | _____ |

_____

_____

| T > | _____ |

_____

_____

MY GOAL

_____

_____

S ⟩ _____

_____

_____

M ⟩ _____

_____

_____

A ⟩ _____

_____

_____

R ⟩ _____

_____

_____

T ⟩ _____

_____

_____

MY GOAL

_____

_____

S ⟩ _____

_____

_____

M ⟩ _____

_____

_____

A ⟩ _____

_____

_____

R ⟩ _____

_____

_____

T ⟩ _____

_____

_____

MY GOAL

_____

_____

S >
_____

_____

_____

M >
_____

_____

_____

A >
_____

_____

_____

R >
_____

_____

_____

T >
_____

_____

_____

MY GOAL

_____

_____

S > _____

_____

_____

M > _____

_____

_____

A > _____

_____

_____

R > _____

_____

_____

T > _____

_____

_____

MY GOAL

_____

_____

S > _____

_____

_____

M > _____

_____

_____

A > _____

_____

_____

R > _____

_____

_____

T > _____

_____

_____

MY GOAL

_____

_____

| **S** | _____ |

_____

_____

| **M** | _____ |

_____

_____

| **A** | _____ |

_____

_____

| **R** | _____ |

_____

_____

| **T** | _____ |

_____

_____

By learning that the SMART goal will provide you with clarity, motivation, and focus, you can soon learn to implement it with every other goal you have – not just this one.

Increasing Engagement in Positive Activities

Science has always suggested that positive thinking is a skill everyone can learn. It is also the main focus of this book. But when it comes to actually doing the work, a lot of people shy away from it. Before thinking that it "takes too much work" to do it, think about the near future. Visualize yourself doing things you want, things that make you feel complete and happy. Just the thought of it makes you happy, doesn't it?

Well, think about how much better you will feel if you actually increase your engagement in positive activities. Just stop and think about what makes you happy. Do you have a hobby that makes you feel fulfilled? Do you have an interest that makes you lose track of time? It can be anything – as long as it puts a smile on your face. It can be drawing, going out with people, watching a movie, reading a book, meditating, running, or photography – all cards are on the table!

By increasing engagement in positive activities, you learn how to stay present in the moment. Your mind does not wander around, creating negative scenarios and falling into the same depressing vortex over and over again. Rather, it instead focuses on what you can do better. As insignificant as this may sound in the beginning, indulging in such activities can help you shift your mindset after a while.

BEHAVIORAL ACTIVATION WORKSHEET

I have found that the most successful way to indulge in behavioral activation is by making a worksheet. Trust me, it is as simple as it can get. There is not much complexity to it, and you don't even have to dedicate a lot of time to it. A few minutes of your day is enough.

Take a pen and write down all the things you love. I mean, things you truly love. They can be of any area of your life. For example, you can write the following.

I love my pet.

I love that I get up early every morning.

I love that I work on myself at least once a week.

I love that it's summertime.

I love watermelon.

You see? This can be anything as long as you focus on the good things. There is always something good and something to be thankful for, and by indulging in this exercise, you accentuate it.

_____

_____

_____

_____

_____

ACTIVITY EXPERIMENT

The next exercise for today is focused on the question – *what would you do if you knew the <u>outcome</u> would be the best possible scenario?*

Experiment with a particular activity. Say you want to improve your mood and focus; running three times a week is an excellent way to do that. But you feel like you're going to fail as soon as you begin. Well, I am all up for changing your thoughts, so let's do it. I know that if you've never run before, your mind will immediately go to thinking you'll fail. Let's entertain that thought for a minute. Why do you think you will fail? Because if you never ran before, how would you know? True, you need to have a certain level of physical preparedness to run, but you also need to run to have physical preparedness. It is a circle, and one cannot go without the other.

Once you realize this is the same for all activities you want to indulge in, you will start looking at it a bit more positively. For the sake of this exercise, let's look at the best possible scenario. You will start running three days a week. You will feel incredible, you will look better, and while you're thinking about your future self, you always picture yourself with a smile on your face. That's the best-case scenario I want you to focus on every time you want to start something new. It doesn't have to be running exactly – it can be anything you want as long as it is an activity that will make you happy.

Activity: _____

The Best-Case Scenario: _____

_____

_____

_____

Activity: _____

The Best-Case Scenario: _____

_____

_____

_____

_____

Activity: _____

The Best-Case Scenario: _____

_____

_____

_____

_____

Activity: _____

The Best-Case Scenario: _____

_____

_____

_____

_____

Activity: _____

The Best-Case Scenario: _____

_____

_____

_____

_____

Activity: _____

The Best-Case Scenario: _____

_____

_____

_____

_____

Activity: _____

The Best-Case Scenario: _____

_____

_____

_____

_____

POSITIVE ACTIVITY CATALOG

This last exercise for this chapter is connected to the previous one. After you do your best with the smallest positive activity and you see the results, you will want to do another activity and then another one. As you stack these up, one at a time, you end up creating a catalog of everything you're doing to improve yourself.

All you need to do here is to remember to write everything down. Write down the activity, how it made you feel, and how often you indulged in it. This is sort of a journalling process except we call it a catalog of positive activities. Give it a few months to really see the results. Let's say you've indulged in several activities in the past period, and then you stopped to look back on how far you've come. Everything you've written down will be the catalog you refer to – each time you need inspiration or a little boost to move ahead in life.

Activity: _____

How it Made me feel?: _____

_____

Times done: ☐　☐　☐　☐　☐　☐　☐　☐　☐　☐　☐

—o—◇—o—

Activity: _____

How it Made me feel?: _____

_____

Times done: ☐　☐　☐　☐　☐　☐　☐　☐　☐　☐　☐

Activity: _____

How it Made me feel?: _____

_____

Times done: ☐   ☐   ☐   ☐   ☐   ☐   ☐   ☐   ☐   ☐   ☐   ☐

———o—◇—o———

Activity: _____

How it Made me feel?: _____

_____

Times done: ☐   ☐   ☐   ☐   ☐   ☐   ☐   ☐   ☐   ☐   ☐   ☐

———o—◇—o———

Activity: _____

How it Made me feel?: _____

_____

Times done: ☐   ☐   ☐   ☐   ☐   ☐   ☐   ☐   ☐   ☐   ☐   ☐

———o—◇—o———

Activity: _____

How it Made me feel?: _____

_____

Times done: ☐   ☐   ☐   ☐   ☐   ☐   ☐   ☐   ☐   ☐   ☐   ☐

———o—◇—o———

Activity: _____

How it Made me feel?: _____

_____

Times done: ☐   ☐   ☐   ☐   ☐   ☐   ☐   ☐   ☐   ☐   ☐   ☐

Activity: _____

How it Made me feel?: _____

_____

Times done: ☐ ☐ ☐ ☐ ☐ ☐ ☐ ☐ ☐ ☐ ☐ ☐

———o—◇—o———

Activity: _____

How it Made me feel?: _____

_____

Times done: ☐ ☐ ☐ ☐ ☐ ☐ ☐ ☐ ☐ ☐ ☐ ☐

———o—◇—o———

Activity: _____

How it Made me feel?: _____

_____

Times done: ☐ ☐ ☐ ☐ ☐ ☐ ☐ ☐ ☐ ☐ ☐ ☐

———o—◇—o———

Activity: _____

How it Made me feel?: _____

_____

Times done: ☐ ☐ ☐ ☐ ☐ ☐ ☐ ☐ ☐ ☐ ☐ ☐

———o—◇—o———

Activity: _____

How it Made me feel?: _____

_____

Times done: ☐ ☐ ☐ ☐ ☐ ☐ ☐ ☐ ☐ ☐ ☐ ☐

Activity: _____

How it Made me feel?: _____

_____

Times done: ☐ ☐ ☐ ☐ ☐ ☐ ☐ ☐ ☐ ☐ ☐ ☐ ☐

———o–◇–o———

Activity: _____

How it Made me feel?: _____

_____

Times done: ☐ ☐ ☐ ☐ ☐ ☐ ☐ ☐ ☐ ☐ ☐ ☐ ☐

———o–◇–o———

Activity: _____

How it Made me feel?: _____

_____

Times done: ☐ ☐ ☐ ☐ ☐ ☐ ☐ ☐ ☐ ☐ ☐ ☐ ☐

———o–◇–o———

Activity: _____

How it Made me feel?: _____

_____

Times done: ☐ ☐ ☐ ☐ ☐ ☐ ☐ ☐ ☐ ☐ ☐ ☐ ☐

———o–◇–o———

Activity: _____

How it Made me feel?: _____

_____

Times done: ☐ ☐ ☐ ☐ ☐ ☐ ☐ ☐ ☐ ☐ ☐ ☐ ☐

What Did You Learn From This Chapter?

Slowly but surely, you are learning so much about yourself and how you can improve. This chapter was probably a true revelation that there is always a flip side to everything. By learning this now, you keep in mind how to be more assertive and engage in positive behavior.

Let's review what we've learned from here:

- ✧ Explaining what behavioral activation is.
- ✧ What are emotions and feelings, and how they differ from each other.
- ✧ Behavior can be a consequence of feelings, but behavior is always a choice.
- ✧ Setting SMART goals.
- ✧ Increasing engagement in positive activities makes you more present.

It is very easy to let negative emotions and feelings control your behavior. That's probably the reason why most people indulge in it. It takes perseverance, control, and determination to get to the other side – where the grass is greener. I am breaking down the journey into small steps to make things a lot easier for you, and I hope you can already feel the difference! But, as much as I like to say that we're almost there, you still need to do a few things. The next chapter is all about assertiveness training. With it, you will unlock a whole new level of yourself. What are you waiting for? Turn the page!

CHAPTER 09

ASSERTIVENESS TRAINING

"The only limit to our realization of tomorrow will be our doubts of today." –
Franklin D. Roosevelt

Train your brain – that's all you ever need. In the previous chapters, I focused on the importance of looking at thoughts, feelings, and behavior as one. But now, it is time to focus only on the aspect of assertiveness. This will be the tool that will keep you in check every time life gets complicated.

Before we delve into the chapter together, let's talk about assertiveness – do you know what it is? Assertiveness is the quality of being confident and self-assured without being hostile or aggressive. Many people think this is a part of personality, which is why some people have it while others don't. The truth is that this is a skill that you can train yourself to possess. The assertiveness skills can help you respond to any situation better and help you build yourself up into a stronger version of yourself.

Importance of Assertive Communication

Since this is our subject for the chapter, and I have dedicated an entire one to it, why is it so important? Assertiveness, in itself, is something quite a lot of people struggle with. As a young person, you may feel like you fear hurting someone else, appear selfish, show aggression, etc. All of these are reasons why you feel afraid to be confident, to stand up for yourself, and to voice your needs.

In many situations, these fears come from a lack of understanding about assertiveness. To clear things up right from the start, assertiveness is not to be mistaken with aggression – even though both include showing your point of view. The difference is that aggression has a hostile and demanding approach, and assertiveness includes calm and respectful communication.

By explaining them, you can see how important assertive communication is. You will show stability to yourself first and then to the people around you. Then, you will know how to ask for something with confidence and clarity. Finally, you will stop feeling subjugated and powerless and instead step into your full force.

Learning Assertiveness Skills

Rather than boring you with details and theory, I want to focus on practice within this chapter. You are fully aware of what assertiveness is. Now, it is time to start learning how to implement it in your life. Learning assertiveness skills is one of the most effective ways for you to get your message across. Here is how to learn assertiveness:

- ✧ **Think about your style** - are you a more active person, someone who wants their voice to be heard, or are you a more passive person, and tend to stay in the background? Once you determine this, it is time to apply the next steps.

- ✧ **Use first person singular** - whenever you want to talk about something, use "I" as much as you can. This will give off the feeling that you're using statements that connect you, meaning you are ready to take on responsibilities or consequences.

- ✧ **Learn how to say no** - this is very self-explanatory. If you don't want to do or say or feel something, just say no.

- ✧ **Rehearse** - if you have something to say, and you're afraid you're not going to sound right, rehearse it.

- ✧ **Body language** - at all times, you need to be aware of your body language - for it speaks even when you keep quiet. Notice yourself in front of the mirror - and practice poses that are calm and radiate certainty.

- ✧ **Check on yourself** - the last step and the biggest one is checking in on yourself. Your emotions and your thoughts are what matter the most, so at all times, keep them in check. There's no need for you to give off what you think and feel all the time. Instead, take a deep breath, take a step back, and calmly approach every situation.

Actually, learning assertiveness seems easy, right? But why would you learn it if you don't know what you're gaining from it? Understandable. I wouldn't want to abide by anything if I didn't know how it would help me. With that in mind, here is what you will gain from learning assertiveness skills:

- ✧ Better communication – when you are being assertive, you have the best chance to successfully deliver a message across. If you are too much on the aggressive side, then you are more likely to lose the message in the process, as the receiving party will only focus on the aggression they see. It is all about being honest about what you want.

✧ Increased confidence and self-esteem – when you truthfully communicate your feelings and thoughts, you stand up for yourself, your rights, and the core of who you are. This naturally boosts your confidence and self-esteem.

✧ Improved relationships – starting from the relationship you nurture with yourself, moving on to your relationships with the people around you. Assertive communication is usually based on mutual respect and trust, and that is why it is an important aspect of every relationship. Communicating directly and being honest can eliminate any resentment or underlying negative feelings that come from a point of unmet needs.

✧ Less stress – this is my favorite benefit. We are all aware that stress is an unavoidable part of life. But did you know that not putting yourself first can elevate your daily stress levels to uncomfortable heights? A lot of stress for a prolonged period leads to significant changes within your mind and body for the worse. Also, learning to be assertive can make you feel stressed. However, while being more assertive may make you feel discomfort and tension initially, knowing that you are open and straightforward in your communication while considering all parties involved will significantly decrease your stress levels long-term.

Improving your communication abilities does not have to come with a high cost. Sometimes, all it takes is to focus on yourself and learn a few new skills.

Role-Playing Assertiveness Response

Before I go into the exercises, one last bit. Being able to communicate assertively is a skill you need to develop so you can maintain healthy relationships, both with yourself and the people around you. It also helps build up your self-esteem.

Role-playing assertiveness response is assertiveness training. Through it, you get to experience all sorts of things – how you initially want to react when you're met with an uncomfortable situation and how to train your brain to react in a more assertive way.

To understand this in-depth, take a look at the exercises below.

ASSERTIVE COMMUNICATION ROLE-PLAY

This exercise is focused on role play. Learning how to communicate assertively is best done by switching sides. Let's say you are talking to your parents or guardian, and they say that you need to focus on yourself and start standing up for yourself. While this seems reasonable for a parent to say, you act out. You begin to shout and say that you don't want to do anything, that you constantly feel pressured, and you don't know where to begin so you can make yourself better.

With the assertive communication role-play, you switch the roles any way you want. You can either be the parent and understand their point of view and why they are discussing this with you. Or you can indulge in assertive feedback rather than aggression. Either way, this assertive communication exercise is developed to help you change your point of view and teach you how to react more calmly in such challenging situations.

ASSERTIVE COMMUNICATION SCENARIOS

The last exercise for this chapter is connected to assertive communication scenarios. In these scenarios, try to think of something that already happened just to see if you could have reacted better in that situation. Assertive communication scenarios can be truly helpful if you want to retrace your steps back and see how far you've come, or to see how much more you need to work on.

Let me give you a few examples of these assertive communication scenarios.

- ✧ For example, you can start with the feedback you received. It can be anything from feedback at home to feedback at school etc. Something that made you have negative feelings.

- ✧ Or you can move on to declining something you don't want to do. Maybe there has been a situation where you have felt pushed into doing something you didn't want to do, which made you act out later on. We are all human, and when we're cornered, aggression can quickly surface.

- ✧ Criticism is next. You can see it everywhere you go. Sometimes, you even feel it deep down. But oftentimes, it happens that criticism is something we don't take lightly. This especially goes for young people. It can make you feel helpless, and it can make you act out.

These are only a handful of situations where you might have felt like you are doing less than optimal work, or that you're cornered, or you simply feel attacked, and you have the need to fight back. Well, let's turn that around.

Here are 10 scenarios for you to practice. Some of these situations may have already happened to you, while others may not have. For those that you've already experienced, you could try practicing how you would have altered your behavior. Also, for those you haven't experienced, try to think of how you would react in the best possible way.

1. You felt cornered by your classmates for who you are.
2. You had a verbal altercation with someone.
3. Your parents looked at you at dinner, and it felt like there was disappointment in their eyes.
4. You woke up from a bad dream feeling terrible, and that feeling persisted throughout the day.
5. You find yourself thinking that you'll never be good enough.
6. Your teacher confronted you for a lousy job you've done on your homework.
7. People make fun of you because of a certain hobby you have.
8. Every time you look in the mirror you don't like what you see.
9. You voiced out an opinion with your friends, and they laughed at you for it.
10. The feedback you got for a project you worked on was not what you expected it to be.

Now, think of how you already reacted earlier, or think about how you would react in each one of these situations (it was probably not optimal). The next step is to replay that scenario in your mind, but this time, try to turn your reaction around. Instead of bursting out, what would you say to make your response assertive?

Looking back on these types of communication encounters and how you could have improved them will help you better understand the great role assertiveness has in your life. It will also help you look at any situation with a clear mind and readiness to communicate and solve anything that comes your way!

What Did You Learn From This Chapter?

Assertiveness is a skill that will serve you throughout your life. A little bit of theory and a lot of practice can go a long way. Let's review what we learned from this chapter:

- ✧ What is assertive communication.
- ✧ The importance of assertive communication.
- ✧ What you will get by learning assertiveness skills.
- ✧ How to role-play an assertiveness response.

By looking at the logical order of things, once you know how to approach a certain situation in life, you should know how to solve it, too, right? Life gives us challenges every day, and the best way to deal with them is to go toward them – head-on. So, the following chapter will focus on that. I know that you probably already possess some problem-solving skills, but it is time to take a deeper look into it. Let's turn the page and continue learning.

CHAPTER 10

PROBLEM-SOLVING SKILLS

"A problem is a chance for you to do your best." – Duke Ellington

I love that you have picked up this book in your hands because, by this stage, you are pretty much aware of the power within you and how you can do your best at any given moment. We talked about the many challenges you might face and how to identify them, and I added many exercises that can help you get back on the right track.

This chapter offers an entirely different insight into yourself. While I helped you tap into your emotions and feelings in the previous chapters, we will discuss matters of the mind here. Your true power comes from your thinking patterns – if you focus on reshaping them, you focus on creating a better you.

Now, we're delving deep into the subject of problem-solving and how it can help you reform yourself.

Steps for Effective Problem-Solving

The problem-solving skills are an absolute must when it comes to skills you should work on. Once you step out in the world, you will see that having these skills will make the difference between success and failure in everyday situations. These skills can help you navigate the complexities and challenges of life and get accustomed to the ever-changing environment.

But what encompasses effective problem-solving? Is this something you are born with, or something that you can develop over time? You're just in luck because these skills can be developed at any point in life – but as I say, the sooner, the better. Whenever you find yourself in a situation that requires a solution and you don't know where to begin, turn to problem-solving. This can be anything that happens during your day. It can also be anything that happens within you. As we work together to get you up and running, learning the steps that will help you get there is important. Now, I will only mention these steps, and we will discuss them in detail below.

I like to consider these the ultimate five steps to tackling any challenge in your life. These five steps consist of:

1. Identifying the issue
2. Generating all kinds of possible solutions
3. Evaluating those solutions
4. Implementing the chosen solutions
5. Adjusting as necessary

Now, let's break these down and talk about them, one step at a time, starting from the top.

Identifying Problems and Generating Solutions

The first step in the problem-solving process is to have a clear definition of the challenge, issue, or setback. You don't need to do this in an instant. Remember, some situations are a little more complex and require a longer time to decipher them. That's okay. During that period, collect as much information as you can. Because the more information you have, the better and easier it will be for you to identify the cause of the issue at hand. For example, if you constantly succumb to negative thoughts, it is essential to identify where it comes from and how it affects you. Also, it is necessary to underline that it all comes from a lack of training. Once you clearly understand the root cause, you can start developing a solid action plan to address it. It is highly important to include all available information – gather first, act on it later.

By doing this step, you are doing yourself a favor – as you are directly affected by the situation.

By doing this, you take a step back to gain a different perspective and insight.

The second step is all about brainstorming. Finding a few possible solutions to a challenge can sometimes be more difficult than you can imagine. I urge you to stay on course and be persistent, as it is worth it in the end. I would advise that, as soon as you come to this second step, you try to come up with as many solutions as you can. It doesn't matter if they are very unrealistic or not. The point of this step is to teach yourself how to stray from your regular mindset. Brainstorming and generating all sorts of possible outcomes can help you bounce off ideas. Once you delve into deep thinking, you can create such a session that the ideas you generate will be amazing, and you can just keep them in the back of your mind without any judgment or critique. Coming up with a list of possible solutions may take a while or a bit. It all depends on your specific way of functioning. Consider all the options you have thought of and weigh the pros and cons of each option. Given the information you gathered, what seems like the most effective solution to you (out of all the things you came up with)?

Evaluating and Implementing Solutions

The question leads us to the third step, which is evaluating the solutions. Within this step, it is crucial to keep an open mind and always consider a different perspective. Try to step out of your usual way of thinking as much as you can. Take all the time you need during this process, especially in the beginning, because you will need some time to train your brain anyway. While you are on this step, it is important to consider the consequences of all the options you have in mind. Some of the long-term effects may not be up to your liking. That is why you are in the process of evaluating each possible option. Prioritize them based on their feasibility and the impact they may have. While they sound nice in theory, their execution may be more challenging than you can imagine, while other solutions may be instantly implemented. That is why choosing a solution that addresses the challenge directly and effectively is essential. If you need some help in this section, you can always go back to the SMART concept to help you out. The last thing to remember here is that not all may work according to plan, and you should always keep this in the back of your mind – but more on that later.

The fourth step is implementing the solution. Here is when you need to start planning carefully. Everything needs to go as smoothly as possible, and you must know your responsibilities. Designing a layout plan with everything in front of you will give you a better idea of how to execute it. You can see this below in the exercise 25, solution implementation practice.

Monitoring, Adjusting, and How the Overall Process Will Make You Feel

Last but not least, it is always important to track the implementation process. As this is the last step of your problem-solving skills, you can only truly complete this process once you realize that regular check-ins are a must. While you are implementing a solution to any of life's challenges you're faced with, it is vital to address them from time to time to prevent them from becoming bigger or creating an additional challenge. Adjusting the solution is imperative to ensure that whatever you want resolved is on the right track. Sometimes, plans don't go as they're supposed to, and you may end up with a problem that is not fully resolved. The thing is, you need to be flexible while you approach a challenge or an issue. Monitor how your chosen solution works, and if you feel like something could be done better, don't be afraid to make any adjustments. It all comes down to the feedback you get – both from yourself and your surroundings. The solution should completely resolve the issue and fulfill your hopes. Once you notice this is not happening, it is time to take actionable steps. Take a few steps back. If necessary, go to the brainstorming step, and see what else you've come up with. Maybe things will change when you look at the solution from a different perspective. And you will find that something else may work better instead.

It is important to be fully invested in the process. This five-step problem-solving process can help you overcome any obstacles you face. Remember that it is all about defining the problem, analyzing it, and getting all the necessary information – those are the first steps. Then, by understanding the root of the issue, you come up with a few solutions and go for the one that seems the most logical at the moment. If by any chance something doesn't work out, back to the drawing board you go!

I love it when people are being practical about something. That's why I tend to focus on creating the ultimate mind-spirit balance. But, to do that, we always need exercise. The following exercises you see will provide you with an incredible way to get in touch with yourself and activate that problem-solving part of your mind.

PROBLEM-SOLVING STEPS PRACTICE

Another way to name this exercise is "a real-life example." You need to practice the problem-solving steps over and over again. In this first exercise, I encourage you to start doing this whenever you are faced with a challenge because there is no better way to master problem-solving skills than to begin utilizing them right there – on the spot!

Depending on your situation, you may have to wait a little longer for such a situation to arise. If that's the case, then give this practice a nudge. Think of any past situation that has been haunting you for a while now. Write it down. From this perspective and this point in time, how would you approach it? Write that down too. Now that you have more knowledge in your arsenal, would it be easier for you to tackle it? Why? Also, once you've settled it in your mind, how did that make you feel? Follow the problem-solving steps below and start practicing.

1. Identifying the issue.

2. Generating all kinds of possible solutions.

3. Evaluating those solutions.

4. Implementing the chosen solutions.

5. Adjusting as necessary.

1. The Problem: _____

2. Possible Solutions: _____

_____

_____

_____

_____

_____

3. What is Good/Bad in Each of the Solutions?: _____

_____

_____

_____

_____

_____

4. The Solution I Will Implement: _____

_____

_____

_____

_____

_____

_____

1. The Problem: _____

2. Possible Solutions: _____

   _____

   _____

   _____

   _____

   _____

3. What is Good/Bad in Each of the Solutions?: _____

   _____

   _____

   _____

   _____

   _____

4. The Solution I Will Implement: _____

   _____

   _____

   _____

   _____

   _____

   _____

1. The Problem: _____

2. Possible Solutions: _____

_____

_____

_____

_____

_____

3. What is Good/Bad in Each of the Solutions?: _____

_____

_____

_____

_____

_____

4. The Solution I Will Implement: _____

_____

_____

_____

_____

_____

1. The Problem: _____

2. Possible Solutions: _____

_____

_____

_____

_____

_____

3. What is Good/Bad in Each of the Solutions?: _____

_____

_____

_____

_____

_____

4. The Solution I Will Implement: _____

_____

_____

_____

_____

_____

1. The Problem: _____

2. Possible Solutions: _____

_____

_____

_____

_____

_____

3. What is Good/Bad in Each of the Solutions?: _____

_____

_____

_____

_____

_____

4. The Solution I Will Implement: _____

_____

_____

_____

_____

_____

SOLVING COMMON PROBLEMS

Practice makes it perfect. Instead of pulling yourself down into the vortex of negative behavior, realize there are many ways to train your brain. One of those ways is to keep posing small challenges for yourself every day. These challenges do not have to be ones of the past or ones you have to make up. But rather, these could be challenges you can find anywhere you turn.

What do I mean by this? Well, more than mere puzzles, of course! Solving common problems such as puzzles or brain teasers can help you challenge your mind. But the real thing to incorporate here is a small scheme that can help you get out of your negative thought pattern every time. If you are unsure that you are thinking "out of the box" to the widest extent, then these teasers can help you out.

Here are a few common issues that every teenager faces:

1. A face filled with spots or pimples.
2. Feeling left out in social situations.
3. Feeling overwhelmed with school.
4. Not wanting to do homework every day.
5. Having very low self-esteem and a bad body image.
6. Difficulty connecting with friends.
7. Difficult connecting with siblings and/or parents.
8. Struggling at school.
9. Struggling to fit in in social situations.
10. Feeling unmotivated.
11. Not knowing what to do with yourself and your future.
12. Frequently arguing, with everyone.

Now, let's elaborate on one of these in this exercise. Let's go with number 3 - feeling overwhelmed with school.

The first step you're going to take is to identify the issue - which we have.

The second step is thinking about possible solutions. In this case, you can try to limit your distractions or ask for help.

The third step is to evaluate the solutions. For example, if you ask for help, you may learn more, and become better (one of the pros), but you may feel like you are losing your independence (one of the cons). Limiting your distractions seems like a pretty good idea so far.

The fourth step is to choose the best solution - which is in this case limiting the distractions.

The fifth and final step is to implement the solution. Always start small but do this every day. Start with 10 minutes or half an hour a day and work your way up - as long as you feel good and are comfortable with the process.

Now, go ahead and do some practice yourself.

1. The Problem: _____

2. Possible Solutions: _____

   _____

   _____

   _____

   _____

3. What is Good/Bad in Each of the Solutions?: _____

   _____

   _____

   _____

   _____

   _____

4. The Solution I Will Implement: _____

   _____

   _____

   _____

   _____

   _____

   _____

1. The Problem: _____

2. Possible Solutions: _____

_____

_____

_____

_____

_____

3. What is Good/Bad in Each of the Solutions?: _____

_____

_____

_____

_____

_____

4. The Solution I Will Implement: _____

_____

_____

_____

_____

_____

_____

1. The Problem: _____

2. Possible Solutions: _____

_____

_____

_____

_____

_____

3. What is Good/Bad in Each of the Solutions?: _____

_____

_____

_____

_____

_____

4. The Solution I Will Implement: _____

_____

_____

_____

_____

_____

1. The Problem: _____

2. Possible Solutions: _____

_____

_____

_____

_____

_____

3. What is Good/Bad in Each of the Solutions?: _____

_____

_____

_____

_____

_____

4. The Solution I Will Implement: _____

_____

_____

_____

_____

_____

_____

1. The Problem: _____

2. Possible Solutions: _____

    _____

    _____

    _____

    _____

3. What is Good/Bad in Each of the Solutions?: _____

    _____

    _____

    _____

    _____

    _____

4. The Solution I Will Implement: _____

    _____

    _____

    _____

    _____

    _____

1. The Problem: _____

2. Possible Solutions: _____

_____

_____

_____

_____

_____

3. What is Good/Bad in Each of the Solutions?: _____

_____

_____

_____

_____

_____

_____

4. The Solution I Will Implement: _____

_____

_____

_____

_____

_____

_____

1. The Problem: _____

2. Possible Solutions: _____

   _____

   _____

   _____

   _____

3. What is Good/Bad in Each of the Solutions?: _____

   _____

   _____

   _____

   _____

   _____

4. The Solution I Will Implement: _____

   _____

   _____

   _____

   _____

   _____

   _____

1. The Problem: _____

2. Possible Solutions: _____

_____

_____

_____

_____

_____

3. What is Good/Bad in Each of the Solutions?: _____

_____

_____

_____

_____

_____

4. The Solution I Will Implement: _____

_____

_____

_____

_____

_____

_____

1. The Problem: _____

2. Possible Solutions: _____

_____

_____

_____

_____

_____

3. What is Good/Bad in Each of the Solutions?: _____

_____

_____

_____

_____

_____

4. The Solution I Will Implement: _____

_____

_____

_____

_____

_____

_____

1. The Problem: _____

2. Possible Solutions: _____

_____

_____

_____

_____

_____

3. What is Good/Bad in Each of the Solutions?: _____

_____

_____

_____

_____

_____

4. The Solution I Will Implement: _____

_____

_____

_____

_____

_____

_____

1. The Problem: _____

2. Possible Solutions: _____

_____

_____

_____

_____

3. What is Good/Bad in Each of the Solutions?: _____

_____

_____

_____

_____

_____

4. The Solution I Will Implement: _____

_____

_____

_____

_____

_____

_____

1. The Problem: _____

2. Possible Solutions: _____

_____

_____

_____

_____

_____

3. What is Good/Bad in Each of the Solutions?: _____

_____

_____

_____

_____

_____

4. The Solution I Will Implement: _____

_____

_____

_____

_____

_____

_____

Try to do this with every issue you face in life. It is mind-altering how useful these steps can be.

You can still indulge in daily crossword puzzles, sudoku, chess, or anything you find interesting. These games are a fantastic way to enhance your logical thinking. But this exercise is the one thing you need to pull yourself back up. Sure enough, after a while, you will notice yourself thinking outside the box constantly.

SOLUTION IMPLEMENTATION PRACTICE

This last exercise is all about implementing a little bit of everything you've learned so far. The practice of implementing a solution includes understanding the challenge or issue, setting some clear objectives, designing the solution, and allocating the necessary resources to make it happen.

To solve a problem, you need to know how to approach it in a way that would result in a successful resolution. The thing is, as I mentioned earlier, you can't always be sure if what you have in mind as a potential solution would work or not. As the last exercise, this is the simplest one of them all – just try. Give it a go! I know that there may be many things blocking you from making a decision or thinking clearly, but as we are nearing the end of this book, you have to be honest – we did cover almost all of them, right?

So, what I want you to do is to choose one single problem you currently have in your mind. Then go through all the problem-solving steps. Once you have the solution you want to implement, then go and give the solution you have in mind a try. Even if it fails, today's chapter taught you that you can always go back to the brainstorming step and assess the situation from the beginning. Because the solutions you may come up with could be the best ones, but nothing will really happen if you never act on them.

What Did You Learn From This Chapter?

In this chapter, I am hoping to have given you the liberty to think positively with your mind. To challenge yourself every single time and hopefully to have nudged you in the right direction. Without challenges, there is no growth.

Let's make a short recap of what you've learned here:

- ✧ You learned the five steps of problem-solving skills.
- ✧ You had an exercise on how to implement the problem-solving practice.
- ✧ An exercise you need to implement daily – solving common problems.
- ✧ The last exercise that simply nudges you to begin.

So far, this book has been about uplifting you and pushing you forward in life. I can imagine what it must be like for you right now. You finally started believing that you can do anything you set your mind to, and you can create a better and more positive version of yourself. But what will happen if you fall back to your old self? Is there still a voice in the back of your mind telling you that you have a chance of failing, that everything would have been for nothing?

The book's last chapter is about permanently cementing everything you've learned so far. It is about preventing a relapse (should you get to that point). You see – I really did think of everything. I have been where you are and know what you're going through. So, turn the page, and let's take the final steps toward creating a better you – together!

CHAPTER 11

RELAPSE PREVENTION

"Life is very interesting. In the end, some of your greatest pains become your greatest strengths." – Drew Barrymore

With this lovely quote, I open up the book's last chapter. To be honest, Drew Barrymore could not have said it better – turning the pain into your strong side is one of the many joys in life. It is what makes you stronger, more resilient, calmer, more centered, and happier overall.

While all of this is true, word for word, you are still a human and a young one at that. You're still learning. Who knows how many times you're going to fall in life before you lift yourself back up? Each time that happens, you will probably want to get right back into the negative mindset, completely dismissing the CBT approach and everything you've worked so hard for. I understand – you may be faced with extremely challenging situations, which can damage all the progress you've made.

But that doesn't mean you should give up. On the contrary, it means that you should have something to fall back on. I understand where your fear is coming from. Maybe that little voice still tells you that you can never improve, even if you went through this entire book and completed all the exercises with flying colors.

Even if your conscious mind notices the change, your subconscious mind may still make you believe that you are not worthy of anything good. This is known as the turning point in the process, and it is when most people relapse.

Because your progress is important, I decided to dedicate this last chapter to relapse prevention. Let's discuss how to handle yourself in tough times.

Recognizing Warning Signs of Relapse

When you have undergone a program or have used an approach where your sole focus has been yourself, you may feel encouraged once you step out into the world. However, some of you may hesitate about everything because of fear. You may be scared that you will fail and return to your old self. I know that no one wants to have an immediate fear of failure once you step out into the unknown. That is why it is essential to create a relapse prevention plan. It will help you learn how to avoid relapse and will help you gain even more skills on how to handle yourself. Ultimately, it will be the final trick you will have up your sleeve that will keep you in check.

When you've worked so hard to make a better person out of yourself, you walked a long and challenging journey. With each step, you got out of your comfort zone, and you assessed the situation over and over again. The level of self-awareness increased, and everything about you unfolded in stages – right before your eyes. The unfolding part gives you a part of the answer. This is the first thing you need to look into if you have the fear of relapse. The more acute the self-awareness is, the easier it will be to spot any issues.

Ultimately, there are a few signs that can apply to anyone when we talk about relapse. They are:

⟡ **Emotional relapse** – the denial tends to be strong here. Emotional relapse is the most serious form of relapse here because, after all, we are focusing on thoughts, feelings, and behavior. You may notice feeling isolated and being emotionally reclusive as the first signs. Other than that, you start not being involved in any day-to-day activities, having negative views about yourself and others around you, having difficulty sleeping, and having a reduced concern for personal hygiene.

⟡ **Mental health** – you start lacking the resistance you worked so hard to obtain. Instead of focusing on the good, taking a step back, and assessing every thought and situation that needs your attention, you stop doing this. You slowly start going back to your old habit of immediately jumping to the wrong and negative conclusions. You notice how the exercises and knowledge you've gained over the past period of time slowly start to slip away from you. Your mental health stops being your priority, and you abide more and more by your past thinking patterns.

Noticing the warning signs of relapse can make you both aware and unaware at the same time. How come? Well, the unaware part is that voice that keeps telling you everything will go wrong, and you're not worth it. The aware part is that you know that you can do better, but you feel like you are constantly pulled under the surface.

Developing a Relapse Prevention Plan

Observing the warning signs I just mentioned is a step in the right direction. To fully prevent yourself from stepping back into your old habits means taking the warning signs seriously. The thoughts that cross your mind don't always need your attention or action. A part of developing a relapse prevention plan means controlling your levels of stress.

Learn to recognize each time when your stress levels go up and are unchecked – especially if you are dealing with anxiety issues. Experiencing anxiety means that you are dismissing the path of dealing with stress healthily.

The main part of your relapse prevention plan should be lowering stress levels. Thankfully, there are a few ways you can naturally achieve this. Here are some examples:

✧ Regularly exercising or indulging in physical activity of your liking.

✧ Keeping in touch with your friends and family and giving them a little bit of your time.

✧ Making a list of feel-good movies and songs that you can turn to every time you feel an onset of negativity creeping up on you.

✧ Always focusing on the positive mindset rather than the negative.

✧ Maintaining a healthy diet, filled with nutrient-dense foods.

✧ Journaling, or any other way of writing down the good things that come to your mind.

✧ Celebrating all the milestones you achieve in life, be those small or large.

Since I am ending this list on a celebratory note, I think it is high time to start looking into the strategies, right? The other biggest part of creating a solid relapse prevention plan is creating strong strategies that will help you maintain success. In other words, let's give the spotlight to the bright side of life!

Strategies for Maintaining Progress Over Time

Over time, it is critical to maintain effectiveness and progress. It is not just about reaching a certain point and then remaining there. No. You will develop as a person throughout your life. During this time, you will keep discovering new things about yourself. You will push your limits and strengthen your boundaries. You can't remain in the same spot your entire life – and you won't.

A part of relapse prevention is the list of strategies that can keep you on the right track every single time. And I am talking about much more than open and honest communication with yourself and with others. I am talking about seeing the good, focusing on the good, and achieving the good.

The trick is to keep yourself motivated. Why are you doing all of this? To create a better version of yourself. Do you want to keep working on this? Yes. Why? Because it makes you feel better and achieve more. Do you need to feel pressured about it? Absolutely not!

Find something that will truly motivate you. At this point, I can give you a little nudge in the right direction. Below, you will find a list of a few techniques or strategies that I have learned about along the way that have helped me remain on track. In order to keep on going, try implementing at least a few of them. That way, you'll know you will have done everything for yourself.

All of these are very easy to do. See for yourself below!

1. **A reward** – reward yourself for all the times you have overcome a certain challenge. As you work on yourself and your goals, you will constantly step out of your comfort zone. You will face an increasing number of challenges and give much effort to overcome them. As that happens, reward yourself each time you make it through. Whether it is a milestone you've set for yourself or the consistency you've maintained, never forget to treat yourself.

2. **Relax** – in all fairness, you can't constantly work on yourself. Everybody needs some time to relax, and you are no exception. You may have just gone through an emotional rollercoaster – that means you did quite a demanding job keeping yourself up! So, when you notice that a calmer period is coming, or you just feel like you need to recharge, give yourself that time. This type of recharging can be anything – from drawing yourself a bath to enjoying a hot beverage – anything that can relax you.

3. **Prepare for the day** – the best way to tackle things is not only one at a time but also one day beforehand. By creating a list of the things you need to do the following day, you can have a clear picture of your responsibilities and divide them into smaller sections. By doing this, you can overcome them very easily. Once you know success is guaranteed, nothing is stopping you!

4. **Be realistic and own yourself** – as I mentioned in the SMART goal frame, your goals should always be realistic. You need to be honest with yourself about how much time you would need to achieve or complete something. What I didn't mention is that you should always own your goals. Do whatever you want to carry out because something might constantly push you back or tell you not to do anything. Take responsibility for your actions and carry them out to the very end – you will be glad you did so.

5. **Indulge in a power hour** – when you feel like you have a lot more energy, focus it on something you've been putting on the back burner for a while. This could be any type of tedious task or something you didn't want to face yet. By putting things in the front line while you have energy, you take advantage of the perfect situation. Instead of doing nothing and then beating yourself up because you've done nothing at the time when you felt you could be active, you're doing something productive. This task could be anything – because you'll see that you will feel lighter as soon as you complete it.

These are only a handful of strategies you can implement to lift any remaining weight off your shoulders. They will slowly pave the way for progress. Before I wrap things up, remember this – progress is still progress, no matter how slow you move. And before you know it, time has passed, and you will look back only to see you've come a long way.

What Did You Learn From This Chapter?

As the last chapter of this book, its goal was to complete the circle – and give you the last bits of information you need to help you on your journey to reinventing yourself. Here is what you learned from it:

✧ The progress you make is as important as you say it is.

✧ Relapse can happen to anyone – there are a few warning signs that point to it.

✧ It is your responsibility to stop the relapse from happening by utilizing the relapse prevention plan.

✧ Other than prevention, you can always focus on the good – try using the strategies for maintaining progress over time.

I can only hope that the biggest thing you learned from this chapter is not to beat yourself up every time. Life will happen to you, whether you want it to or not, and you will not be prepared for what it gives you most of the time. However, you must remember how strong you are through all the challenges and especially, the curveballs. You can achieve anything you set your mind to and easily become the best version of yourself. There is no need to fear what's yet to come because whatever it is, through the power of this book, you can overcome it.

CONCLUSION

"I am the master of my fate; I am the captain of my soul." – William Henley

With this wonderful quote in mind, I would like to bid you one final adieu. As we reach the end of our journey together, I want to reflect on everything we've learned. Now, I am not going to do the regular "let's review what we've learned" since we did that at the end of each chapter. No. I will help you reflect on these lessons, as they will be the most valuable life lessons you will ever learn.

Through this book, you realized there is a way for you to shape your future and yourself, and you learned about all the different strategies you can implement to make that happen. Together, we highlighted the importance of self-control and accentuated your potential for continuous personal development. What you learned here is more than just another skill set. It is the cornerstone of creating a successful, fulfilling, and happy life. Once you realize that you have no trouble mastering self-control and that the CBT approach is the most successful one, you will have gained complete power over your life.

Making deliberate choices that align with your goals and values and what you aspire to be is important.

Managing your time is important.

Resisting falling back into your old ways is important.

Pushing through the most challenging times is important.

Self-control and CBT have helped you achieve just that. By utilizing the tools you found in this book, you will commit to life-long learning and self-improvement. I can only imagine the feeling you got while reading this book – that feeling comes from realizing that we are constantly evolving. There was always room for improvement and development. You just had to find a way to do that. At the end of the day, it is all about abiding by a growing mindset and opening yourself up to all life can offer.

Through all the steps you made while reading this book, you noticed that they are still significant, no matter how small they are.

Being a teenager is difficult. Being a teenager in the 21st century seems like the biggest challenge – especially when you're the teenager in question. I can understand that. I did understand that. That's why this book was filled with information that was helpful to you. You learned how to create new habits and keep yourself away from a life that was difficult and negative.

Before we part ways, I leave you with this – always surround yourself with people who are good for you. Always try to look on the bright side. Remember that the choices you make today pave the way for the person you will become in the future. Having full control over yourself and constantly learning is not something you achieve once – but rather something you work on every day. You are willing to make a change, and I know you have both the patience and the determination to make that change possible. Cultivate your mind and move forward through life. Carry the lessons from this book with you and allow them to guide you to create and control the life you've always wanted!

EMILY CARTER

DBT
WORKBOOK
for Teens

Easy & Proven Ways to Manage Anger, Anxiety &
Stress, Improve Communication Skills, and Develop
Healthy Coping Skills for Better Emotional Regulation
Using Mindfulness & DBT

INTRODUCTION

"Life is a balance of holding on and letting go."

– Rumi

You are about to begin a journey of self-discovery. I know you. You've come from a challenging place and want to see how to deal with whatever life throws at you differently. Being a teenager is one of the most challenging things you have gone through in life so far. As you navigate this exciting phase, you notice changes happening all around you – the dynamic in your family changes, your friendships grow and change, you enter a new school environment, and you also change and grow as a person, as well. You've probably even felt lost and insecure at times. That's why I'm here to give you a hand.

Don't think of this book as another self-help book. Think of it as a friend – one who will guide you through this exciting chapter of your life designed specifically for you. Here, you will learn what it takes to be a teenager in this world and how to find yourself, center yourself, and to simply – be yourself. The skills I focused on in this book are based on Dialectical Behavior Therapy (DBT). This powerful approach can help you manage your emotions and build your entire life from the ground up.

Understanding Dialectical Behavior Therapy

Dialectical Behavior Therapy, or DBT, is a type of cognitive-behavioral therapy that was originally developed to help people manage their intense emotions. Nowadays, it is the perfect tool for young people like you to develop some strong skills. DBT is built on the idea that two things can coexist and be true at the same time. A good example of this would be, accepting yourself for who you are but also wanting to change yourself. The balance between these two is what DBT is all about.

Right now, you feel like there is a rollercoaster of emotions – one minute, you feel like you are on top of the world, and the next minute, you feel like all is falling apart. The good news is that DBT will help you navigate these highs and lows even when you're struggling with stress, sadness, anxiety, or just the regular changes that happen within you while growing up. The DBT skills can help you collect all the tools you need at your disposal to tackle anything that comes your way.

Before we begin, it is crucial for you to understand that DBT consists of four concepts. These concepts are - mindfulness, distress tolerance, emotional intelligence, and interpersonal effectiveness. We are going to go through all of these concepts together. Just to give you an idea of what each of these represent, here are some brief explanations.

Mindfulness is the art of being fully focused and present in the moment. It consists of observing, describing, and participating without any judgement. It is considered the foundation of DBT. Through it, you can enhance your awareness and allow yourself to recognize your own thoughts.

Distress tolerance is knowing how to survive and cope with difficult situations. Here, it is all about soothing yourself and accepting the situation as it is. Life can deal you with some tough cards sometimes, and distress tolerance is important so that you can learn how to survive during these moments without engaging in harmful behaviors.

Emotional regulation is the ability to manage your emotions in what is considered a healthy way. Identifying and managing your emotional responses is crucial if you want to maintain emotional balance. This way, you can enhance your overall well-being.

Finally, interpersonal effectiveness is knowing how to communicate with other people in a way that exudes confidence and respect. As an aspect of DBT, it can help you navigate social situations and build long-lasting relationships.

All of these concepts tie together to create a comprehensive framework that will help you deal with any kind of emotional challenge that comes your way. As you go through this book, you will notice how strong and important they are.

How to Use This Workbook?

Using this workbook to your advantage will be easier said than done in some situations. But, looking at the bigger picture, you will realize that this book is meticulously divided into sections that focus on the core DBT skills. Every section comes with incredible explanations, is easy enough to understand and implement, and is filled with exercises and examples. These can help you apply what you've learned in real-life situations. To answer your question of how to use this workbook, the best way to do that is through the exercises. They are extremely beneficial, and all you need to do in most of them is to take notes, and sometimes have a partner to talk to (depending on the exercise).

Through the book, you will find many ways to use DBT skills to overcome the challenges you're faced with in life every day. Some of the examples can be your reassurance – you're not alone, and you've never been alone in this.

Before we dive right into the subject, let me tell you something important – you already are as capable and strong as you wish. Just think about this – you are here, reading this introduction, getting ready to read the book that will ultimately shape your life. You are ready to take control. The path is filled with obstacles. It will not be easy. Sometimes, you may want to give up, but I am here to help you power through and make it to the other side. This book is designed to help you every step of the way.

Work through these skills, make mistakes along the way, and allow yourself to grow. Be patient, as change takes a lot of time. Count all small steps you take as victories and get ready to start the journey – because now, it is time for you to turn the page and begin!

Part 1

MINDFULNESS

"To a mind that is still, the whole universe surrenders."

– Lao Tzu

There is a certain connection between your mind and your relationship with yourself and everything else around you. This certain kind of connection you have is special. It is unique, and depending on how well you nurture it, it will either flourish or perish.

In this first part, we will talk about mindfulness and how to stop whatever you are doing and start focusing on yourself. Because remember, the star of this book is you. The work you will be doing while reading is unmatched – and you will only get to realize that once you are done with the last page. I will have managed to describe every aspect you should focus on. Now, it is yours to accept and grasp the term mindfulness with both hands.

But that's not all. In this part, I will help you explore a few other important aspects of DBT - these include the wise mind, the what skills, and the how skills. You might see them as confusing terms now. However, as we delve deeper into the book together, you will notice how all of them are connected. There is not one without the other. It is all about getting a better understanding of what lies ahead for you. While you want to paint the big picture now, remember that any big picture consists of small things. From mindfulness, to the how skills, these are the small, yet significant things you are going to explore.

What Is Mindfulness?

Mindfulness. This word signifies an incredible concept of being fully present in the moment. It elaborates on the fact that your mind is completely present. Whether you are doing something, moving through a certain space, or you are fully invested in what is going on.

For a young mind such as yours, this may seem like a strange concept. You may even ask, "Well, isn't my mind present all the time?" and you are right to do so. It may even sound illogical as a statement, except it isn't. The mind works all the time, and often, it can steer us away from the moment we're currently in. You've probably felt it before – it simply takes off in the middle of a situation, and you start to lose touch with your senses, your body, and so on. As soon as you know it, this is something that can make you feel absent in an instant.

Sit with this for a while, has this ever happened to you? It must have at some point by now. That is why I am starting this book with the concept of mindfulness. Because everything you will ever learn from this point on connects back to it. Mindfulness is more than the human ability to be fully present in the moment – it is the pillar upon which this book is based.

The good thing about mindfulness is that you already have it within you. This is not something you need to work to obtain (like a degree), it is already present. All you need to do is learn how to access it and nurture it.

Are you still feeling a little bit confused? I've created a small list of things that can help you understand the concept of mindfulness. Think of them as facts, something that cannot be changed.

- ✧ Mindfulness is a familiar thing. You already do this every day, but up until now, you haven't been aware of it.

- ✧ Mindfulness is not some special thing you can be or do. You hold a spectacular power to be present within yourself, and you do not need to change to harness it. All you need to do is cultivate it.

- ✧ Mindfulness recognizes your full potential. Every solution that requires change from you should not be implemented. Mindfulness helps you cultivate the best of who you are as a human being.

- ✧ Anyone can do mindfulness – specifically because it has the potential to grow into a transformative phenomenon. You can really benefit from it, and it is an easy thing to focus on.

- You can easily turn mindfulness into a lifestyle. It is more than just a practice. By doing that, you will slowly implement a caring and an awareness approach to every aspect of your life.

- It will spark up your entire life. Mindfulness comes with many benefits, including happiness, improved relationships, better work, wilder imagination, and innovation, as well as effectiveness and resilience.

But of course, you are not here to learn just about mindfulness. We both know that this is only the beginning. Next, you are going to delve a little bit deeper into your mind.

WISE MIND

Wise mind - more famously known as the "aha" moment in DBT. I already mentioned that DBT is an abbreviation for dialectical behavior therapy. It is kind of like a talk therapy that can help you understand your emotions as well as your behavior. Within this book, you are going to learn how to incorporate that into your everyday life. Remember that the whole purpose of DBT is to help you accept the reality of your life and your behavior as well as to help you enjoy it to the fullest extent.

I am aware that until this point, everything sounds completely new to you, but you will soon find out that everything serves its own purpose. And the wise mind is only the first concept for you to understand. Well, a wise mind is not something you have. It is a technique. The wise mind is the core aspect of DBT, and it is based on the concept that there are three states of mind – a reasonable mind, an emotional mind, and a wise mind.

The wise mind represents the absolute optimal state. This is the place where emotions and rational thinking come together. The wise mind allows an individual to make a solid and sound decision based on both, so it is something that aligns with their goals and values. As a technique, the wise mind is very successful and powerful because it can help you strengthen your mind, especially when you are feeling a little distressed. It includes mindfulness exercises so you can make the most out of any situation.

The good thing about the wise mind is that it comes with many qualities and characteristics. By cultivating it, you can navigate many challenges that come your way. Here are some of them:

- You get to work on your intuition. The wise mind technique can help you get a better understanding of what comes within you and can guide you toward taking the appropriate action.

✧ After using it for a while, your ability to clearly see any situation or issue is improved. You are objective and don't allow strong emotions to overwhelm you.

✧ The wise mind is the perfect way to incorporate some balance into your life. The reason behind this is to incorporate both the rational and the emotional aspects, helping you find the exact middle between them.

✧ As you incorporate the wise mind technique into your life, you open yourself up to an authentic experience. Instead of being led by external factors, you delve deep into your true, authentic self.

✧ A life of compassion is what follows. Cultivating the wise mind means you will foster a feeling of empathy, understanding, and compassion – both toward yourself and others.

It seems that navigating challenges will be easy after reading this, right? We are only at the beginning, so let's move on to discovering how to integrate both the reasonable and the emotional mind.

As a concept, the wise mind relies on the merging of the reasonable and the emotional mind. The reasonable mind is the analytical one, the one that looks at every situation logically, while the emotional mind represents the intuitive aspect of it all. When you combine the two together, you can make sound decisions.

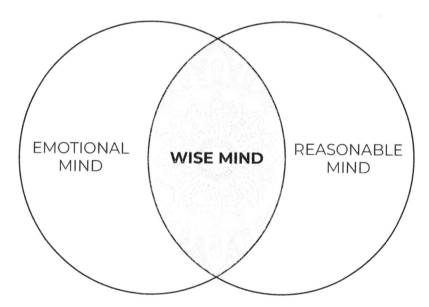

There is an importance behind doing this. By balancing the reasonable and the emotional mind, you can start effectively solving problems and making decisions. Why is that so? Well, think about it. Say you need to make a decision. A large one. If you only look at it from a logical point of view, you may come to a very robotic and detached solution. But on the other hand, if you only include your emotional side in it, you might make an impulsive and irrational decision.

That's why I love to focus on both aspects. While doing that, you discover a whole new part of yourself too – a balanced one. Using the wise mind means you consider your goals and values, but also your well-being. And once you find it – you never go back.

You learn that when emotions are the only thing driving your decisions, you may become moody and reactive and act in a way that is not really typical for you. As you are a teenager, I can understand how emotions can get in the way sometimes. That's probably the main reason why you started reading this book in the first place. Without the help of a little bit of logic, you will only rely on your impulsivity.

It is time to take a look at the first exercise.

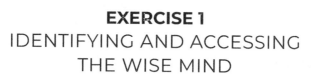

EXERCISE 1
IDENTIFYING AND ACCESSING THE WISE MIND

The first of the many exercises you will find throughout this book is identifying and accessing the wise mind. As you can see, we already explored the topics of reasonable and emotional mind – now it is time to put them both to good use!

As you can see, cultivating mindfulness is a crucial thing if you want to access the wise mind. You need to be present in the moment and be attentive – fully aware of your feelings, thoughts, and body. I mentioned earlier that it is all about balance – the perfect combination between emotion and reason. Here is how you can identify and access your wise mind.

It is all about using mindfulness. Find a space where you feel comfortable and do the following (you can either sit down or do this standing up):

⬦ Take a minute to pause and take a deep breath.

⬦ Clear your mind from everything, and focus on you, both physically and mentally, in that moment.

⬦ Focus on the current thing that constantly occupies your mind. This can be anything - an idea, a plan, or maybe an emotion.

⬦ Sit with it for a minute and recognize it fully. Allow yourself to recognize the sensations you have with that idea or thought in your mind.

⬦ Now, it is time to access the wise mind.

⬦ Ask yourself, "How can I benefit from this plan/idea/action/thought? Is this connected to my wise mind?"

◇ Allow yourself to listen to both the emotion and the logic. The answer is somewhere in between. If it helps, take notes.

◇ Before you finish this thought process, check if the decision you are making causes you any imbalance of emotion or reason. Remember, the wise mind should also give you peace of mind.

If you don't know how to check in with yourself, it is always good to follow the breadcrumbs – your body. I have noticed that many people, especially young people, experience the wise mind in the center of their body or between the eyes. To complete the process, try to allow yourself to enter a meditative state. Try to intentionally bring awareness to these body parts and see how you feel. Notice the thoughts and the feelings. If you are making the right decision, you will feel calmer, centered and ready to get back into reality.

_____

_____

_____

_____

_____

_____

_____

_____

_____

_____

_____

_____

_____

_____

_____

_____

_____

_____

_____

_____

_____

_____

As you continue reading, you will discover a lot of new things about yourself. And I will be there every step of the way, making it easier for you to understand the process of balancing yourself and your emotions. The next thing we're going to look into is the mindfulness skills. These are considered the foundation of all DBT skills. They are also known under a different name – the what skills and the how skills. Remember earlier in the chapter, when I mentioned this? Well, first off, we are going to start with the what skills, and then we are going to move on to the how skills.

WHAT SKILLS

The issues that are addressed with these mindfulness skills can help you know who you are, what you want to do with your life, and how to obtain it. These skills can even help you control what's going on in your mind. The "what" part from the what skills refers to the ways of practicing your thinking – what you do to take control over yourself. The three ways that I'm about to share with you are important, and all of them can help you whenever you are dealing with an issue or need a change. They are - observing, describing, and participating. I will go into detail for each of them below.

01.

Observing

Observing is about being present in the moment and opening up all of your senses to every experience - your touch, sight, smell, taste, and hearing. The lens of your senses can be extremely powerful, and during the observation of the present moment, you utilize all of them. When you observe, you experience without ever labelling the experience. In the beginning, you may find yourself struggling with this, and that's okay. After a while, you will notice the quiet benefits of this skill. You will learn how to observe without your mind talking as much.

It will be difficult for you to watch thoughts go by, as there is always a little bit of temptation included, which is also something that can help you get "caught up" in the experience. When you get caught up, this may mean you are becoming obsessed, where you preoccupy yourself with something, and you can't stop thinking about it. With the power of observation, the goal is to stand back a little bit. I do not want you to detach from the situation entirely but rather take a step back and try to view it objectively.

Another thing here – I know it is tempting for you to react to every thought you have in this situation – especially to the negative ones. These thoughts can make you want to leave a specific situation. But the challenge of being observant means experiencing something without judging whether it is good or bad. In this situation, you let all the thoughts go by.

EXERCISE 2
BODY SCAN

Let's make two exercises connected to this observing skill. In this first exercise, I advise you to sit down, or even lay down on a yoga mat or a carpet. Try to completely relax and feel yourself, your entire body. Focus on your breath and notice how your body inflates and deflates with every breathing cycle. Now, you should do a body scan. Start from the top (or from the bottom) and work your way through every part of your body. Really feel and pay attention to every part of your body - arms, legs, torso, hair, neck, everything.

Now, notice your thought pattern. You are a teenager, so chances are – there is something about yourself that you don't like. Say, for example, you don't like your legs. As soon as you think about them, you immediately have negative feelings. By using the power of observation, notice these thoughts – but allow them to flow through you rather than being stuck with them. It may take you a while to get there, so I recommend you practice this whenever you get a chance.

When I want to connect with myself, I always start from the bottom and work my way up. If you don't know where to begin, this is a good starting point. Start from the feet and feel them (one at a time). Consider this to be almost of a spiritual practice. While you observe, you also connect on the highest possible level. The goal here is to be connected with every part of your body, know all its edges and how they make you feel. Now, we were talking about the feet. Start with whichever one you like, and really feel it. Is it in pain, is it pulsating (maybe if you've walked for a longer time before you did this exercise)? Acknowledge any sensations you feel around it - is it cold, hot, or incredibly comfortable? Do you have a sock on your foot? How does that feel too? This exercise is all about becoming more aware of sensory experiences - and ultimately, more accepting of them. This exercise is about training the mind rather than relaxing it. After a short while, you will see how it makes you feel a little more centered, and helps you connect to any sensations you're feeling without judging them.

EXERCISE 3
OBSERVING THE SURROUNDINGS

It is interesting to see how many things surround us. These things are incredible – just take a look at what surrounds you at the moment. It seems almost incredible, right? In this exercise, it is about observing your environment. For example, if you are at home, during the day, or in the office, find a sunny spot. Give it a minute and notice the sun's rays penetrating through the windows and illuminating the room. Allow the opinions to wash over you once again, and to let them flow.

On the other hand, if you are outside, try to be even more observant. Do the surroundings change often (meaning – are you a part of a crowd)? Or maybe you're in a park? Observe with all of your senses, and allow the feelings to sink in.

02.

Describing

The next skill we're talking about is describing. This, in simple terms, means putting into words what you have observed. However, it still means describing an experience without any judgment.

This act of describing the responses and the things that happen around you (or to you) can provide you with the ability to label events and behaviors. When you start describing a situation that makes you feel a certain way (either good or bad), it helps you observe it more objectively and make a clear connection between yourself and what surrounds you or what is happening.

The goal here is to use the skills of observation and description together to help you stay in the present moment. Together, they will provide you with the focus you need.

EXERCISE 4
DESCRIBING THOUGHTS, FEELINGS, AND SENSATIONS

It is important to learn how to describe everything you think and feel – and not consider those things as facts. Your state will constantly change, and for example, if you feel afraid, it does not necessarily mean that there is a real danger around you. So, in this exercise, you will learn how to describe your thoughts, feelings, and sensations.

Pick one thing that you do every day – your morning or night routine, cooking a meal, walking, or playing with your pet – yes, this can be anything. Start by observing the experience while you are doing it. As you notice every single detail (even some details you have missed before), start describing the experience without judging it. For example, you might be one of those people who don't close the toothpaste after using it – and you might associate that with a feeling of laziness or indifference. Try to remove these "obstacles" and just describe to yourself what you are doing. Describe the experience, the sensations, every little thing.

_____

_____

_____

_____

_____

_____

_____

_____

_____

_____

_____

_____

_____

_____

_____

_____

_____

_____

_____

_____

It is quite a revelation when you look at what you have described. This will give you a sense of who you are, what interests you, and what you notice the most, as well as give you an insight into your thought pattern. Except in this situation, it will look as if you have taken a step back and you are looking at the situation objectively – meaning you're on the right path.

EXERCISE 5
"I FEEL" STATEMENTS

Now, take things a step further – and feel.

During this exercise, we are going to label emotions. There are probably at least a handful of times in life when you felt disappointed, happy, sad, angry, content, etc. In this fifth exercise, you will learn how to verbally describe your feelings in a given moment.

This is an exercise you can do next time you find yourself in a situation that makes you feel a certain way. Until now, you have most likely relied on the factor of the emotional mind, leading to a possible outburst in many situations. But now, try to do this exercise. Something happens to you – maybe a friend or a sibling tells you something you don't like, or a situation starts making you feel uncomfortable. Rather than an outburst and creating an even bigger situation, try to step back and – use the wise mind. Observe whatever you think and feel during that given moment, and then state it. Make the "I feel" statement. Say, "I feel sad you acted that way", or "I feel disappointed in you."

Let's try to put this into perspective by examples. The "I feel," statements would be ones that reflect your present state, but they should be ones you realize will pass and will be resolved with time. So, here are a few examples of when a bad scenario presents itself before you. This is the best time to use these statements. You can also use the following for practice.

1. When you get caught up in a verbal altercation with a friend.
2. When you notice that your parents are pushing you to your limit.
3. When you have a misunderstanding with your sibling.
4. When you expected someone to do something for you, and they failed to deliver.
5. When someone promised you something, but they didn't fulfill it.

6. When you feel cornered by a teacher or educator because of a certain thing you did or didn't do.

7. When you are all alone with yourself, and you have this surge of negative feelings coming on.

8. When your romantic interest is not interested in you anymore.

9. When you feel trapped in a social situation.

10. When your best friend does something to you, intentionally (or not).

These sayings come from a valid point – but saying them out loud not only helps you create a better communication channel with someone else but also with yourself. These sayings are also a reflection of what is happening at the moment. They are not facts; they are just thoughts or feelings, so there is no need to cling to them like facts. I would encourage you to put them on paper as this is the easiest way to exercise them. Write down the "I feel" statements and keep doing that until you feel comfortable with yourself to communicate them with the people around you.

Situation: _____

I feel... _____

_____

_____

Situation: _____

I feel... _____

_____

_____

Situation: _____

I feel... _____

_____

_____

_____

Situation: _____

I feel... _____

_____

_____

_____

Situation: _____

I feel... _____

_____

_____

_____

Situation: _____

I feel... _____

_____

_____

_____

Situation: _____

I feel... _____

_____

_____

_____

Situation: _____

I feel... _____

_____

_____

_____

Situation: _____

I feel... _____

_____

_____

_____

Situation: _____

I feel... _____

_____

_____

_____

Situation: _____

I feel... _____

_____

_____

_____

Situation: _____

I feel... _____

_____

_____

_____

Situation: _____

I feel... _____

_____

_____

_____

Situation: _____

I feel... _____

_____

_____

_____

Situation: _____

I feel... _____

_____

_____

_____

Situation: _____

I feel... _____

_____

_____

_____

Situation: _____

I feel... _____

_____

_____

_____

03.

Participating

The final "what" skill we're going to dissect is the participating skill. It means completely immersing yourself in a certain activity. It means jumping head-first and allowing yourself to be involved in the moment. Doing this helps you to let go of self-consciousness and be completely present in whichever activity you're indulging in. When you participate with awareness, you can completely enjoy the moment without having to overthink every step of the way or be "half-present" in the moment. Participating is an excellent skill to use if you are feeling stressed.

In order to participate, all you need to do is actively practice the other skills and then immerse yourself in this one. Instead of closing this cycle with dissociation and not really remembering or enjoying something, do the opposite. Participate. This is the perfect way to start actively practicing these DBT skills until they become a part of who you are.

EXERCISE 6
MINDFUL PRACTICE

That leads us to the sixth exercise. Mindful practice means being active and aware. For this exercise, try to do something that you do often (like washing the dishes, eating, or something else). But this time, try to pay full attention to everything. Concentrate as hard as you can and notice every single thing you're doing. Then, try to do every single thing as well as you can. Take washing a piece of fruit as an example. Take the fruit (let's say it's a pear), go to your kitchen sink, and turn on the faucet. This is something you unconsciously do every time - but in this case, try to feel the whole process. Do you turn the water all the way to the coldest or the hottest point? Or do you maybe rinse your piece of fruit with lukewarm water? How does it feel? Notice the water going through your hands and between your fingers, onto the skin of the pear. Notice how gentle you are so you don't damage the fruit. Be as specific as you can while doing this task. Then, take a pen and write down how this made you feel - being mindful and completely present in the moment.

Activity: _____

How being mindful made me feel: _____

_____

_____

_____

Activity: _____

How being mindful made me feel: _____

_____

_____

_____

Activity: _____

How being mindful made me feel: _____

_____

_____

_____

Activity: _____

How being mindful made me feel: _____

_____

_____

_____

Activity: _____

How being mindful made me feel: _____

_____

_____

_____

Activity: _____

How being mindful made me feel: _____

_____

_____

_____

Activity: _____

How being mindful made me feel: _____

_____

_____

_____

Activity: _____

How being mindful made me feel: _____

_____

_____

_____

As I mentioned earlier, the basis of everything in this book revolves around the concept of mindfulness. The skills we're looking into together are all connected to it, and they are considered the foundation of DBT. After reading through the what skills, you are probably aware of what I'm talking about. You've probably noticed that the issues addressed by these skills will help you realize who you are and what you want out of life. These skills will also help you control what's happening in your mind, resulting in you living in the moment and focusing on the now.

HOW SKILLS

The second set of skills we will tackle are the how skills. These are just as important as the what skills, and their focus is helping you practice mindfulness. DBT has truly paved the way for any person to develop themselves into the form they want, and these skills are the perfect beginning to that adventure! To deepen your practice, you should follow these three skills that I have outlined for you below. They are – nonjudgmentally, one-mindfully, and effectively.

01.

Nonjudgmentally

The first one is being nonjudgmental. As people, all we do is judge – especially teenagers. But if you are a person who is constantly judged for your behavior, looks, or anything else – you will probably understand this the most. After all, you are in the middle of those teenage years where, frankly – kids can be mean.

I am sorry to be the bearer of bad news, but judgment continues throughout your entire life. You judge others, but mostly, you judge yourself. The thing is, you need to understand that judgment as a form can possibly lead to the creation of a highly hostile environment – both inside and outside your body. It can lead to guilt, shame, sadness, and so much more.

That's why I would like to dedicate some time to learning how not to judge. The point here is to allow yourself to observe everything you've observed until now but open up to a different kind of thinking. It is not about withholding your judgment but rather understanding it. Observe your thoughts as if you are observing a different person. Treat yourself more gently. The judgemental thoughts will slowly start to fade away because, at given moments, you will begin practicing the most powerful act – of letting go.

EXERCISE 7
PRACTICING SELF-COMPASSION

I mentioned that the most judgment you are ever going to receive in your life is judgment from yourself. As human beings, we are all flawed, but it seems like we keep forgetting that at times. That is why I designed this exercise – to remind you that, if you want to make sure you're viewing the world with compassion, you need to begin with yourself.

Say you're trying to observe a situation, and it is just not working out for you. You keep getting distracted, and other things keep popping up in your mind. You start to spiral, and before you know it, you blame yourself for your entire behavior without ever giving yourself the benefit of the doubt.

The exercise is as follows – you notice that you are starting to go down that rabbit hole, but you don't know how to stop. Start by noticing every sentence that goes through your mind and every negative thought about yourself. With each sentence, take a step back and analyze it. Here's a small example of it. You start thinking about that friend who let you down or said something mean to you. Then, you start thinking about whether they actually don't like you (or maybe they never did?). This is the time when you need to stop going down the rabbit hole, because you are practically spiralling - you start thinking you don't have any friends, or that this particular friend doesn't care about you, and so on. Bring yourself back to the surface by reminding yourself that anyone can have thoughts and feelings that do not coincide with yours at some point.

Then, ask yourself this – are each of those spiralling thoughts true? Or is it something that is derived from the emotional mind (which is usually activated when we don't have full control over a situation)? Remember to do this every time you feel like your self-compassion levels are low. Below, you can find some lines to take notes.

EXERCISE 8
CHALLENGE JUDGMENTS

Challenging yourself about yourself is one thing – but challenging yourself about judgments towards the outside world is a whole new thing. In this exercise, let's try to do that together, shall we?

Say you're in a situation where you're meeting a new person – and you instantly start to judge them. Once you notice yourself doing this, it means you are on the right path of mindfulness. Notice all the thoughts going through your mind and witness how they form. Question them. Why are you thinking this? Is the person standing opposite you really that bad? Or is it something that may have derived from another experience you've had with another person in the past – that reminded you of them? It is important to start recognizing these thoughts in your head. Don't forget to take notes of your observations.

_____

_____

_____

_____

_____

_____

02.

One-Mindfully

The second one is one-mindfully. This is a skill that will come up as you are reading this book in one way or another. The idea behind it is that whatever you are doing, you should be doing one thing at a time. It is about finding mindfulness in everything you do. For example, if you are learning, reading, or working, do that. Don't play music in the background. Try not to turn the TV on or have some kind of other noise happening. Or when you're with someone else, say a friend, try to be with them, present in the moment, instead of constantly looking at your phone.

The idea behind this is that you can give your full attention to something and do your best to maintain it. Doing this will help you stay in the present moment rather than having your attention divided all over the place. So, you see, mindfulness truly has a lot to do with the level of awareness you bring into your life. Focusing on being present in the moment, giving your undivided attention to what you are doing – there is no greater feeling than that. Most of us, all through our lives, are distracted. Whether it is by images, feelings, thoughts, or even worries – we constantly try ways to steer clear of the present moment. Once you get used to this, it's a little challenging to put everything away and focus on only one thing.

Being one-mindfully is an excellent way to pull your attention to what is happening at the moment. With it, you can absorb the information and take part in the present.

However, the most important thing to remember here is that you always need to be patient with yourself. It takes time to master this skill, and while some of you may achieve this in a shorter time period, others may need some more time. In the beginning, if you're having trouble focusing on a task, try to remove all the distractions from your surroundings. Observe everything that surrounds you and pinpoint the things you need to remove. Choose one thing that you'd like to focus on and start doing it slowly. With time, this will become an unconscious process.

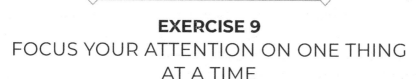

EXERCISE 9
FOCUS YOUR ATTENTION ON ONE THING
AT A TIME

That is precisely why I have chosen this to be an exercise as well. In life, sometimes you need to stand still and let go of every thought and emotion. It is with this exercise that you're going to do just that. Let's try focusing your attention on one thing at a time.

Stand in the middle of a room. You don't even have to do anything – just watch. Now, choose a couple of objects around the room. Then, try to focus on one subject (say, a chair). Take a deep look at the chair and try not to think of anything else. Notice the materials, the patterns, the shapes – pay full attention to the chair. At that moment, you should completely forget about the other items you've chosen or that there is anything else in the room. After you've observed one thing, try to shift your focus to another thing. Do this process with a few objects just to get started. Before you know it, you will be able to do this in a heartbeat, with everything.

03.

Effectively

The third one is effectively. As a word, effective is something you're going to hear a lot. The goal here is to know you're effective every time you focus on what works. Instead of thinking whether something is right or wrong, you should focus on understanding how to accept and work with a situation as it is. Effectively means allowing yourself to let go of the need to be right. When you are determined to be right, it may cloud your judgment and make you come to the wrong conclusion or decision. Being determined to be right all the time can be a very challenging thing.

Effectiveness is knowing how to tolerate and accept a situation or a person you don't really like. Effectiveness is knowing you are right but still letting go because fighting something and proving how right you are don't really align with your values anymore. You are simply – better than that. By accepting a situation where you know you can't change things, you show the actual signs of growth.

EXERCISE 10
ALIGNING ACTIONS WITH VALUES AND GOALS

For the last exercise of this chapter, you are going to need a pen. The goal is to access your values, and then make goals based on them. But, to assess your values, you need to start somewhere, right? Well, start by thinking about the values that you hold in your life. Now start writing. Let's go step by step.

Think about what matters most to you in life. Write down 5-10 values that come to mind. These can be anything. Here are some examples:

- ✧ I value respect for myself and others.
- ✧ Gratitude for what I have is important to me.
- ✧ I believe in the strength to overcome challenges.
- ✧ I value honesty and being true to myself.
- ✧ I care deeply about kindness and helping others.

MY VALUES

1. _____

2. _____

3. _____

4. _____

5. _____

6. _____

7. _____

8. _____

9. _____

10. _____

Based on the values you wrote down, create goals that reflect them. Here are a few examples:

- ✧ If you value respect, a goal could be to strengthen your relationships.
- ✧ If you value success, you might set a goal to achieve something specific in your studies.
- ✧ If you value gratitude, your goal could be to practice it daily.
- ✧ If you value honesty, a goal could be to communicate more openly with people.
- ✧ If kindness matters to you, a goal might be to volunteer or support a cause regularly.

MY GOALS

1. _____

2. _____

3. _____

4. _____

5. _____

6. _____

7. _____

8. _____

9. _____

10. _____

Now, write down actions you can take to reach your goals. These should be small, specific steps that align with your values. For example:

- ✧ Respect - make an effort to listen more in conversations.
- ✧ Success - break your big goal into smaller tasks and tackle them one by one.
- ✧ Gratitude - start a gratitude journal and list three things you're thankful for each day.
- ✧ Honesty - practice expressing your thoughts clearly, even when it's difficult.
- ✧ Kindness - offer help to someone in need or do something nice for a friend or stranger.

ACTIONS

1. _____

_____

2. _____

_____

3. _____

_____

4. _____

_____

5. _____

_____

6. _____

_____

7. _____

_____

8. _____

_____

9. _____

_____

10. _____

_____

It is important to answer this truthfully as it can help you align your actions with your beliefs and values. In most cases, the answer is straightforward. You either take some action that aligns with these values, or you don't. The exercise is to create goals that align with what you believe in. The action should match your value. If it doesn't, think about what you need to change in order for that to happen. Write that down, and then remind yourself that you have a goal every time your mind feels like it starts to go down a rabbit hole.

What Did You Learn in This Chapter?

This is a chapter that only opened the doors for you toward a whole different world. Out of everything you've read, here is a summary of what you learned in part 1:

✦ The concept of mindfulness.

✦ The power and the characteristics of the wise mind.

✦ The importance of what skills – observing, describing, and participating.

✦ The importance of the how skills – non-judgmentally, one-mindfully, and effectively.

As we close the part on mindfulness, we embark on an adventure – and right into the second part! There, we are going to discuss everything connected to distress tolerance – what it is, learning how to refine it – everything. So, turn the page – and let's discover some wonderful new things together!

Part 2

DISTRESS TOLERANCE

"The real man smiles in trouble, gathers strength from distress, and grows brave by reflection."

– Thomas Paine

In the first part of this book, we began by highlighting mindfulness. I did mention that mindfulness will be the foundation upon which you will build yourself up. So, this second part is about something that is closely connected to the topic of mindfulness. It is a sort of an extension of mindfulness.

Let's start from the very beginning. If you have never heard or thought about it until today, we will discuss distress – and everything connected to it. Later on, as the chapter unravels, we will also include much more information linked to it. All of this will help you regulate your emotions and increase your interpersonal effectiveness.

What Is Distress Tolerance?

Have you ever asked yourself if you are a person that gets agitated quickly? I mean, you are a teenager, so this is kind of "a given". But how do you perceive yourself? Considering we have removed the factor that you are in your teen years?

Distress tolerance is your ability to manage perceived emotional distress. It includes making it through an emotional episode without worsening the situation. People who are dealing with low distress tolerance may become a little overwhelmed whenever they come face to face with a stressful situation. Sometimes, when this happens, they may even turn to a very unhealthy or destructive outlet that would help them cope with it.

But the thing is – everyone experiences stress every once in a while. You've probably found yourself experiencing stress, too. You can experience stress over everything – a fight at home, bad grades, lost romantic interest, etc. No matter how small or large this stress is, it can affect your ability to manage that particular situation. Sometimes, you can notice how it's more difficult for you to manage strong negative emotions such as guilt, anxiety, fear, shame, anger, and sadness. The stronger the emotion is, the more difficult it is to control it.

Poor distress tolerance can be a very challenging thing. The first thing you need to do in this situation is to identify the emotions you're experiencing. However, as a teenager who doesn't have that much experience on the topic, identifying such strong emotions may be terrifying. The relief you may get from a self-destructive measure is only a short-term one. The truth is that every distressing emotion can make matters worse and pile up feelings of guilt and shame, ultimately leading to you being even more upset.

Thankfully, there is some good news behind all this! After all, that's why we're here. There are many techniques we can work on together to help you cope with the intense emotions you have. These healthy distress tolerance outlets are perfect! With their assistance, you can create a long-term outlook on dealing with every challenging thing in your life.

Increasing your distress tolerance can be an effective way to help yourself regulate your impulsivity and anger. This can come with many other benefits, ultimately leading to you living a calmer, happier, and more serene life.

Before we go into the techniques to work on, let's look at the factors a bit. Oftentimes, you need to realize that what you are feeling is okay, but it has not been within your control because you were not aware that such a background exists with emotions in the first place.

For example, there may be biological influences on distress tolerance. The temperament you have may just be the indicator of the level of difficulty you're met with each time you face a challenging situation.

Another example is distorted beliefs. Suppose you are intolerant when it comes to challenges. In that case, you may find yourself thinking you're always upset about something, that you will never feel better, and that everything is terrible, or you hate everyone – or everyone hates you. These types of thinking patterns can make it more challenging for you to come up with upsetting events. While these are automatic thoughts, they often result in avoidance, withdrawal, and even self-harm.

I know that, while reading this, you already felt a little bit distressed, but don't worry. The reason why we go deeper into this subject together is to help you come out the other side better, stronger, and happier. With that in mind, let's move on to the distress tolerance techniques.

Distraction

The first one is distraction. This can be a very easy way to take action and thus increase your distress tolerance level. It usually includes various methods that can help you take your mind off of things. The different methods can be as follows:

✧ Distract yourself by doing something you like – when times get tough, turn your attention to something you really like to do. It can be anything, as long as it is an activity that will help you become fully present in the moment.

✧ Distract yourself by focusing your attention on someone else – it is about realizing that sometimes, more than just one person goes through a difficult period. Depending on your situation, there will often be other people involved. Some of the distractions you can indulge in include people watching (sitting outside on a bench and quietly observing people), calling someone (a friend or a relative, just to check on them, and see how they are), or going outside and physically meeting someone.

✧ Distract yourself by doing chores – probably the most effective (and used) approach of all is distracting yourself by throwing yourself into work. There is a certain satisfaction in completing a task, something you cannot feel with anything else. So, when you're facing a difficult situation, it is time to find all the things you've put on the back burner and complete them. The chores can be anything – from rearranging your clothes to doing your dishes, redecorating – anything that will make you feel like you are doing something important – because you are.

While we discuss these simple yet effective distraction methods, it is important to realize that they are here not only to help you cope but to help you in the long run as well. Consider utilizing them whenever you feel stuck or have a strong sense of negative emotions washing over you. I must warn you – it will be challenging in the beginning! You may not be able to focus on one thing at a time or anything because you still haven't completely succeeded in controlling your emotions, but don't worry! Practice makes it perfect, and the sooner you start, the better!

And while we are on the topic of practicing, it is time to move on to the next exercise.

EXERCISE 11
IDENTIFYING HEALTHY AND UNHEALTHY DISTRACTIONS

This one is connected to how you perceive things as good and bad. We already learned that distractions are coping mechanisms – but some can have a positive effect, while others can negatively influence your overall life. In this exercise, I am going to help you differentiate between them and pay close attention to what is good and what is bad.

Take out a pen and paper, or use the worksheet below, and imagine a scenario where you are challenged in a certain way. You've faced a difficult situation, and now you need to know how to healthily cope with it. But also, before you start writing things down, consider everything you've read so far in this chapter.

Now begin – divide your piece of paper by drawing a vertical line down the middle of it. On the left side, write healthy; on the right, write unhealthy distractions. Keep that scenario in your mind. It may even help more if you have multiple scenarios or past events just to compare your behavior. In some cases, you may have turned to things such as sleeping a lot, avoiding the issue, shutting down, overeating (or not eating enough), and so on. These are all the unhealthy distractions you've participated in – so you can put them in the right section. Now think about all the cases where you faced the issue at hand; be understanding, indulge in physical activity, or talk to someone about it. All of these things are healthy distractions, and they can actually help you cope.

Healthy Distractions

Unhealthy Distractions

_____

_____

_____

_____

_____

_____

_____

_____

_____

_____

_____

_____

_____

_____

_____

_____

_____

_____

_____

_____

_____

_____

_____

_____

_____

_____

_____

_____

_____

_____

Even though these might not have necessarily been the things you wrote down, you get the idea. To know which of all the responses should go in the left and which ones should be in the right section, think about this – there is a certain result that comes with every little thing we do. This is an essential thing to remember when it comes to distractions. The result may be you end up feeling better – or worse. That's how you know what is healthy and what is an unhealthy way to cope with things. Out of all the things that crossed your mind, how many of them have truly made you feel calm and better? Focus on them because these are the good things, the productive distractions.

Radical Acceptance

Has it ever happened to you to face a situation that is so difficult you thought it would be impossible to accept it? Maybe you had a falling out with your best friend, or a very bad grade, or a fight with your parents. This can be anything that has made you feel like everything around you is falling apart, and you can't really deal with it. This is where the second skill comes in handy – and it is radical acceptance.

Sometimes, trying to cut out all the unnecessary drama in life is advisable. It is also advisable to accept a situation as it is. After all, there is a lot of relief behind that, so why not try it? Things are not in your control anyway, and there is no harm in letting go. By doing this, you practice radical acceptance.

Think of it this way – you are not accepting the pain or approving of it in any way. On the contrary, you simply allow yourself to focus on what is in your control and what you can do. It is all about creating a shift in your energy. Rather than preparing for war and leading with your emotions, you start to plan your next move and do that with a calm and clear mind.

You should accept radical acceptance if you're willing to go through life's challenges stronger than ever. As a part of DBT, it is a technique that includes embracing the present moment. The situations you may find yourself in the middle of during your life can be highly challenging. Some of them may even be borderline unbearable. Radical acceptance comes into place when things seem almost impossible. I'm talking about situations where most people would run from. Radical acceptance means facing all these challenges without trying to avoid or change them.

So, how does radical acceptance function?

The thing you need to realize here is that it is not about acceptance. You cannot just be okay with a situation that is obviously far from optimal, right? Radical acceptance is just acknowledging a situation – as it is, without any judgment. At that moment, you stop fighting reality. I know that this is a lot easier to read about than to do in actual life, but the more of it you accept, the more resilient you become. This technique is created to help you build some tolerance against distress. Because this is where the real magic happens, radically accepting reality, with all its painful parts, can help you open the door to personal transformation and growth.

Radical acceptance comes with many benefits. All you need to do is truly commit to it. The few reasons why you are developing this as a skill, are to start cultivating self-compassion, increase your tolerance to distress, to no longer fight what cannot be changed, to improve your ability to cope and solve issues effectively, to stay away from harsh judgment, and deepen your capacity to accept things in all areas of your life. Picture radical acceptance as a threshold you need to cross to get to the other side happier. But, in order to achieve this, you will need to practice it. I have prepared a couple of exercises for you to try. But before that, let's talk a little about how to practice radical acceptance.

All of this may seem simple in theory, but it can be quite challenging in practice. But, to master it, you still need to practice it. To do that, here are a few steps I always like to incorporate. These steps have helped many other people as well as myself, so I am sharing them with you so that after much practice, they can become your "second nature".

- ✧ You may discover you are constantly fighting against your reality (complaining or wishing that everything was different).
- ✧ Then, you start acknowledging what reality is, even if you don't really like it. You notice that you can't change anything about the situation.
- ✧ You make the choice to accept the situation as it is and breathe into the discomfort of it all.
- ✧ You start embracing self-compassion. There are many painful emotions as you go through the process, but you suddenly realize that beating yourself up about it will only make things worse, not better.
- ✧ Finally, you start to shift your focus. At that exact moment, you ask yourself what the next thing you can do to be effective and take better care of yourself is.

The trick with radical acceptance is that you need to start small and know how to cope properly. The change process is long, so you also need to be compassionate and patient with yourself. If you need some more time to master this – take the time. Don't put pressure on yourself. Go through the exercises I have prepared for you and guide yourself toward the new realm of acceptance and understanding.

EXERCISE 12
ACCEPTING DIFFICULT EMOTIONS

This exercise is about embracing change and accepting the things that cannot be changed. Radical acceptance is not always easy, but that doesn't mean you can't incorporate it into your life – starting today. Think about it this way – there are a few statements you can say whenever you are faced with a challenging situation. After all, the most difficult part of radical acceptance is to go through and feel the emotions, no matter how hard it is.

Take a pen and paper, or use the worksheet below, and sit down. Think of a situation where you felt like your entire world was turned upside down. Think of the most difficult situation you've ever been in and the feelings that you have. If you haven't gone through the process, you might still notice the negative emotions surfacing. Accepting difficult emotions is about knowing how to handle them. Now, you're going to start handling them by using coping statements.

To get you started on this, here are a few examples:

- ✧ I am able to accept the present moment as it is.
- ✧ I know I will get through this no matter what.
- ✧ I will survive, and this feeling will pass.
- ✧ I can't change what happened in the past, but I can learn to let go and focus on the present.
- ✧ Fighting my negative emotions only makes them stronger. I now allow them to wash over me and pass.
- ✧ I can choose to create my own path despite the negative history.
- ✧ I don't need to judge, just to take the appropriate action toward the future.

✧ I can get through all the complex emotions, even though they seem like the most difficult thing to do at the present moment.

You can either use these, create your own coping statements that would work best for you, or make a mix of both. Some of the examples you can take from your own experience include:

✧ My fallout with my friend does not define me as a person.

✧ When I look in the mirror, I choose to see the good.

✧ My bad grade does not mean that I will fail at everything.

✧ I love myself no matter what.

✧ My romantic interest may not be interested in me anymore, and that's okay.

Either way, these can be an excellent reminder that tomorrow will be better than today and that you already have all the tools to accept difficult emotions.

Situation: _____

Coping Statement: _____

_____

_____

Situation: _____

Coping Statement: _____

_____

_____

Situation: _____

Coping Statement: _____

_____

_____

_____

Situation: _____

Coping Statement: _____

_____

_____

_____

Situation: _____

Coping Statement: _____

_____

_____

_____

Situation: _____

Coping Statement: _____

_____

_____

_____

Situation: _____

Coping Statement: _____

_____

_____

_____

Situation: _____

Coping Statement: _____

_____

_____

_____

Situation: _____

Coping Statement: _____

_____

_____

_____

Situation: _____

Coping Statement: _____

_____

_____

_____

Situation: _____

Coping Statement: _____

_____

_____

_____

Situation: _____

Coping Statement: _____

_____

_____

_____

Situation: _____

Coping Statement: _____

_____

_____

_____

Situation: _____

Coping Statement: _____

_____

_____

_____

EXERCISE 13
DIFFICULT SITUATIONS

As you can realize, radical acceptance is a skill that gets better the more you practice it. In this exercise, together, we are learning how to cope with difficult situations. To improve your engagement in radical acceptance, you need to know how to take the proper steps in a difficult situation. Here are the steps – all you need to do is memorize them and try them out next time you come face to face with an almost impossible situation.

1. Think about resistance. Certain cases act like triggers; notice them. It is only in those situations that you cannot accept something.

2. When something difficult happens, remind yourself that you cannot change the situation.

3. Then, remind yourself that things are absolutely out of your control.

4. Think about what would happen if you started to accept the situation as it is. Imagine what it would be like to receive the problem.

5. Suppose it is not possible to do that. In that case, you can always utilize some relaxation strategies such as journalling, self-reflection, and mindfulness practices to help you understand your emotions and what you're going through.

6. Allow yourself to feel safe in your skin and feel all the emotions.

7. Observe what kind of an effect they have on your body. Does your chest feel tight? Do you need to breathe deeply? Is there any pain?

8. Always remember that life is still worthwhile, even with a lot of pain in it.

9. Practice this acceptance process whenever you feel like you have some issues with a particular situation.

These magnificent steps can help you stop thinking about how things could have been and help you start thinking about the things that are at the moment. These steps will help you stay present. To know when these steps are best used, here are a few example situations for you. These include situations that you might have already been in by now. If not, they will give you a perfect starting point so you can brainstorm some situations that actually have happened to you. As you read them, think about something similar happening to you. You can also use the lines below to make some notes.

- ✧ When you have an argument with a friend at school, and you feel a lot of emotions.
- ✧ When you want to explain something to someone, and it looks as if they don't understand you - and you get frustrated about it.
- ✧ When something you see happening reminds you of a certain situation that happened to you.
- ✧ When it looks like you may need some help to repair something.
- ✧ When you come face to face with a challenge.

_____

_____

_____

_____

_____

_____

_____

_____

_____

_____

Self-Soothing

In life, you're always going to face some ups and downs. There will be plenty of moments of happiness, but also there will be some tough times too. Before I go into the following technique, this is a gentle reminder for you – you live in a very fast-paced world. As humans, we are not created to endure as much as we do. So, when you're feeling emotionally distressed, just keep in mind that it is okay.

That leads me to the topic of self-soothing. DBT is designed in such a way to help you navigate tough situations with so much ease. It teaches you how to be constructive and deal with every situation healthily. Out of all the tools and techniques we're going to cover in this book together, this one is both the most effective and the most challenging. The self-soothing means using all the senses you have to bring calmness into your existence. It comes with a set of sensory strategies (the two exercises in this section will help you with that), so let's get started.

The interesting thing about self-soothing is that it is connected to the distress tolerance. When you are in the middle of a situation that causes some intense emotions, the one helpful thing is to try to relax in the moment using your senses. In these moments, self-soothing can help a lot because you feel highly overwhelmed, and you need a pleasant sensation to calm down. Self-soothing skills focus on the five senses of taste, hearing, smell, sight, and touch. In those moments when you feel incredibly distressed, you might find it difficult to navigate through this and get back to your senses. However, you can always rely on self-soothing skills.

Get ready to go through some trial and error while you practice this. Still, in the end, you will experience the ultimate stress relief from it. The goal here is to practice this for as long as you need until you are confident you can turn to them whenever you need them.

Since it is about engaging the five senses, let's take a look at each of those senses individually, shall we? Below, I am sharing some suggestions with you. These can be your starting point as you go through your soothing journey.

◇ Let's start with sight. Whenever you feel distressed, turn to something that means a lot to you – for example, take a look at a picture of your partner (if you already have one), your family, or your pet – as long as you feel the love overflowing you while you look at it.

◇ Move on to the sound. In a stressful situation, all people, especially teenagers, have found sound to be the most soothing thing they can turn to. Put on some music and allow the feeling of calmness to wash over you.

✧ Taste something. A simple thing such as chewing your favorite gum can help you recenter and feel much better instantly. Your favorite meal may just help you bring yourself back to yourself again.

✧ Try using your smell. Another incredible thing about different scents is that they remind us of different things. To calm yourself down at a given moment, you can always turn to your favorite perfume, lotion, or spray. There is a certain mindfulness to smelling something that reminds you of good times.

✧ The final one is touch. A soft blanket, a favorite toy, or your most comfortable clothes – touching something that feels comfortable is one of the best ways to calm down in a stressful situation.

Self-soothing as a concept seems relatively straightforward, but when the time comes for you to actually utilize it, it may feel like it's a little more than just challenging. That's why I've created two excellent exercises where you can get the most out of this skill.

EXERCISE 14
RELAXATION

There is a little bit of science behind the relaxation exercise, specifically because it is paired with muscle relaxation. Allow me to explain this a little more. Lay down, or sit down comfortably in a chair, and completely relax your entire body. Now, to fully relax your muscles, try to breathe in and out deeply and slowly, and slow down your heart rate with it, too.

Focus on one group of muscles and try to tighten them. Hold for a few seconds, and then relax. Allow them to rest for a few seconds before doing that again. Each time you tighten and relax your muscles, you slowly release the tension. Go into detail, and as you inhale and exhale through the process, feel your muscles relaxing, one at a time. Once you notice that one group of muscles is relaxed (for example your arms), you can move on to the next group of muscles and so on. As soon as you know it, your entire body will feel completely relaxed.

EXERCISE 15
BUILDING A SELF-SOOTHE KIT

Before I moved on to the exercises, I mentioned the five senses – touch, sight, hearing, smell, and taste. This exercise can help you combine them in order to create a self-soothing kit that is a perfect fit for you. Let's put the words into action!

Take a pen and a piece of paper (or use the worksheet below), and on one side, write all the five senses. Now, with the help of the examples I presented above, start to brainstorm. Dedicate some time to each sense and think about what calms you down. Try writing down a few things next to each sense. For example:

Sound – the sound of waves crashing on the shore, the sound of my favorite playlist, etc.

As soon as you're done writing this and brainstorming about each sense, take a look at what you've written. Right now, you have, in your hands, your own self-soothing kit. It is designed by you, for you, and as long as you are completely honest while writing it, this can help you every time you feel distressed. Think of this as your first-aid kit. Whenever you find yourself in a challenging situation, simply go back to it, open it up, and use all the power that is placed inside of it.

Sight _____

_____

_____

_____

Sound _____

_____

_____

Taste _____

_____

_____

Smell _____

_____

_____

_____

Touch _____

_____

_____

_____

Pros and Cons

Moving on to the pros and cons. I know the thought that crossed your mind right now – the pros and cons are relatively easy to do, and you already know what they are. But not in DBT terms. The pros and cons of DBT are very different from the mainstream pros and cons we all know. *The way DBT views pros and cons is by focusing on tolerating vs. not tolerating or coping vs. not coping.* In other words, pros and cons in a distressing situation using DBT means looking at all the consequences of all the potential actions you may take.

Since the exercise here would be a little bit larger, we can move on to it together. Study the method and discover how to make the most of this DBT skill.

EXERCISE 16
PROS AND CONS WORKSHEET

The best way for me to describe this skill is by putting it in motion. Picture a difficult situation – it can be something you make up as you go or a past situation that stuck with you. It can be anything – a challenge at home, school, or friends. Now, think about your initial response to that situation. Is it filled with outbursts, with a lot of emotions, and with a response that you could barely control? This is something we're trying to change through this exercise.

Write down the initial response that automatically came to your mind. Now, it is time to create the pros and cons worksheet. Divide your piece of paper into two sections and write the pros in one and the cons in the other section. You can also use the worksheet below.

Now, when you write the pros and cons of this specific situation, you will do that by utilizing DBT. Answer these questions:

- ✧ How can you step out of this situation with success?
- ✧ Can you get what you want out of it?
- ✧ Are you used to being in distress?
- ✧ What would happen if you spoke up?
- ✧ How can you tweak the initial response to get better results?

Write all the answers down and separate them into the cons or the pros section. As you look at the piece of paper with all the emotional and logical things included, you end up realizing that there may be more to the story (taking a look at things from the other side's perspective) and that you can always choose what you act on (emotions, logic, or both).

Here are a few example situations for you:

1. You have a fight over different opinions with a friend.
2. You get scolded by your parents for something you did or didn't do.
3. You failed to deliver a project at school.
4. You bailed on your friends without explanation.
5. You had a fight with your sibling.

Let's take one of these situations as an example for our answers. For example - failing to deliver a project at school. How can you respond to that? Let's take a look at a few example answers:

1. You may come up with a constructive answer that shows the reality of the situation.
2. You may panic and start crying.
3. You may communicate with your teacher and ask them if you could finish the project and deliver it at a later date.
4. You may blame someone else for you not being able to complete the project on time.
5. You may break down completely and argue with your teacher.

Now, think of the consequences of each one of these answers. For some answers, the consequences are good, and for some, they are bad. You can easily categorize them. To make the most out of every situation in the long run, you need to respond calmly and honestly. That way, you can act on both logic and emotion.

Situation: _____

Initial Response: _____

_____

Pros: Cons:

_____   _____

_____   _____

_____   _____

_____   _____

_____   _____

Situation: _____

Initial Response: _____

_____

Pros: Cons:

_____   _____

_____   _____

_____   _____

_____   _____

_____   _____

Situation: _____

Initial Response: _____

_____

Pros: Cons:

_____   _____

_____   _____

_____   _____

_____   _____

_____   _____

_____   _____

Situation: _____

Initial Response: _____

_____

Pros: Cons:

_____   _____

_____   _____

_____   _____

_____   _____

_____   _____

Situation: _____

Initial Response: _____

_____

Pros: Cons:

_____   _____

_____   _____

_____   _____

_____   _____

_____   _____

_____   _____

Situation: _____

Initial Response: _____

_____

Pros: Cons:

_____   _____

_____   _____

_____   _____

_____   _____

Situation: _____

Initial Response: _____

_____

Pros:

_____

_____

_____

_____

_____

Cons:

_____

_____

_____

_____

_____

Situation: _____

Initial Response: _____

_____

Pros:

_____

_____

_____

_____

_____

Cons:

_____

_____

_____

_____

_____

Situation: _____

Initial Response: _____

_____

Pros:

_____   _____

_____   _____

_____   _____

_____   _____

_____   _____

_____   _____

Cons:

Situation: _____

Initial Response: _____

_____

Pros:

_____   _____

_____   _____

_____   _____

_____   _____

Cons:

What Did You Learn From This Chapter?

As we slowly close this chapter, this is the part where we reflect upon everything we've discovered together so far. While your journey is just getting started, you have done an amazing job up to this point. Let's see what you can take away from this part with you:

- ✧ What is distress tolerance, and how to increase it.
- ✧ Distraction as a powerful distress tolerance technique – and how you can utilize it.
- ✧ Radical acceptance – one of the pillars of DBT and a skill that can serve you the most.
- ✧ How to come to terms with difficult situations by incorporating the self-soothing skills – what are they, how powerful are they, and how easy it is to use them.
- ✧ The magnificence of making a pros and cons worksheet – they are very different from the pros and cons you're used to.

As the mind becomes stronger and healthier, so does the body. Until now, we have focused on bringing together all aspects of DBT and utilizing them in your mind. In the following section, we will shift our focus and gain a whole new perspective on things. Turn the page and start the next chapter – because it is all about properly dealing with your emotions!

Part 3

EMOTIONAL REGULATION

"I don't want to be at the mercy of my emotions. I want to use them, to enjoy them, and to dominate them."

– Oscar Wilde

It is always important to keep your emotions in check. As you can see from what you read so far, you can't really shut them out. Emotions are important, and they are a healthy way to express yourself. But when is it "enough" of emotions? Until now, we have talked about matters of the mind, but now we get to talk about matters of the soul.

You communicate with yourself and with other people through emotions. It is an excellent way to create relationships and approach situations. But as a teenager, you may not always know how to control your emotions. Sometimes, they come in large shipments, and you don't know what to do with them all. So, you unload them. You unload them on yourself, and on the people around you. At the moment, while you're doing that, it even feels like a storm is happening inside of you. But once the moment has passed, you look at things differently, from another (calmer) perspective, and you may notice that you've created chaos.

It is just as challenging to control your emotions as it is challenging to control your thoughts. That's why, in this part, you will uncover everything you need to know about your emotions. I will start from the very beginning, so get ready – because it is quite an interesting process to go through!

What Is Emotional Regulation?

Emotional regulation means taking action to alter the intensity of any emotional experience. Many of you may think that this is a way to hide and suppress your emotions when it cannot be farther from it. Emotional regulation means having the ability to have full control over your emotions through many approaches.

As you go through your life, you will notice that some people are better at regulating their emotions. These people seem to have a higher emotional intelligence, and it may seem like they are fully aware of their experiences within and the experiences of those around them. These people seem naturally calm.

While this is true – these people are calm – they still experience a fair share of negative emotions. They have just managed to regulate their emotions properly. Emotional regulation is not something you have or don't have – it's something you improve and master over time. In life, you will face many challenges and difficulties, which can take their toll on your physical and mental health.

This is why emotional regulation is so important. Slowly, you are reaching the stage of adulthood, and as an adult, you are expected to regulate your emotions that fit with the "socially acceptable way of handling them". It is known that when emotions get the best of us, sometimes they lead to issues.

The thing is, there are many things that can influence emotional regulation. Every stressful situation you've ever had to deal with provoked powerful emotions from within. I have mentioned this a few times throughout the chapters.

Now, you are aware that you may hurt relationships by not taking charge of your emotions. It is the kind of emotional volatility that can make a change for the worse. You may end up saying or doing things you never meant to do in the first place.

Other than having an overall negative impact on any relationship, feeling overwhelmed can cause unnecessary struggles and suffering. If you don't start dealing with it, then you will have to deal with a lifetime of not having new opportunities and experiences.

It is all about maintaining a positive reaction - that's what this chapter will delve into. The thing we're learning here is how to properly respond to a challenging situation, and together, we are going to cover a few important things.

First, we're going to start with opposite action, and a few exercises that can help you develop it. Then, we are going to move to learning how to focus on the positive. Finally, we are going to focus on ourselves, and our physical health as well.

Opposite Action

Putting those words into action is something you will start doing now! It is time to fully control your emotions and discover the power of emotional regulation! Opposite action will teach you how to do just that!

When all emotions are activated, they make us respond in a certain way. It seems like we are almost pre-programmed to do that with all of them. The opposite action is a skill that can help you respond completely the opposite of how you normally would. This is how you get ready to act and take control over yourself. Of course, this means focusing on the negative emotions only whenever you want to take the opposite action.

That leads me to the first exercise of this part. Here it is below.

EXERCISE 17
RESPONDING OPPOSITE TO INTENSE EMOTIONS

It is all about learning how to recognize and deal with your emotions. Yes, it will take a lot of practice to make this happen, but this exercise is an excellent starting point. Once combined with the other ones from this chapter, they bring together all the aspects of emotional regulation you need to know and practice.

For this exercise, think of five emotions you feel most of the time. Keep in mind that they should be negative emotions. Write them down on a piece of paper, or on the worksheet below, and write how they make you act. Now, after you're done with that, write down the opposite reactions of these emotions. It is a kind of role-playing where you think of the opposite reaction to your intense emotions. For example:

When you feel shame, you have the need to hide.

But the opposite of shame is keeping your head up and facing anything head-on.

When you feel depressed, you feel like you want to curl up and stay away from the world.

But the opposite of that is going out, getting active, and staying in touch with everything and everyone.

When you feel anger, you want to attack or defend yourself.

But the opposite is to show concern and kindness – or simply walk away.

Create this list and stick to it – especially if you want the negative emotions to go away and for you to feel less uncomfortable. This is the perfect skill – along with the belief you hold within that this kind of exercise will work!

Emotion: _____

Action: _____

_____

Opposite Action: _____

_____

Emotion: _____

Action: _____

_____

Opposite Action: _____

_____

Emotion: _____

Action: _____

_____

Opposite Action: _____

_____

Emotion: _____

Action: _____

_____

Opposite Action: _____

_____

Emotion: _____

Action: _____

_____

Opposite Action: _____

_____

Focusing on the Facts and Problem-Solving

Problem-solving seems like a relatively easy thing to do. Once you are met with an issue, you need to figure out the best course of action and then proceed to resolve it. The thing is, while it all sounds good "on paper", it's not that easy to do in life. Sometimes, you may find yourself in situations where there isn't really a way out – at least, that's how it seems in the beginning. I am here to tell you that problem-solving, as a technique, cannot truly exist if it is not connected with the former one – and that is focusing on the facts. Fact-checking and problem-solving skills as a part of DBT are essential and should be looked into immediately.

The main goal of this skill is to help you manage and regulate your emotional response by looking at the facts and the facts only. It is about examining the facts supporting your feelings, assumptions, and thoughts. This process can help you differentiate between judgments and interpretations. And if you haven't been aware of it by now – these two can often distort emotions. Focusing on the facts as a DBT skill can help you both with emotional regulation and with distress tolerance. You will see, once you finish this book, that all of the skills and techniques you will uncover here are connected.

Now, let's do some work! Here are the steps you need to take in order to check the facts when it comes to DBT:

- ✧ Identify the emotion. Look within yourself to find out what you are feeling and why you are feeling that particular emotion.
- ✧ Identify the event next. What happened to you that triggered the emotion you're dealing with at the moment? Can you pinpoint that?
- ✧ Clarify your thoughts. A certain chain of thoughts started roaming around your mind as you felt those emotions. Identify those thoughts –they could definitely be connected to a belief you hold on to.
- ✧ Start looking at the facts – and checking them. Evaluate the situation and whether the emotion and intensity match the facts of your situation.
- ✧ Create a new response. After you look at the emotions and the facts, it is time for you to check if they align. If they don't (which will probably be the case), you need to change your emotional reaction and create one that suits the facts better.

As you can see, this is the perfect DBT skill for a teenager – because you are the ones who struggle with emotions the most! Also, you are the ones who have the most difficulty distinguishing between the reality of a situation and your thoughts. Fact-checking means improving your emotional intelligence. Fact-checking can help you draft healthier responses to any kind of situation.

And, if you think that this is not something that's created for you – think again. This DBT skill can be used by anyone who needs some assistance managing their feelings, emotional responses, negative thoughts, or anything else. While this is an incredibly powerful tool for adults who want to improve their emotional intelligence, teenagers can benefit from it in the same way. After using this skill for a while, you will notice that you can resolve conflicts better, you can improve your overall well-being and enhance your mental strength. While I am on the topic of how this skill can help, why not look at all the benefits that come from it? Here, I am sharing some of the best ones with you, hoping to get you practicing this skill as soon as possible!

- ✧ Your emotional intelligence will improve. As a skill, fact-checking can help you better understand your emotions and the triggers behind them, thus resulting in improved self-awareness on an emotional level.

- ✧ You will stop reacting as impulsively. Granted, your parents probably say this will happen to you once you step out of the teenage era and into adulthood, but this is not always the case. It is all about analyzing if the emotions fit the facts. Doing this can help you reduce any overreactions and emotional responses that are not adequate for the situation you're dealing with.

- ✧ You will improve your problem-solving skills. A clever approach once means a clever approach again. After some time, this kind of clever approach will help you get a clearer scope of the situation and will give you the assistance to make rational decisions and seek effective solutions.

- ✧ You will improve your relationships with the people around you. Once you have a better understanding of your emotions, you will lead not only with your mind but also with empathy. As you understand that, your connections with the people around you will grow stronger and better.

- ✧ You will enjoy improved mental health. Nowadays, it seems like mental health is a topic often communicated among people – and for a good reason. By implementing this approach, you can strengthen your overall mental health and maintain it at an optimal level.

- ✧ Your self-confidence will skyrocket! Yes, I do mean this! When you do good, you see good, and you are good, you will end up feeling good! Gaining control over your emotions will lead to increased self-esteem and much more confidence when you handle a challenging situation in your life.

So, you see, the sole act of focusing on the facts will help you go a long way, especially because it will help you become a little more rational and turn to that corner of your mind that we mentioned earlier – the wise mind. Speaking of which, let's move on to the exercises connected to the fact-checking aspect of DBT.

EXERCISE 18
CHALLENGE IRRATIONAL THOUGHTS

When you're focusing on the facts, it means that you are challenging everything you believe in. It's true – this is when your entire belief system is being broken down. So, in order to start that up, you will need to challenge every irrational thought that goes through your mind. Let's talk about checking the facts.

Sit down and think of a situation where you had arrangements with people, and you've been looking forward to spending time with these people. Now, imagine that, in that particular situation, the people you were supposed to meet cancelled on you at the last moment. Now, think about how that would make you feel. Would you feel nervous, sad, or angry? Or maybe some other feeling you associate with when facing such an event? As soon as the emotions surface, it is time for you to do that fact-checking. Here are the steps you're going to take.

1. Identify the emotion first. For example, in this case, you might feel very angry.

2. Identify what caused you to feel that way. The cancelation of plans.

3. Start describing the event. How did you feel when you initially heard that? What was the first thing that crossed your mind? Did you start thinking that they don't appreciate your time, or they're just pulling your chain, or they don't care about you, and they never have?

4. Start with your interpretation. Go deeper into what you thought and felt. Why does this make you feel this way? Go deeper and find the reason.

5. Now check the facts. Has this been the first time these people have cancelled on you? Or maybe you've cancelled them a few times before, and they seemed fine with it? Did they apologize to you?

6. Come out with the facts. After you start rationalizing a little bit, things will easily start to put themselves into perspective. It is completely understandable to feel annoyed, disappointed, or even sad about the entire new situation, but the situation is really not that important to be that angry about it. You slowly start to realize that the extreme response you have does not match the severity of the situation – especially if there is a reasonable explanation behind it.

7. Start formulating a new response. How would you react the next time such a situation happens to you? Would you know how to properly formulate your response? Remember that while it is always okay to feel slightly disappointed, that is not an excuse to blow the situation out of proportion. It is all about checking the facts and then comparing them to your current emotions, thoughts, and feelings.

This exercise of checking the facts will help you rationalize and will help you calm yourself down every time you feel like a strong surge of emotions is coming to the surface. Here are a few situations when you can use this:

1. Whenever you feel anxiety about a social event.
2. When you are having an argument with a friend (or just had one).
3. When a crush rejects you.
4. Whenever you feel like your parents are criticizing you a lot.
5. Whenever you fail an exam.

Emotion: _____

Reason for the Emotion: _____

Describe the Event: _____

_____

_____

_____

Go Deeper: _____

_____

_____

_____

Facts: _____

_____

_____

_____

Your New Response: _____

_____

_____

_____

_____

Emotion: _____

Reason for the Emotion: _____

Describe the Event: _____

_____

_____

_____

Go Deeper: _____

_____

_____

_____

Facts: _____

_____

_____

_____

Your New Response: _____

_____

_____

_____

_____

Emotion: _____

Reason for the Emotion: _____

Describe the Event: _____

_____

_____

_____

Go Deeper: _____

_____

_____

_____

Facts: _____

_____

_____

_____

Your New Response: _____

_____

_____

_____

_____

Emotion: _____

Reason for the Emotion: _____

Describe the Event: _____

_____

_____

_____

Go Deeper: _____

_____

_____

_____

Facts: _____

_____

_____

_____

Your New Response: _____

_____

_____

_____

_____

Emotion: _____

Reason for the Emotion: _____

Describe the Event: _____

_____

_____

_____

Go Deeper: _____

_____

_____

_____

Facts: _____

_____

_____

_____

Your New Response: _____

_____

_____

_____

_____

EXERCISE 19
PROBLEM-SOLVING TECHNIQUES

The second exercise is connected to the aspect of problem-solving. The truth is that how you feel about a problem is more important than the actual problem. This is a saying you will learn to be true after this exercise. Sometimes, when you come face to face with a certain situation, you may feel insecure and unable to solve the issue at hand. Whenever you don't know how to proceed, you need to come back to this exercise. Well, this is not particularly an exercise but more of a set of techniques you can use to find yourself on the other side – with any situation or issue solved. Take failing an exam as an example:

1. Feel better about it – to start feeling better about failing the exam, you need to know how to regulate the emotions that surface. This may look like the opposite of what your gut is telling you, but it works. By exposing yourself to an uncomfortable situation, you may start to regulate your emotions better.

2. Tolerate it – here, I'm not talking about keeping quiet about the situation and turning a blind eye, but rather tolerating a situation you probably cannot change at the moment. This is the time to identify the problematic feelings and thoughts you have and try to bring yourself back to the present moment.

3. Stay in the current position – this may come as a shocker, mainly because we are working toward creating an attitude that will help you control your thoughts and emotions, but it is true. Sometimes, you may need a minute to deal with the shock of a certain situation. In this case, if the situation happens to be that serious or shocking, think of it this way – give it a minute. If you are not ready to rationalize and shift your perspective, then simply don't. Allow yourself the time you need to become calm and collected.

There are many people out there who believe that solving an issue can only have two outcomes. Sometimes, things are not as black and white as they seem, so whenever you feel like it, give yourself the time to calm down before you start exploring the right solution. Here are a few situations when you can make that happen:

1. Whenever you're coping with some friendship issues.
2. Whenever you feel like you have peer pressure.
3. Whenever school is starting to get to be too much for you.
4. When you have a conflict with a teacher.
5. When you struggle to properly manage your time.

Focus on the Positive

Easier said than done, right? But the thing is, increasing positive emotions is an essential part of creating an overall good life. Thankfully, there is an aspect of DBT that focuses just on that. Other than teaching you how to regulate and deal with negative emotions, it encourages you to focus on the positive ones. Focusing on the positive means providing you with more skills to help you manage emotions rather than the alternative – being managed by them. By doing this, you will even reduce your chances of negative emotions (and vulnerability caused by them) and will start building a positive emotional experience.

You need to understand here that you are not trying to put the positive emotions in place of all the negative feelings you've had. You are learning how to put them both in the same place. They should coexist, and as long as they do, it means you understand that sometimes the negative emotions will rule, and sometimes the positive emotions will rule – but no feeling is final.

That means building up the positive emotions does not mean you completely dismiss or remove the negative ones. You are simply expanding your experience. Now, in the beginning, this may be very challenging for you, especially if you have learned to focus on the negative for a long time. Thankfully, everything can be undone, and with the help of this DBT skill, so can the constant negative thinking.

To help you out, just so you can get started, there are a few ways to build positive emotions – both by including emotional experiences in your life. The first is focusing on short-term experiences, and the second is focusing on long-term experiences.

Let's try to differentiate them, shall we?

Short-term experiences are positive ones that are usually already a part of your everyday life. You may not give that much attention to them because they are something you do every day, but they make you feel good. This could be anything from walking in a park, watching your favorite TV show, talking to a friend, going for a run or a swim, or taking a bite out of your favorite meal. It is in these small things that we tend to find the true joy of life. When you do something you love, it fills you up with positive emotions. And no matter how difficult life may be for you, these positive emotions that come from short-term experiences mean a lot and can make a big change. The more you do them, the more positive energy you will create around you.

Long-term experiences are usually made up of positive things that have a long-lasting impact on the quality of your life. These are the things that are considered to make life worth living. For example, one of the things you can say to be the biggest positive long-term experience is your list of goals. Think about it – no matter what you do in life, you have a goal every day when you wake up. A driving force that gets you out of bed. For some people, this may be a combination of a few smaller goals, and for others, it may be one big goal that they have set their heart on. Your goals can be anything – from developing a new skill to learning how to craft something to moving to a different city or country, learning a new language, getting into college, getting the job of your dreams, etc. Here, the possibilities are endless. Think carefully about what would make your life more pleasant and happier. After you have the answers, turn those answers into goals and start working toward a better and brighter future.

Another thing that I'd like to include here is the relationships. Out of all the long-term experiences you may have in life, relationships are one of the most impactful things you can count on. Starting from a relationship with yourself and moving on to a relationship with the people around you, this is an important area of your life to work on. It can help you create a more positive future for yourself. You have probably seen this happening to some of your classmates at school – they have no issue developing any kind of relationships – whether they are personal or professional. This sometimes comes easy for some people, but for others, it can be a little challenging. Chances are, if you are reading this book, you are probably a part of the latter group – but that's okay! That's why I am here – to help you work through all the troubles you have and create a better version of yourself, as well as a happier life.

You can do both – reach out for new friendships and work on the existing ones. While both can be difficult at times, both are worth it. For example, working on the current relationships you have may be connected to anyone – from a friend to a sibling to a romantic interest. These are the people you spend a lot of time with. After working on maintaining a strong relationship with them, you can notice how your feelings improve. As this is a long-term commitment, you get a long-term positive experience out of it. Instead of letting your happiness depend on one person, try to cultivate many different relationships.

The second example is when you're trying to create a new relationship. This can be extremely difficult. The trick here is to find a place where you can do a joint activity with other people, such as dancing, bowling, singing, etc. Once you visit that place often, you will find yourself in the middle of a familiar crowd. Spark up a conversation with someone you think you can "click" with as a friend and make your way from there.

By this time, you should know what cultivating a positive emotion and experience means. In addition, we will turn to some fantastic exercises I've prepared for you to set you up for success!

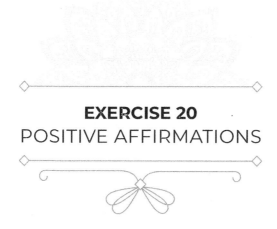

EXERCISE 20
POSITIVE AFFIRMATIONS

When times get tough, it is all about focusing on the positive. For this exercise, you are going to do just that – try to focus on the positive. Only in this case, you will start with no one other than yourself. If you have not noticed this by now, all negative emotions come from a place of negative belief about ourselves. Once you realize that and try to shift your perspective, your environment and you will change as well. I have found that, with the power of positive affirmations, you can do anything you set your mind to – including changing your entire mindset from a negative to a positive one.

Look at yourself in the mirror as you do this. The first time you stand in front of your mirror is going to be a difficult one. Why? Because you will need to think of ten good things to say about yourself. These can be good things in terms of your mind, smile, energy–anything you can think of. Talking positively to yourself is an excellent way to start focusing on the positive. It can help you reprogram your mind and start looking for the good things everywhere you turn.

Now, while you stand in front of the mirror, talk about some things about yourself – some positive things. Say them out loud as if they are already a part of your reality – even if they are not. Here are a few examples just to get you started:

1. My mind is wonderful.
2. My energy is addicting and fantastic.
3. All good things come my way without exceptions.
4. Whatever I attract, I become.
5. I feel constantly happy and fulfilled with my life.

You have the creative freedom to add anything you want to this list – the longer and more specific you make it, the better. Do this exercise every day so you can start feeling the results very soon!

MY POSITIVE AFFIRMATIONS

_____

_____

_____

_____

_____

_____

_____

_____

_____

_____

_____

_____

_____

_____

EXERCISE 21
GRATITUDE JOURNALING

For the second exercise, you are going to need a journal. This can be a regular notepad, a real journal, or even the notes app on your phone. As long as it is something where you can write constantly and go back to see what you've written, you're good. To get started, you can also use the worksheet below.

Take a pen and start writing. I suggest you do this every day. Notice everything happening around you and to you - and accentuate the positive each time. Even on those uneventful days where nothing really happens, it is your task in this exercise to find something for which you are grateful. At the end of each day, write down all the things you're grateful for that day. Allow this to become a practice. Try not to skip a day. Remember that being grateful doesn't necessarily mean something good has happened. You should always be grateful for the things you already have and who you already are.

For example, you can be grateful for another good day where you learned how to master your negative emotions. You can be grateful for everything you already have in life – a healthy body, mind, family, friends, etc. Or you can even be grateful for the small things in life that actually make a lot of difference – like a sunny day or if someone holds an elevator door for you. This gratitude journaling exercise can help you look at all the positive things in life. By writing them down, you focus on them so much more that, before you know it, this will become your default way of thinking.

Date: _____

Today I am Grateful for... _____

_____

_____

_____

Date: _____

Today I am Grateful for... _____

_____

_____

_____

Date: _____

Today I am Grateful for... _____

_____

_____

_____

Date: _____

Today I am Grateful for... _____

_____

_____

_____

Date: _____

Today I am Grateful for... _____

_____

_____

_____

Date: _____

Today I am Grateful for... _____

_____

_____

_____

Date: _____

Today I am Grateful for... _____

_____

_____

_____

Date: _____

Today I am Grateful for... _____

_____

_____

_____

Date: _____

Today I am Grateful for... _____

_____

_____

_____

Date: _____

Today I am Grateful for... _____

_____

_____

_____

Date: _____

Today I am Grateful for... _____

_____

_____

_____

Date: _____

Today I am Grateful for... _____

_____

_____

_____

Take Care of Your Body

A healthy mind requires a healthy body. These are words to live by. As someone who has invested so much into dealing with your emotions, realizing how to keep them going is the most challenging thing. What not many young people realize is that exercise does you a lot of good – not just for the body, but for the mind as well. There are a few things in life that are always a recommended option, and physical activity is one of them.

To take care of your body means to treat it with caution. Listen to it every time it tries to tell you that it's full when it comes to food, that it needs a stretch when you've been sitting down for too long, and that it is time for a little bit of pampering after a long day of studying. DBT focuses mostly on the mind, but it is always important to keep up with your body too. And to get into that, it is important to follow the next exercise.

EXERCISE 22
BUILDING AN EXERCISE ROUTINE

As soon as you start thinking about getting active, here is an exercise that can help you get in the right mindset. Start by looking into some options. When it comes to working out, think about what you like – is it cardio exercises, weightlifting, running, yoga, pilates, swimming, or something completely different?

Pick something that you want, something that you enjoy, something you feel good about. Then, just start doing it. I know it sounds pretty simple, but when you come to think of it, it really is! Dedicate at least 10-15 minutes at first, just to get into the routine, and then start dedicating some more time from your day to it.

After a while, you will start feeling like you have support – something that helps you be even more focused on the positive. Taking care of your body instantly puts you in a good mood, and after a while, you can see how that reflects on the outside, too. Write down every exercise you do, write down how many times a week you've exercised, and write down how it made you feel to work out to such an extent that you now feel spectacular!

This exercise is designed to help you exercise and give you the most out of your journey to create the most spectacular version of yourself!

_____

_____

_____

_____

What Did You Learn From This Chapter?

It is time to close another chapter filled with extremely powerful DBT skills! I know that this one was a tad longer and a little denser with information, so let's try to take out the best from it. Here is a little summary of what you learned in this chapter:

- ✧ What is emotional regulation, and how does it affect your overall quality of life.
- ✧ Opposite reaction and how to take control of yourself.
- ✧ Solving issues by focusing on the facts – giving yourself clarity in situations when your judgment seems clouded.
- ✧ The power of positivity.
- ✧ The power of exercise on your overall emotional and mental state.

In this chapter, I covered everything about managing your emotions and keeping up with the positive things in life. After you turn this page, a different world awaits! The next part is all about interpersonal effectiveness – from social skills to boundaries. It is time for you to discover the final aspect of DBT so you can shine! Let's go into the details and round up our incredible journey together!

Part 4

INTERPERSONAL EFFECTIVENESS

*"To effectively communicate, we must
realize that we are all different in the way we
perceive the world and use this understanding
as a guide to our communication with others."*

– Tony Robbins

Together, we have come to the last part of this book. So far, DBT has taught you plenty, but now, it is time to take all that knowledge that was always within you and turn to the final bit – interpersonal effectiveness and how to use it. During this part, you will notice what it is like to work on some aspects of your personality you might not have thought about until now. It is time to focus on what you can improve –yourself. Through the power of interpersonal effectiveness, you will become the version of yourself you're striving toward.

But for now, maybe one thing is on your mind only – what is interpersonal effectiveness? I took the liberty of explaining that to you before we go into further detail.

What is Interpersonal Effectiveness?

When it comes to relationships, everyone can be tricky. Even when considering the relationship, you are developing with yourself, you need to work hard – because you can be tricky, too. The trickiness part comes from the fact that not everyone knows how to use the power of the wise mind. Because as soon as it becomes a part of a relationship, you know you are in for constructive communication. Constructive communication is the key to success in all your relationships – with yourself, your family, friends, etc.

With this in mind, interpersonal effectiveness is about asking what you want or even saying no to someone while keeping your self-respect and the relationship intact. It is all about having a conversation (a relationship) with someone; no matter the outcome, you still feel good about yourself. Interpersonal effectiveness does not mean you need to twist your words and be diplomatic every time until you get what you want. It does not even mean you should get what you want every time. But it means that you should be happy with the outcome and yourself every time. It is about being proud of how you communicated things to that point where you feel good about yourself but still see the situation objectively. After all, you should not applaud yourself if you mishandle a communication or a relationship issue, right?

Essentially, interpersonal effectiveness means that you have found a calm yet strong way to express your needs while maintaining your integrity. In this case, the most important thing you can do is ask what you want or need and say no to a situation that doesn't suit you.

This entire section is an integral part of DBT because it can show you exactly how you affect your relationships. By now, you know that all communications and relationships are important. But did you know that the outcome of those communications and relationships is important as well? The outcomes affect your well-being, your self-esteem, and your sense of purpose. Now that you know all this, would you still be able to continue your relationships as you did until this point?

Social Skills

A lot of young people don't know how to ask for something, but rather make demands about it. Some adolescents even ask for things in a way that is confusing or don't ask at all. Interpersonal effectiveness skills are helpful here – they can make you focus on the most effective way to create and maintain a relationship. That is why I love this section; it is dedicated to the power of social skills.

Social skills are something everyone has. Some of you may have more of them, some less – but it is ultimately something embedded in our systems as human beings. We all need to communicate and create relationships with other people. This is something that cannot be done without some strong and healthy social skills. Let's explain this a bit better.

Think of any relationship you have as a tree. The better the relationship is, the bigger the tree grows. The stronger it is, the more incredible it looks. But this tree needs a system to support it while it is growing. The roots grow just as much as the leaves! Think of this every time you create or try to maintain a relationship with someone. For that relationship to grow, you need to focus on the roots. DBT, including the social skills, helps you with that. It can help you realize how to build strong roots, maintain relationships, and be effective at it.

The goal is to develop these social skills to help you become a better person. While I would love to get into the DBT interpersonal effectiveness skills right away, let's just look at it from a different angle – from the benefits point of view. Once you develop the social skills you need, here is what you will experience:

1. Improved communication

Considering interpersonal effectiveness means considering another method of communicating your feelings and thoughts clearly and respectfully. When you learn how to express them effectively, you can reduce any misunderstandings you have with the people around you, and you can build stronger and better relationships with everyone. How to do this? Don't worry; this is the part that I decided to focus on the most, and the three exercises cover the three aspects of this. They are *active listening* (when you fully concentrate on the other person and what they are saying, understanding their perspective and all), *resolving conflicts* (this is when you can be assertive and address an issue in a way that is constructive and helps you focus on finding a solution), and *empathy* (this is the part where you are respectful of both yours and the other party's feelings, thoughts, and emotions).

2. Boundaries

Teaching yourself how to establish boundaries in your personal and professional life will help you go a long way in the future. It will also help you understand other people's boundaries as well. This will help you come to terms with yourself and will prevent you from getting into conflicts in interpersonal relationships.

3. Improved self-respect

The DBT skills you will learn here will enhance your self-respect, as you will notice that you make choices that align with your values and self-worth. This will give you the ability to stand up for yourself in tough situations.

4. Less stress, more emotional intelligence

I mentioned empathy just a few sentences before this, and while I have created an entire exercise about it, you need to understand how deeply this will impact you. When you use interpersonal skills and strengthen them, you can navigate through relationships with ease, which will lead to less emotional strain and less anxiety. In turn, this will show great empathy and higher emotional intelligence. You learn how to understand and recognize your emotions and those of the people around you, so don't be afraid to open up!

Let's move on to the exercises for this part.

EXERCISE 23
ROLE-PLAYING – ACTIVE LISTENING

One of the key components of DBT is practicing active listening. Since the exercises here have the objective of helping you create the best version of yourself, I suggest you do some role-play for all the exercises for today. You will need a few materials for this particular one – a quiet space, another person who can help you with the exercise, a timer or a stopwatch, and a scenario (but this is optional).

Before you go into the exercise, it is important to accentuate how helpful active listening is in any relationship. It is more than just hearing the words; it is remembering and responding to them accordingly. This is an essential skill in every DBT aspect, and it can ensure that all misunderstandings are minimal. Active listening includes asking clarifying questions and letting the other person speak while you give them your full and undivided attention.

For this exercise, choose to be the listener, while the person sitting across from you would be the speaker. Then, they will start talking about an issue with you. This can either be an imaginary issue or a real-life issue. Here is an example scenario:

You were organizing a party, and you didn't invite them. Now, you get to hear how they feel and what they think about it. Listen to them talk, but really hear what they have to say. Answer their questions and share your opinion on the topic, too. Talk about your initial responses (especially yours) and note how everything made you feel. Talk about the challenging parts of active listening and what you learned. Also, think about how you can apply this exercise in real life. *Time your responses to a minute or two just so you can avoid getting stuck in unnecessary info.*

There are more scenarios such as this one - here are a few examples just to get you going:

1. You wanted to talk about your feelings, but you got shut out in the middle of the conversation.

2. They felt like you didn't listen to them when they were talking.

3. You were supposed to go to school together, but you forgot to pick them up.

4. You asked them if they wanted to go shopping with you, and they declined.

5. You asked for help from them for a school assignment, and they didn't help you.

They did a favor for you, but never even got a thank you from you.

EXERCISE 24
ROLE-PLAYING – ASSERTIVENESS

The second exercise has a different objective. Assertiveness is something you need to develop if you want to learn how to express your thoughts and feelings directly, respectfully, and honestly. This exercise is about refraining from being aggressive or passive while doing so.

Again, for this exercise, you will need another person who will actively participate. You will need a space where you can do the exercise and a timer so you can time your responses.

Assertiveness is the middle ground in communication. It means setting clear and respectful boundaries. It also means maintaining a steady tone of voice and manner, maintaining eye contact, and being honest yet respectful.

In this situation, you can be both the speaker and the listener. The scenario can be anything you like – from a fictional one to a real-life one. If you are the listener, then you will have to respond to the reaction of the speaker (they choose a scenario where they express a need or stand up for themselves). After you're done, you can switch the roles.

As an example scenario, let's say you borrowed something from them and didn't return it. In this role-playing exercise, you will need to understand the needs of the speaker. Listen to their, "I" statements, where they express their needs and feelings, and adhere to the clear boundaries they set. If you feel like you cannot do the last one, then it is okay to talk about it until you find a middle ground. Throughout the exercise, try to maintain a calm and steady voice and keep eye contact at all times.

Note that, during this exercise, you and the person sitting across from you may not be able to see eye to eye. This role-playing exercise has a goal to provide a realistic response – which may be one of three things – acting positively, asking for further clarification, or acting negatively. But no matter the response, you should maintain the assertiveness.

To make the most out of this exercise, I recommend you be both the listener and the speaker. Here are a few sample scenarios:

1. Trying to refuse a request from the person sitting opposite you.
2. You talked about them behind their back, and they found out, now they're confronting you with it.
3. They treated you unfairly, and now you are confronting them.
4. You try to set boundaries with them.
5. You ask them for help with a certain assignment or homework.
6. They pressured you into staying out later than you were supposed to.

Once the exercise is done, look within and note how you felt when you expressed yourself. Did you learn something about your communication style? How challenging was it for you to maintain your assertiveness at all times? Finally, think about how you can apply assertiveness to your life because you may have just learned something new and positive about yourself through this exercise.

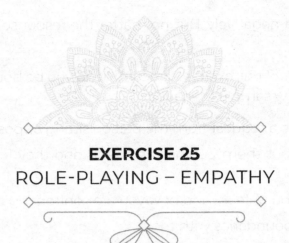

EXERCISE 25
ROLE-PLAYING – EMPATHY

The last exercise from this part is all about empathy. Some of you may already know what empathy is – it is the ability to feel what the other person is feeling. It is the ability to put yourself in their shoes and understand their origin in a certain situation. Empathy is a very important skill that every teenager should develop. That's why I recommend a role-playing exercise here – so you can get the most out of it.

You know the drill – you need another person, a quiet space for the exercise, a partner, and a timer so you can measure your responses. But in this case, the first thing you will do is start discussing the concept of empathy. Empathy is the ability to understand another person's feelings. Also, it is not about fixing an issue or a concern. It is not even about giving advice! Empathy is a part of a healthy relationship and the base for effective communication. It can help a person feel understood and supported.

The components of a conversation filled with empathy include reflecting emotions back to the speaker, avoiding being judgmental or critical, offering validation about their feelings, and listening to them actively. Empathy is an important part of every relationship you form in life, and it can help you in many social interactions.

Create a scenario where the speaker needs support. For example, let's say that the person opposite you is upset because they had an important exam, and they failed it or didn't perform as they expected. This is an emotional thing for them, and it is your job as the listener to hear what they have to say – whether that is anxiety, frustration, anger, sadness, or something else.

It is your job to listen to them attentively while they are speaking. They describe the situation in detail, and it is your job to reflect back to them what they say and offer support. Try to avoid giving them advice as this is not a very good approach. After the time has passed and you shared some empathy with them, switch the roles. It is important for you to understand what it's like to be on both sides of the situation. This way, you will know how it feels, you will know what the most challenging bit was, and you will learn something about yourself – how you handle these kinds of situations and in which areas you can improve. Finally, you will learn how to apply empathy in your real-life relationships.

To get you started, here are a few example scenarios how you can practice that:

1. You failed a test, and you want to talk about it.
2. They are being bullied and they just want you to hear them out, because it is a difficult time for them.
3. You are anxious about a presentation and want to talk about it.
4. They are struggling with body image issues.
5. You simply want to talk about your day and your challenges.

You felt left out in a certain situation and want to be understood.

Setting and Maintaining Boundaries

Boundaries are the limits we set for ourselves in relationships and interactions with others. They define what is acceptable and unacceptable behavior towards us, helping to protect our emotional well-being and maintain healthy relationships. Setting and maintaining boundaries is crucial for everyone, but it can be especially important for teenagers as they navigate friendships, family dynamics, and the pressures of school life.

In DBT, boundaries are seen as essential for emotional regulation, self-respect, and effective interpersonal relationships. Learning how to set and maintain boundaries can help you feel more in control of your life, reduce stress, and prevent feelings of resentment or frustration.

Boundaries can be divided into several categories, each of which plays a vital role in maintaining healthy relationships:

Physical boundaries: These relate to your personal space and physical comfort. They determine how close others can get to you physically and what kind of physical contact is acceptable. For example, you might feel uncomfortable with hugging someone you don't know well or prefer to have your own space when studying.

Emotional boundaries: These involve your feelings and emotions. Emotional boundaries protect your emotional well-being by helping you avoid being overwhelmed by others' emotions or taking on their problems as your own. For example, you might set a boundary by telling a friend that you're not comfortable discussing a certain topic that triggers anxiety for you.

Intellectual boundaries: These involve your thoughts, ideas, and beliefs. Intellectual boundaries protect your right to have your own opinions and beliefs and to respect those of others. For example, you might set a boundary by asking someone not to criticize your ideas or beliefs in a disrespectful way.

Time boundaries: These involve how you manage your time and prioritize your activities. Time boundaries protect your time by helping you balance different aspects of your life, such as school, extracurricular activities, and social life. For example, you might set a boundary by saying no to a social invitation because you need to study or rest.

Material boundaries: These involve your personal belongings and financial resources. Material boundaries protect your possessions and money by ensuring that they are used or shared in ways that you're comfortable with. For example, you might set a boundary by not lending your favorite book to someone who tends to lose things.

Setting these boundaries is essential for several reasons:

Self-respect: Boundaries help you show respect for yourself by acknowledging your own needs and limits. When you set boundaries, you say your comfort and well-being matter.

Emotional protection: Boundaries protect you from being overwhelmed by others' demands or emotions. They allow you to take care of your own emotional needs first, so you don't burn out or become resentful.

Healthy relationships: Boundaries are the foundation of healthy relationships. They help ensure that both you and others know what is expected and what is off-limits, reducing misunderstandings and conflicts.

Stress reduction: Clear boundaries reduce stress by preventing you from taking on too much responsibility or feeling pressured to meet others' expectations. This can lead to a more balanced and fulfilling life.

Since boundaries are an important part of life, it is imperative to know how to implement them. These can help you grow into the person you want to be. Let's move on to the exercise bit.

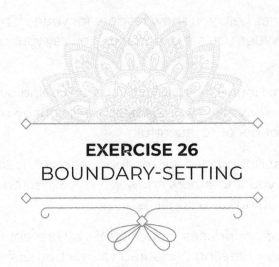

EXERCISE 26
BOUNDARY-SETTING

The first exercise is all about creating healthy boundaries. If you do not know how to properly place them in your life, let me remind you that you are not the only one. Many people, such as yourself, are probably struggling to do the same. But the difference is that you have this book in your arsenal – one you can easily pass on to someone you notice is in need of it. In DBT, setting and maintaining healthy boundaries is an essential part of becoming a strong version of yourself. That is why this exercise is crucial.

You will need a pen and paper to write things down, and other than that, you're good to go! Before you start writing things down, understand that boundaries are exceptionally important. They are the limit that can help you protect yourself from any emotional, mental, and physical damage. They can help you manage your relationships with yourself and the people around you – mostly because they are based on mutual respect and understanding.

Write down all the times you felt like someone challenged you to do something that is out of your comfort zone – for example, when you hung out with your friends, and they dared you to do something you didn't really like doing. That is your boundary. You probably didn't want to say no to that just because you didn't want to look like a coward or a weak person at the moment, but deep down, you knew that it was not something you liked doing. Write about how you would react if you knew that you could set a boundary at the moment. Would anything be different?

Reflect on that – how would it feel to set a boundary? Would it feel like something you can gain confidence from? Or would it feel like a big challenge? Remember that the good thing about challenging yourself, in this case, is that you not only learn new things about yourself but also learn how you may handle a situation in which you are expected to do one thing but would prefer to do the complete opposite.

Think about the aspects of your life for which you want to set boundaries. For example, these aspects may be connected to school, to your friends, or even to yourself. Setting a boundary is not an action you do only once – it is a continuous process you will keep doing – it requires ongoing attention. While you write down the things you are setting boundaries to keep a note that you will constantly need to remind yourself how to practice them, and basically focus on taking care of yourself.

_____

_____

_____

_____

_____

_____

_____

_____

_____

_____

_____

_____

_____

_____

_____

_____

_____

_____

_____

_____

_____

_____

_____

_____

_____

_____

_____

_____

_____

_____

_____

_____

_____

_____

EXERCISE 27
BOUNDARY COMMUNICATION

It is one thing to set boundaries for yourself, but it is a completely different thing to try to communicate those boundaries with the people around you. If you want to practice effectively communicating these boundaries, DBT suggests you practice that. Because no matter what you do in life, practice makes it perfect. You need to know how to empower yourself and clearly express your boundaries at every given moment. That is why this exercise is created solely for that intention.

For this exercise, I recommend that you sit down with someone (maybe a parent or an older sibling) so you can fully grasp the scope of what it is you are trying to do. The exercise is a conversation with them where you express your feelings. Try to sit them down and explain what is happening – how you feel, what makes you uncomfortable, or what awakens some negative emotions or thoughts within. Stay focused on the topic and be assertive. Let them know that your final goal is to know how to communicate your boundaries.

Now, think about an aspect of your life where you want to set a boundary. This could be anything – something that has been bothering you, something that has been making you uncomfortable, or something you've wanted to change. Talk to them and explain the entire situation. For example, this can be trying to stop someone at school from bullying you. While you are explaining, use a calm tone and a steady voice. I know this may be difficult for you at first but think about what you may gain from it. These exercises are designed solely for your consideration and are here to help you improve. And in time, after practicing them, you will.

Now, after you've communicated your issue, I recommend grabbing a pen and paper and writing down how the conversation made you feel. Did you feel confident about it? What was the most challenging part of the process? Would you think that, in real life, when you communicate this, you might get a response that would put you back to square one? If so, how would you react to prevent yourself from going back? It is through these questions of self-reflection that you will be able to learn how to better stand up for yourself and know how to deal with future situations.

_____

_____

_____

_____

_____

_____

_____

_____

_____

_____

_____

_____

_____

_____

_____

_____

_____

_____

_____

_____

_____

_____

_____

_____

_____

_____

The DBT interpersonal effectiveness skills are the final part we are going to cover in this book. They are specifically designed to help you get what you need from a relationship while being respectful of yourself and the people around you. Relationships can be very challenging and tricky, and at any point, you might come face to face with some unstable and extremely negative emotions.

That is why I am sharing the effectiveness tools: DEAR MAN, GIVE, and FAST.

Objectives Effectiveness: DEAR MAN

Starting from the first one, DEAR MAN is something that can help you achieve a certain goal or objective – no matter what that is. As you can probably notice, DEAR MAN is an acronym, and it stands for:

Describe the current situation

Express your feelings

Assert yourself

Reinforce

stay **M**indful

Appear confident

Negotiate

When it comes to the use of DEAR MAN, you first need to make sure of what you want. The clarity of your argument will be based on the clarity of your thoughts. So, if you want to start determining what you want or need, give some time to your priorities. It's okay that, at certain times in life, you feel overwhelmed. But this feeling of being overwhelmed can help you remove all the low-priority demands. Start considering doing things only because you want to do them, not because you *should* do them.

Also, consider asking for help when you need it. At the end of the day, you need to come to terms with the fact that you don't have to do everything yourself. You can even use the DEAR MAN to ask someone else for help – it all depends on your goals. Here are some goals that you might have in mind:

1. You want to stand up for your rights and want to be taken seriously.
2. You want to resolve a conflict.
3. You want to have your opinions and thoughts to be taken seriously.
4. You want to request something from someone in a way that they will do it.
5. You want to refuse to be a part of an unreasonable situation and refuse a certain request.

However, there is something to remember here. Even with the DEAR MAN technique, note that you can't have it your way all the time. You can't get everything from people constantly. Sometimes, your techniques will be put to the test, and you will need to increase your interpersonal skills; other times, they will fail completely. That's okay. In these situations, it is important to go back to distress tolerance because you know that what you want is impossible to get.

While this is a little bit tricky to understand right now, I have created an exercise for each of these techniques. That will give you the clarity you need.

EXERCISE 28
DEAR MAN

What's interesting about all these exercises is that no matter what you want to achieve, you always go back to the wise mind I mentioned at the beginning of the book. There is no better mindset than the wise mind, so whenever you want to do this exercise, go into that state and then begin.

For this exercise, you will need a pen and paper and a friend, sibling or parent – someone you completely trust. Take the pen and paper and write out the acronym vertically. Each letter represents a certain aspect you're going to focus on. This way, you will have the opportunity to spend as much time as you need on the most challenging letter. Before you begin, make sure you are comfortable.

Sit down with the person you've chosen to be your partner and think of a situation you want to discuss. Start from the beginning – here is an example of how the conversation should flow:

Let's say you sat down with a friend who gave you a hard time and maybe even made fun of you in front of other people. Now, start going through the letters.

D – Describe the situation from your point of view and clarify what you are asking them. In this case, you're asking them not to do that to you anymore. But, since you are wise, try to only state the facts. That means you have to limit yourself to not judging the situation, who and what caused it, and whether it is good or bad.

E – Express your feelings about the situation. Avoid transferring the blame to them but let them know how you feel. Go from the assumption that they don't know how you feel (because that is usually the case). Think of this as your opportunity to openly tell them how you feel.

A – Assert yourself – tell them what you want. In this case, you want to stop being made fun of in front of other people. Be clear and concise so that there is no misunderstanding. Do not assume that the person sitting across from you is able to read your mind.

R – Reinforce your statement. That way, you will make sure there is a positive outcome to your request. I recommend that you reinforce there would be a positive outcome if they agree with you and a negative outcome if they don't – that way, you are more likely to get an affirmative response.

M – Mindfulness of your goal. The person sitting across from you will not be mindful of your goal – that's why you should do that yourself. Don't get distracted from the conversation and, if you need to, start repeating things – be just like a broken record. If they attack you, ignore their attacks. Repeat yourself until you make your point and notice they have understood you.

A – Appear confident, as if you are in charge of the situation. You may not be at first, but you will lean into it as time passes. Exude confidence in your posture, your tone of voice, and your words.

N – Negotiating is key. You can be as confident as you want, but you also need to be flexible. If you want to get something, you need to be willing to give something, too. Focus on your goal but be practical about what will work. Make way for communication and find a mutual solution to the issue.

Just to help you get going, here are 5 example scenarios:

Asking to spend some more time together.

Ask them for some extra help on something.

Ask to spend less time together.

You feel like you need to raise a particular subject with them and talk about it.

Ask them to include you more in their social activities

Describe the Situation _____

_____

_____

Express Your Feelings _____

_____

_____

Assert Yourself _____

_____

_____

Reinforce Your Statement _____

_____

_____

Mindfulness _____

_____

_____

Appear Confident _____

_____

_____

Negotiate _____

_____

_____

D _____

_____

_____

E _____

_____

_____

A _____

_____

_____

R _____

_____

_____

M _____

_____

_____

A _____

_____

_____

N _____

_____

_____

D _____

_____

_____

E _____

_____

_____

A _____

_____

_____

R _____

_____

_____

M _____

_____

_____

A _____

_____

_____

N _____

_____

_____

D _____

_____

_____

E _____

_____

_____

A _____

_____

_____

R _____

_____

_____

M _____

_____

_____

A _____

_____

_____

N _____

_____

_____

D _____

_____

_____

E _____

_____

_____

A _____

_____

_____

R _____

_____

_____

M _____

_____

_____

A _____

_____

_____

N _____

_____

_____

D _____

_____

_____

E _____

_____

_____

A _____

_____

_____

R _____

_____

_____

M _____

_____

_____

A _____

_____

_____

N _____

_____

_____

Relationship Effectiveness: GIVE

Let's move on to the second exercise, which is all about relationship effectiveness. I cannot remind you enough how challenging it can be to deal with unstable emotions. During these times, one wrong step in communication can damage a relationship beyond repair. That is why the technique GIVE will provide you with the help you need to keep your relationship intact, even in those times when you have an argument.

GIVE is another acronym that will help you obtain some skills that are important for all those times when you don't know how to act in an argument but still want to meet your goal or objective. Each letter represents a certain aspect you're going to focus on. Here is what GIVE stands for:

Gentle

Interested

Validate

Easy manner

To provide you with a little more clarity on this one, think of the GIVE as a how skill and of DEAR MAN as a what skill. DEAR MAN is more about what you do, and GIVE is more about how you do it (the same thing will apply to FAST, but more on that later on. However, since all these skills are connected, you will subconsciously improve your DEAR MAN skills by using the GIVE skills.

A part of the relationship effectiveness is to tend to your relationships as regularly as you can. You should not allow any issues or troubles to pop up and should remain there – like an elephant in the room. Instead, GIVE is your opportunity to address them as soon as they happen. By doing this, you use all the skills you've learned from this book to prevent any issues from becoming bigger and eventually blowing up. This technique also helps you end any toxic relationships because it shows you it is not necessarily a good thing to continue doing something you don't want and give a person the attention they probably don't deserve.

GIVE is, just like DEAR MAN, all about goals. Before you start your communication, it is important to be clear about what you want. Sometimes, you may want a person to accept you more. You may want to stop them from rejecting or criticizing you as much. Some of the goals you may have in mind include the following:

1. You want to act in a certain way so the other person will give you what you want.

2. You want to act in a certain way so the other person will not feel wrong about you rejecting their requests.

3. You want to act in a certain way to balance the good of the short-term goals with the good of the long-term goals.

So, you see – this one is all about balancing your relationships with the goals you have for yourself and your life. You should not sacrifice who you are just to get the respect of others – which, at the end of the day, you probably don't even need. The only time you should commit to something is when you want to. As we lean into GIVE and learn the FAST technique, you will see how these three techniques should be used at the same time and balanced effectively.

EXERCISE 29
GIVE

For this exercise, think about how you want to be treated in a situation during a discussion. Do you want to be yelled at, or do you want to be treated with kindness? How would you imagine the conversation will flow if you want to be treated with kindness? This exercise consists of you getting a pen and paper, as well as someone to discuss with. Here is how you can use the acronym.

First, write it down on your piece of paper.

G – Remind yourself that people respond in a gentle manner better than they do to yelling. That's why, no matter what you want to discuss, as long as you present it well and approach them with kindness and respect, you know you have opened a steady line for communication. Avoid being snarky, making threats, and passing judgment on them. Tolerate it if they want to say no to you and give them time to respond to what you said to them.

I – Being interested is another thing you should focus on. Has it ever happened to you that sometimes someone doesn't listen to a word you say? You see their attention is being pulled to a different side, and you get a little angry about it. Well, you should give as much as you get. Being interested may be a challenging thing for you, but in this case, it is only fair to listen to their point of view, too. Maintain eye contact, don't interrupt them, and carefully listen to what they have to say.

V – Show the other person that you've listened to their side of the story by completely understanding them. Validate their point of view and try to put yourself in their shoes. Even in those times when you think they aren't making much sense, try to find the grain of truth and reason for what they are saying. Be non-judgmental and be that in a loud way. Validate their feelings, wants, opinions, and difficulties (which, remember, does not mean you have to accept them). Oftentimes, someone just needs to feel heard and seen, and that paves the way for a potentially solid relationship.

E – Easy manner means trying to be as friendly and as easy-going as you possibly can be. You can even use humor to ease into the conversation and relax the other person. You should not guilt-trip them but rather have a good attitude, especially if the other person may feel hurt by your request. Give your best to accept their response and maintain calmness.

Here are a few scenarios to get you started:

1. Support your friend when they're having a bad time.
2. Resolving a conflict you may have with them.
3. Comforting them after they get a bad grade.
4. Talking about a sensitive issue.
5. Helping them whenever they feel anxious about something.

Gentle _____

_____

_____

Interested _____

_____

_____

Validate _____

_____

_____

Easy Manner _____

_____

_____

G _____

_____

I _____

_____

V _____

_____

E _____

_____

G _____

_____

I _____

_____

V _____

_____

E _____

_____

G _____

_____

I _____

_____

V _____

_____

E _____

_____

G _____

_____

I _____

_____

V _____

_____

E _____

_____

G _____

_____

I _____

_____

V _____

_____

E _____

_____

G _____

_____

I _____

_____

V _____

_____

E _____

_____

Self-Respect Effectiveness: FAST

The last technique is FAST. It is very easy to get lost in the moment and lose yourself in the whirlpool of emotions while you are having a conversation or an argument with someone. And before you know it, you have bent to their will without ever having the intention of doing that. This is where the last technique – FAST, comes into the picture. As you can see, it is a self-respecting effectiveness skill, and it is one we will dissect together in depth. FAST can help you maintain your self-respect during a discussion, conversation, or argument with someone.

Yes, you guessed it, this is an acronym as well. It will teach you how to act every time you are faced with a challenging situation, yet you are determined to meet your goals without sacrificing yourself in the process. Here is what FAST stands for:

be **F**air

no **A**pologies

Stick to values

be **T**ruthful

I mentioned earlier that FAST is just like GIVE – it is a part of the how skills that will help you have an objective and successful discussion. For this technique, you must remember that nobody can take away your self-respect – unless you give it up willingly. I noticed something, especially with young people such as yourself, that self-respect is based on the quality of your relationships with other people. By using this skill, you learn how to tend to your relationships skillfully.

As with the two previous techniques, before you begin your conversation, you need to keep your goal in mind. Doing this will help you remain focused and clear on what you want. And remember, the focus here is maintaining your level of self-respect. With that in mind, here are a few goals as an example for you:

1. You want to like yourself.
2. You want to feel effective and capable.
3. You want to act in a way that makes you feel moral, respected, and valued.

Before we move on to the exercise, I would like to share the wise words of Eleanor Roosevelt – *"No one can make you feel inferior without your consent."*

EXERCISE 30
FAST

We have made our way to the last exercise of the book – and boy, is it a good one! For this final exercise, you will need to practice in the same way you practiced with the other two exercises – you need a pen and paper and someone to talk to. Again, you can choose anyone you want – it can be a sibling, a parent, or a friend. Only this time, note that it's helpful to practice FAST when you're not in the middle of an argument so you can first get used to it. Then, as you do, you can start using it in real-life situations when things get a little more intense.

Take out your pen and paper, write the acronym vertically, and go through the letters one by one.

F – it is all about being fair. When you think of a situation you want to discuss with the person sitting opposite you, you need to be fair when describing it. After all, while you still want to put whatever it is you feel or think about the situation on the table, you still need to be mindful of their wants and needs, too. Stick to the facts and avoid judgment but remain fair to yourself.

A – if you don't have to, don't apologize. Putting yourself in a position when you want to ask for something is not a reason to apologize. Having a different opinion or a point of view is also not a reason to apologize. It is okay for you to take up space. The only situation where you need to apologize is when you have made a mistake and want to get things right. Apologizing means you are wrong. Taking up space and having an opinion is not wrong. Apologizing for doing all this will only make you lower your self-worth and self-respect. Also, it gets on other people's nerves.

S – stick to your values as much as you can. I know that it can be scary to ask for a change (or to ask for anything, for that matter). At the time, it might feel like the person you're talking to may stop liking you if you ask them for something. Through my years of experience, I have noticed that this is often the case, especially with young people – and that is why I am accentuating it now. Don't let fear be the overwhelming feeling, and don't compromise just to avoid conflict or to please the other person. Doing this will only make you like yourself less in the long run.

T – lastly, make sure you are always truthful to yourself. Stick to the facts and avoid stretching them out too thin. If you start noticing a dishonesty pattern within yourself, remember to cut it out. In the long run, this pattern will make you like yourself less and less and will diminish your self-respect. There is no need to make judgmental statements – only the facts are enough. Also, being truthful means being grounded and not acting helpless. Even in those times when you feel insecure and scared, try to stand firmly on the ground with both feet.

Here are a few example scenarios to get you started:

1. Trying to say no to peer pressure.
2. Make your voice heard in a group project, where you only know the person sitting opposite you.
3. Asking more time to finish a task.
4. Dealing with unwanted criticism.
5. Setting boundaries with the person sitting opposite you.

With FAST, there are some instances where being truthful may be a destructive thing for the relationship. To guide yourself through this tricky process, I suggest you include a wise mind to guide you whenever you feel like it is appropriate to do so.

It is incredibly interesting to learn that these techniques are part of what makes you an incredible, stable, calm, and happy person. I would love to see you give them all a go because there is so much you can learn about yourself from them!

Be **F**air _____

_____

No **A**pologies _____

_____

Stick to Values _____

_____

Be **T**ruthful _____

_____

F _____

_____

A _____

_____

S _____

_____

T _____

_____

F _____

_____

A _____

_____

S _____

_____

T _____

_____

F _____

_____

A _____

_____

S _____

_____

T _____

_____

F _____

_____

A _____

_____

S _____

_____

T _____

_____

F _____

_____

A _____

_____

S _____

_____

T _____

_____

What Did You Learn From This Chapter?

As the final chapter in the book, I believe that things are wrapping up quite nicely. I know this was a long one and that we had a lot to cover here, so let's do a short recap of everything you learned through this chapter, shall we?

- ✧ What is interpersonal effectiveness.
- ✧ Social skills and the power of creating and maintaining relationships.
- ✧ What you will gain by developing your social skills.
- ✧ The power of boundaries; different types of boundaries – why setting them and maintaining them is important.
- ✧ The first of the three techniques – DEAR MAN – is all about the effectiveness of objectives.
- ✧ The second of the three techniques – GIVE – is all about the effectiveness of relationships.
- ✧ The third of the three techniques – FAST – is all about the effectiveness of self-respect.

This chapter may have been the longest one, but it was essential to go through it together so I could help you go through this wonderful journey to yourself. All of the techniques you've learned here are something that will soon become invaluable to you. I know it will be difficult to deal with them at first – it may have seemed like the more you read this book, the more challenges you will have. But there is nothing better than stepping out of your comfort zone when you know it is the path toward creating the best version of yourself.

That being the case, I can't wait for you to turn the page so we can complete our time together on a high note!

CONCLUSION

Congratulations! You've made it to the end of this book! I am happy to say, however, that your journey to your true self is something that will continue long after you've completed reading this. I wouldn't even be surprised if you come back to the book every once in a while. By exploring and practicing the skills of DBT, you will take a significant step toward understanding yourself better, managing your emotions more effectively, and building healthier relationships (with yourself and the people around you). This is no small feat—learning and applying DBT skills takes courage, dedication, and a willingness to grow. You should be incredibly proud of yourself.

Take a moment to reflect on everything you learned in this book. Think back to when you first started reading this book. Do you feel like you can face some life challenges better now? Do you think you have a better scope of your emotions? How have you changed through this book? How can you manage your life better from now on?

Up until this point, you may have been faced with times when you didn't know how to react or hoped for a different outcome than the one you got. That's okay. Learning how to get through these situations equals growth. What matters here is that you are committed to learning and applying these skills, every time things are hard.

The skills you've learned in this book are tools that you can carry with you for the rest of your life. They're not just for times of crisis or extreme emotion; they can be integrated into your everyday routines, helping you to live more mindfully, manage stress, and communicate more effectively. But, to make the most out of them, you need to know how to make that happen.

Try to practice these skills as often as you can. For them to become a part of who you are, you need to practice them as often as possible. Set some time aside every day and revise the techniques you've learned here. The more you practice them, the easier they will be for you.

Practice with mindfulness. As you learned in the book, mindfulness is the foundation of DBT, and to take full advantage of this, you need to keep being fully present and remove judgment from your thoughts and feelings. Use the toolbox of skills you've taken from this book every time you face a challenge. Consider how you can make the most out of each situation.

Reflect on your past experiences and notice how you start to use the DBT skills in your life. Put some finishing touches and keep moving forward while constantly evaluating your progress. Also, don't forget to ask for help when needed. If you feel like you need some assistance in overcoming a challenging situation, remember that you are not alone. You can always come back to this book and revisit a chapter or a segment alone, or with a friend, sibling or anyone you like.

As you continue to grow and develop, remember that the skills you've learned in this book are just the beginning. Life is full of opportunities for learning and self-improvement. By staying open to new experiences and challenges, you'll continue to build resilience, deepen your self-awareness, and strengthen your relationships.

DBT is not about perfection; it's about progress. It's about finding a balance between accepting yourself as you are and striving to become the person you want to be. It's about understanding that you have the power to shape your own life, even in the face of adversity.

You've embarked on a journey that many never take — self-improvement and emotional growth. You've shown that you're willing to face your challenges head-on, learn new coping methods, and build a life that reflects your values and aspirations. This is a remarkable achievement, and it's something you can carry with you as you move forward in life.

As you close this book, know that the skills you've learned are yours to keep. They are tools that can help you navigate the many twists and turns that life will inevitably bring. Whenever you face a new challenge or feel uncertain about the future, remember the progress and strength you've discovered within yourself.

You are capable, resilient, and worthy of the life you want to create. Keep believing in yourself, practicing your skills, and moving forward. The journey doesn't end here — it's just the beginning. Your future is full of possibilities, and you have the tools to make the most of them.

Thank you for allowing this book to be a part of your journey. Wishing you all the best as you continue to grow, learn, and thrive.

COPING SKILLS WORKBOOK

for Teens

How to Manage Anger, Anxiety & Stress,
and Use CBT and DBT Exercises for Lifelong
Emotional Regulation

EMILY CARTER

INTRODUCTION

In today's day and age, it can be quite challenging to be a teen. The interesting bit is that, while you are young, you can't wait to get to those crazy teenage years. But once you do, it's not exactly what you expected - I know, we've all been there. You have a lot of freedom and a lot of opinions, and you want to express every little thing that pops into your head. However, you can still feel something within you, like something's not right.

You feel like you don't have enough space to process all kinds of emotions. It starts to feel like your teenage years are about to be a rollercoaster. One minute, you feel like everything is great, and the next, you are overwhelmed by everything surrounding you. You have to meet certain expectations from your family (in terms of how you should behave, what grades you should get, etc) When you go to school, the same expectations happen there as well. Then, of course, there is also peer pressure (which somehow always seems to be present). At the end of the day, life starts to feel like it is too much for you to handle. You feel stressed, anxious, and just unable to process everything around you, especially when things sometimes happen too fast.

Well, I am happy to tell you that you are not alone in this.

I am even happier to tell you that I will help you get through this!

I designed this book with the sole purpose – for you to have a practical guide that can help you navigate life's challenges. You will do that using Cognitive Behavioral Therapy (CBT) and Dialectical Behavior Therapy (DBT). These two evidence-based approaches have helped millions of young people gain control over their emotions, build resilience, and improve their relationships. These techniques aren't just for therapy sessions. They are also skills you can use in everyday life. They can help you handle stress, anxiety, sadness, and anger and even help in those moments when everything just feels like it's too much.

CBT helps you recognize and change unhelpful thought patterns. If I take a wild guess here, these negative thoughts probably make you feel worse. Ever notice how one negative thought can spiral into a full-blown bad day? Well, CBT gives you tools to catch those thoughts and reframe them - so they don't take over. DBT, on the other hand, will help you work on balancing emotions, improving communication, and learning to stay calm in difficult situations. Basically, these skills help you handle life.

I am happy to share this workbook with you - mostly because it isn't about a series of lectures or just a bunch of unrealistic advice. I made it interactive, practical, and for real life – your life. Each chapter includes exercises, techniques, and activities that will help you apply these coping skills in a way that makes sense for you (I know this may sound confusing now, but once you start the chapters, it will make much more sense). So, no matter what you deal with – anxiety, self-doubt, or you just want to build healthier habits, here you will find a step-by-step guide that will help you be more in control.

Oh, and one last thing before we begin – you don't have to be in a crisis to benefit from these skills. In fact, the best time to learn these healthy coping strategies is before things get out of control. But, even if you do feel like you are on the verge, remember this – as long as you have this book in your hands, everything will be alright. Think of this workbook as a toolkit for your mental well-being. You can turn to it every time you need support, clarity, or just a reminder that you have the power to navigate through whatever comes your way.

No one expects you to have life figured out. As a teenager, I felt the same way, but as soon as I grew up, I realized that most of the things were just a result of not knowing how to control myself. But with the right skills (the ones I included in this book), you can learn to handle stress and regulate emotions. You can build a balanced and fulfilling life. You can work through this book on your own or with a supportive adult – just know that every small step you take is a step toward emotional strength and a better you.

Are you ready to take control of your emotions, develop better coping strategies, and build the skills to handle whatever life throws at you? Let's begin together!

UNDERSTANDING CBT AND DBT

"You have power over your mind – not outside events. Realize this, and you will find strength."

– Marcus Aurelius

We all learn, grow, and understand. It is a part of the wonder called life, and we are all aware that there are always some ups and downs. We embrace every challenge and overcome every obstacle that comes our way. But what happens when things become a little too much for us? Does it mean that we cannot cope with anything anymore? Does it simply mean we're tired?

As a teenager, I can fully understand how you feel. You already deal with all these kinds of feelings, thoughts, and emotions, and it feels like it is bad enough that you can't regulate them on a daily basis. The thing is, as soon as anything happens to you, you start to feel like you're spinning out of control! This may have happened to you once, twice, or more than a few times, and after each time, you feel disappointed in yourself.

Well, I am glad you're here because, from this point on, I will help you embark on a journey of self-discovery. However, to properly do that, let's break things down – one at a time. This first chapter is all about easing you into the process.

We will start by explaining some basic terms.

What is CBT?

The first thing we're going to do is explain the concept of CBT. Yes, you have probably guessed it already – there is a difference between CBT and DBT. Before you go much further into detail and exercises, I believe this is the right way to start learning things.

CBT is like a therapy session – one that can help you manage all your symptoms by helping you change how you think and how you behave. Basically, it is based on the concept that your thoughts, feelings, and emotions are all connected – and that too much negativity can make you feel trapped. The goal of CBT is to help you deal with any issue you may have, and just help you cope with life overall in a more positive way. CBT can help you break down the larger issues into smaller tasks. It constantly looks for practical ways to help you make that happen.

This approach has been proven effective in treating many issues and even mental health conditions. You may be dealing with anything from anxiety, OCD, panic attacks, and phobias to PTSD, insomnia, and even chronic pain – CBT can help you cope, even handle whatever it is you think is unresolvable.

In terms of emotional regulation, CBT works in such a way that it helps you break down everything about your problems into three sections – your feelings, your thoughts, and your actions. As you analyze every single section, you try to work out whether all of what you're experiencing (or at least a part of it) seems unrealistic. You realize the effect this has on you. By doing this, you work out how to change your thoughts and the behaviors that are not of much help to you. Also, you learn how to manage the problems you have and prevent them from having a negative effect on your life (especially your emotions).

The funny thing about CBT is that we all do this at some point in our lives. Some of us focus on this without putting too much thought into it. Others put a lot of energy into it. Whatever the case, CBT is an approach that can help anyone with any kind of issue – especially because the techniques used are very easy! Some of the most popular examples of CBT techniques include journaling. Writing down what you feel, think, and experience throughout the day can help you step back and look at whatever is happening from a different, calmer perspective. Some other quite popular techniques include breathing exercises, role-playing, mindfulness, setting goals, and doing certain physical activities. Do any of these sound familiar? That's because CBT is based on putting the focus on yourself and pulling away from negativity while focusing on logic.

That did not sound bad, right? I know that this is still uncharted territory for you, but don't worry – I am here to guide you every step of the way.

What is DBT?

On the other hand, DBT is somewhat of an altered CBT approach. While it focuses on the same goal (to make you feel better and become a better version of yourself), the approach is a little bit different here. DBT's main goals are to help you live in the present moment, fully embrace it, and develop a healthy way of coping with stress. It also helps you learn how to regulate your emotions and improve your relationships with the people around you.

DBT is very well known among people who need help with emotional regulation. This approach relies on a certain set of principles, including distress tolerance, interpersonal effectiveness, acceptance and validation, behavior change, biosocial theory, and emotional regulation. These principles have the power to help you create a certain core mindfulness and regulate your emotions.

Now, what is the difference between CBT and DBT? It seems like I have talked plenty about it. But, at this point, it still sounds like the same thing, right? It is okay to be a little confused right now, especially because there is so much for you to learn!

The difference between CBT and DBT is what you learn during the process. The other difference is knowing how the treatment is delivered. Both of them are equally powerful approaches. Here, the thing is – it all comes down to your personal needs. There are many differences between these two, but the approach is the main one. With CBT, you focus on your behavior and your patterns of thinking. And on the other side, with DBT, you focus on your relationship with yourself and the people around you.

The bottom line is that both of them can help you deal with different mental challenges. Again, it all comes down to the approach you prefer. In some cases, you can even go as far as to focus on both of them and use both approaches – if you feel like you could benefit from both. And that is exactly why we're here! These two approaches (when combined) can help you work out wonders!

Benefits of Using CBT and DBT

Both Cognitive Behavioral Therapy and Dialectical Behavior Therapy stand out as powerful, evidence-based approaches. Believe me when I say – these approaches offer hope and healing, but what makes them the pillar of modern mental health care is that they can adapt to each individual need. Sounds fascinating, doesn't it? I would love to talk about their effectiveness for a little bit (bear with me on this one), but also share some real-life success stories with you, and finally, how both these approaches can transform your everyday life.

CBT is recognized as a gold standard that can help treat a variety of mental health issues. As I mentioned earlier, this includes anxiety, depression, and post-traumatic stress disorder (PTSD). Now, if you need some actual reassurance that this works, this next part is for you. Research shows that CBT is highly effective if you want to minimize the symptoms. It can help you identify and challenge unhelpful thought patterns and behaviors. According to a meta-analysis by Hofmann et al. (2012) published in *Cognitive Therapy and Research*, CBT significantly outperforms other therapeutic approaches (in the treatment of depression and anxiety disorders).

On the other hand, DBT was originally developed to treat borderline personality disorder. However, it also expanded its reach to address issues such as substance use, eating disorders, and other mental health challenges. Because of its dual focus, you get to experience the most results. Here, you combine acceptance strategies (mindfulness) with change strategies (emotion regulation, distress tolerance, and interpersonal effectiveness). A 2023 study by Vijayapriya and Tamarana published in *Research in Psychotherapy* journal showed how DBT may lead to significant improvements in emotional regulation and interpersonal development in individuals who have higher mental health needs.

Both therapies offer structured, actionable tools that empower individuals to take charge of their mental health, making them highly effective for a wide range of challenges.

While statistics and studies are compelling, it's the personal journeys of those who have embraced CBT and DBT that truly bring their impact to life. Here, I would like to remind you to view these with an open mind and heart and to try to understand that their journey has been just as challenging as yours. Also, as you can see from these success stories, these are all shared by people who are well into their adult lives. This is another positive thing for you – because you start to comprehend and work on your issues from an earlier age. I am here to remind you that you are bound to succeed.

Take a look at the success stories.

Emma's Story – Overcoming Anxiety with CBT

Emma, a 32-year-old marketing professional, had struggled with debilitating anxiety for years. Social situations, once joyful, became sources of dread, and her career began to suffer. Through CBT, Emma learned to identify her automatic negative thoughts such as "I'll embarrass myself" – and challenge them with evidence. By practicing gradual exposure to anxiety-inducing situations, she rebuilt her confidence. Amazingly enough, Emma now leads presentations with ease and actually enjoys a thriving social life.

Mark's Journey – He Found Balance with DBT

Mark, a 24-year-old college student, battled emotional dysregulation and impulsive behaviors. DBT taught him mindfulness techniques to stay present and recognize his emotions without judgment. He also mastered distress tolerance skills, such as using grounding exercises during moments of high stress. With consistent practice, Mark's relationships improved (significantly, if I may add), and he found stability in both his academic and personal life.

These stories highlight how tailored interventions in CBT and DBT can lead to profound, life-changing results.

How These Therapies Can Be Applied to Everyday Life

The beauty of CBT and DBT lies in them being the most practical ones. They're not just for therapy sessions. Honestly, they offer tools you can carry into your daily life and handle challenges with resilience and clarity. And at the end of the day, isn't that why you are here? There are a few ways you can include both CBT and DBT into your everyday life. While I have some ideas for you below, I recommend that you use at least one of the CBT and one of the DBT ones (for starters). I will share many techniques with you here. These techniques here, as well as many other ones will be presented in detail, just for you. They span throughout the entire book. Familiarize yourself with the exercises, one at a time, and try to do them once a day. Then, you can try some of the other ideas I've shared. Compare and combine to get the best results. Once you get the hang of it, you will have no trouble doing them every day – even subconsciously.

CBT in Daily Life

- ✧ **Challenging Negative Thoughts –** If you find yourself thinking, "I'll never be good at this," pause and ask, "What evidence supports this thought? What evidence contradicts it?" This shift can help reframe your mindset.
- ✧ **Behavioral Activation –** Struggling with motivation? Break tasks into smaller, manageable steps and commit to action. The act of doing often reignites motivation.

DBT in Daily Life

- ✧ **Mindfulness** – Practice being present during everyday activities, such as eating or walking. Notice the sensations, smells, and sounds around you without judgment.

- ✧ **Distress Tolerance** – When faced with overwhelming emotions, use grounding techniques like the 5-4-3-2-1 method (identify five things you can see, four you can touch, three you can hear, two you can smell, and one you can taste).

- ✧ **Interpersonal Effectiveness** – Use the DEAR MAN framework (Describe, Express, Assert, Reinforce, stay Mindful, Appear confident, and Negotiate) to navigate difficult conversations with assertiveness and respect.

These strategies not only improve mental health but also enhance overall well-being and strengthen relationships. And I'm happy to say – these strategies are only the beginning.

What Did You Learn in This Chapter?

Before we leap into the next chapter (where the true excitement begins), let's take a look at what we learned from this one. After all, this is the basis on which you will only continue to build yourself up as a person.

In this chapter, you learned:

- ✧ What is CBT, how does it work, and some of its most popular techniques
- ✧ What is DBT, how does it work, and its principles
- ✧ What is the difference between the two
- ✧ The benefits of using these two approaches
- ✧ How you can use the approaches in everyday life

Now, turn the page, and let's move on to the next chapter!

UNDERSTANDING YOUR EMOTIONS

"Emotion can be the enemy, if you give into your emotion, you lose yourself. You must be at one with your emotions because the body always follows the mind."

– Bruce Lee

There is so much happening behind the screen that you are (currently) unaware of. The wonderfulness behind the complexity of being human shines bright and illuminates everything. Yet somehow, as individuals, we sometimes remain in the dark. But this is not a bad thing. Without darkness, there cannot be light – and without knowing that something is wrong, you would never know you need to work on it or improve it.

This chapter is all about addressing your emotions. Let's learn together how you can help them work for you instead of controlling you. It is an interesting process to dive deep into yourself and uncover the real truth about yourself. It is such a liberating feeling – you'll see.

The Science of Emotions

Have you ever thought about your emotions as a concept? Do you know where they come from? Some of you may answer this question with the heart, some with the head, and some of you may just shrug without answering. Sometimes you feel sad, and other times you feel happy – this is how all our bodies work. It may come as a surprise but there is some science behind all of this, so stay with me.

In essence, your emotions come from your brain. To be more precise, they come from the limbic system, which is a very complex structure found in the cerebral cortex. This part of the brain is responsible for your emotions, your behavior, and your level of motivation. Think of this as somewhat of the control center of your body. It can interpret various emotional stimulations.

Basically, your limbic system is your EQ (emotional intelligence). It includes the amygdala, hypothalamus, and hippocampus. When all these aspects are combined together, they work to help you regulate your emotions in any given situation. One of the most important structures of the limbic system is the amygdala. Its responsibility is to help you process emotions like anger, fear, anxiety, and aggression (the reason why we're here). What happens is that when you feel threatened, the amygdala sends a signal to the hypothalamus, and this makes you act in a certain way.

So far, this all seems like a relatively logical explanation, but where are the hormones and emotions? There is more to the limbic system than you think. Hormones also play a very important role in how you feel – especially because you are a teenager. All the hormones that you're probably already aware of (dopamine, oxytocin, cortisol, etc) that either make you feel good or not.

But, there is also one final point, where you might suddenly feel angry or scared or even snap at someone – without knowing why. You just can't explain it. Well, in this case, it is all about the environment. Sometimes, your emotions can be ruled by an external factor. This can be anything from your genetics to your surroundings. This is the last bit of the science equation regarding what can influence your emotions and response.

Emotions are complex, and there is no easy way to explain all of them. That is probably why you feel the way you feel right now. But fear not – there is always light at the end of the tunnel. There is no one explanation for your emotions because there is no one answer that could fit everyone. For now, all you need to remember is that emotions are an essential part of what makes you a human. They can help you navigate through life and connect with yourself and with those around you.

Emotional Brain Development

Of course, there is no science behind emotions without emotional brain development. These topics go hand in hand. But, for a teenager, it seems like you have a long way to go in terms of brain development. No, don't take this the wrong way, it's just that science says that the brain of a teen is not fully developed until they reach the age of about 25. So, to get there, you need to first understand how your brain works.

How does the teenage brain process emotions? This is a question your parents or guardians have probably asked themselves many times. Even though they have been teenagers at some point in their lives, this concept seems like a completely unfamiliar one to them. The thing is, the brain of every teenager works differently – and this differs a lot from an adult's brain. Adults tend to think with their prefrontal cortex, which is the rational part of the brain. This part of the brain responds to situations with reasonable judgment and is fully aware of any long-term consequences.

As mentioned earlier, you, as a teen, process everything with your amygdala – which is the emotional part. In every teenager's brain, the connection between the emotional part of the brain and the center for making decisions is still developing – and sometimes, this doesn't happen at the same time. This is why you tend to get emotional at times, and later, you cannot really explain why you acted the way you did. You still feel more than you think.

But why does understanding brain development help in managing emotions? Why would this book help you? If it is normal to feel this way, then isn't the best course of action to just wait it out? Well, no. The thing is, a lot of things can happen to you before you reach the age of 25 or so. You don't have to wait and succumb to the pressure of emotional irregularity until that moment comes. What you can do in the meantime is to try to understand your brain and thus manage your emotions. Yes, the rest of this chapter will be all about that.

Identifying and Differentiating Your Emotions

Identify, differentiate, and manage – these are the three things you will learn over the course of this book. These are considered quite important if you want to learn all there is to know about emotional development. Strong emotional development leads to skills such as social awareness, self-awareness, responsible decision-making, the ability to build relationships, and emotional regulation. These are the skills you may struggle with at the moment. In order to conquer this, you will need to know your emotions – you can do this by acknowledging the three major stages in emotional development.

1. **Identify emotions** – at first, since you are born, it is believed you only have three emotions – happiness, fear, and anger. However, as you grow, so does the palette of emotions you feel. The first thing you need to do whenever you find

yourself in a situation that needs extra attention from your end is to recognize the emotions you feel.

2. **Differentiate emotions** – as you grew, up until this point, you probably realized that there is a way to experiment with emotions – at least, with how you express them. While this is a healthy way of growing up and developing into a healthy adult, this is your time to figure out how to differentiate between knowing how to express emotions healthily rather than in an unhealthy way.

3. **Manage emotions** – we all grow and enter into various social environments where we need to be in control of our emotions. Of course, that doesn't mean you need to act like an animal when you are alone and restrain yourself in public. It means you need to know how to manage your emotions and support your further development in life.

Differentiating Between Primary and Secondary Emotions

Indeed, there is such a thing called primary emotion. Then there is secondary emotion, too. These are very well known by therapists everywhere in the world, but not by the common people – especially not by teenagers. So now I'm going to share them with you so you can get a better idea of what it is that I'd like to teach you.

Primary emotions are the ones that teens typically think about when they think about feelings. These are a kind of emotional response – so-called pure reactions to anything that happens around us or to us.

Secondary emotions are traced to the core emotions, but these are a little bit more complex. Here, you may use a lot of words to describe these feelings. The secondary emotions are the emotions of the primary emotions. While these vary from one situation to the next, they are always a reaction to whatever the first feeling was.

But why do these two matter? Emotional awareness is an essential part of the work that could promote emotional and mental well-being. The concept of secondary emotions can give you the opportunity to understand them better – and use them to your advantage. Differentiating is essential if you want to truly become aware emotionally. This will give you the space to explore yourself over and over and to also explore what you do with your feelings.

And now, let's go into the techniques for naming and understanding your feelings. Some techniques are better than others, but again, it all boils down to what you find to be most useful to you. Let's start unwrapping the exercises!

EXERCISE 1

EMOTION WHEEL

Sometimes, emotions can feel overwhelming or confusing, but this exercise will help you understand and manage them better. You'll use an *Emotion Wheel* – a chart with basic emotions at the center that branch out into more specific ones.

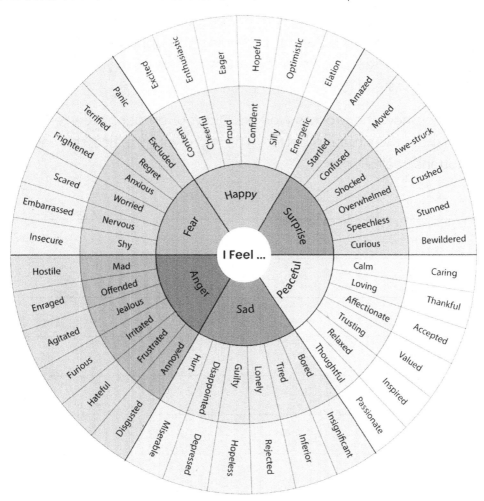

First, take a moment to figure out how you're feeling. Take a look at the Emotion Wheel and pick the main emotion that stands out, like sadness, anger, or fear. Then, dive deeper into the outer parts of the wheel to pinpoint exactly what you feel, like lonely or frustrated.

Once you know what you feel, think about what triggered it. What happened? What are you telling yourself about the situation? How is your body reacting – like a tight chest or shaky hands? Then write this down to get it out of your head.

Then, ask yourself, "Is this thought accurate? Could I be making assumptions?" Just remind yourself that emotions aren't bad – they're just signals. It's okay to feel what you feel. You tell yourself, "It makes sense I feel this way because..." Validation can help you calm down.

Now, you should decide what to do with the emotion. If it's helping you, then go with it. If it's not, try something different, like doing the opposite of what the emotion urges you to do. For example, if you feel angry and want to yell, take a deep breath and speak calmly instead.

Finally, reflect on how the process worked. Did your emotions feel less intense? Did it help you handle the situation better? The more you practice, the easier it gets to handle emotions healthily.

_____

_____

_____

_____

_____

_____

_____

_____

EXERCISE 2

FEELINGS JOURNAL

Keeping a feelings journal is a simple way to make sense of emotions and learn how to handle them better. All you need is something to write with and a bit of honesty.

First, write down how you're feeling right now. Don't overthink it – just one or two words like "anxious" or "excited." Then, think about what happened today that might've made you feel this way. Was it something someone said? Something you did? Write that down, too.

Next, ask yourself what thoughts are connected to this feeling. What are you telling yourself about the situation? Are these thoughts helpful, or are they making you feel worse? Try to challenge anything that doesn't feel true or fair by asking, "Is there another way to look at this?"

Lastly, write what you can do to feel better or to healthily handle the emotion. Maybe you need to take a break, talk to someone, or just let yourself feel it for a while without judging it.

Writing in your feelings journal will help you understand yourself better. The more you do it, the easier it gets to notice patterns and figure out what you need.

_____

_____

_____

_____

_____

_____

_____

The Impact of Emotions on Behavior and Health

Emotions might feel like these big, uncontrollable waves sometimes, but they actually have a lot of power over how we think, act, and even feel physically. Let me break it down.

How Emotions Influence Thoughts and Behavior

Have you ever noticed how being in a bad mood can make everything feel 10 times worse? That's because emotions influence how you see the world. If you're feeling sad, you might start thinking, "Nobody cares about me," even if that's not true. On the flip side, when you're happy, everything feels easier, and you notice the good stuff more. Your emotions shape your thoughts without you even realizing it.

Now, those thoughts affect how you behave. For example, if you're angry, you might snap at someone or say something you will regret later. If you're anxious, you might avoid doing things that scare you, even if they're important. But you can make better choices when you take a second to understand your emotions. Instead of letting them control you, try to pause, think, and decide how you want to act.

The Connection Between Emotions and Physical Health

Here's something wild: emotions don't just live in your head – they also show up in your body. When you're stressed or scared, your heart beats faster, your muscles tense up, and sometimes you may even get headaches or stomachaches. That's because your brain is telling your body, "We're in danger!" – even if the danger is just an upcoming test.

If you stay in those intense emotional states for too long, your body starts to feel the effects. Constant stress, for example, can mess with your sleep, make you feel tired all the time, and even weaken your immune system. On the other hand, positive emotions like joy or gratitude can actually boost your health. They help you relax, sleep better, and feel more energized.

EXERCISE 3

MIND-BODY CONNECTION MAPPING

This exercise can help you notice how your emotions show up in your body so you can understand and manage them better. All you need is a quiet moment and something to write with.

First, pause and think about how you're feeling emotionally. Are you happy, sad, stressed, or something else? Write that down. Then, focus on your body. Do you feel tension anywhere, like tight shoulders or a heavy chest? Is your breathing fast or slow? Write down everything you notice.

Next, think about how your body and emotions might be connected. For example, if you feel nervous, your stomach might hurt, or if you're angry, your jaw might feel tight. Draw a quick outline of a person (stick figures work!) and mark where you feel these sensations.

Finally, decide what to do with this information. If your body feels tense, you might stretch or take deep breaths. If your emotions feel overwhelming, simply remind yourself it's okay to feel this way and try something calming, like listening to music or going for a walk.

Mapping the connection between your mind and body can help you feel more in control and show you how to care for yourself better.

_____

_____

_____

_____

_____

Common Emotional Challenges for Teens

Before we wrap this chapter up with a nice bow, let's talk about some of the most common emotional challenges you face. Don't think that I haven't noticed why you're here. You feel stressed. You feel angry. You feel like you carry the weight of the world on your shoulders. You don't know what to do with it. It seems like everything is falling apart at times, and you can't always make sense of it all.

There are a few common emotional challenges for teens – let's go through them together.

Stress and Its Effects

Stress can hit from all angles. For you, it might be schoolwork piling up, arguments with friends or family, or pressure to meet everyone's expectations. Even stuff like social media or figuring out your future can feel overwhelming. Sometimes, it feels like everything is happening all at once.

When stress gets out of control, your body and mind let you know. You might feel constantly tired, have trouble sleeping, or even get headaches or stomachaches. Your mood can swing wildly, and little things might make you cry or snap. It's like carrying a weight you can't put down.

If you don't deal with stress, it doesn't just go away. It can pile up. Over time, it can make you feel burned out, anxious, or even depressed. It can also mess with your health, causing issues like constant fatigue or a weaker immune system. Learning to handle stress now can help you avoid bigger problems later.

Anxiety in the Teenage Years

Anxiety is that nagging feeling like something bad is about to happen, even when everything's fine. For you, it might be triggered by things like tests, social situations, or big changes like starting at a new school. Sometimes, there's no obvious reason – it just shows up out of nowhere.

When you're anxious, your body reacts. Your heart races, your hands get sweaty, and you might feel shaky or dizzy. Mentally, your thoughts spin out of control, and it's hard to focus on anything else. It's like your brain is stuck in the "what if" mode.

It is common knowledge that everyone worries sometimes. But anxiety is different. While worry usually fades after the stressful thing is over, anxiety can stick around and show up even when nothing is wrong. It feels bigger and harder to shake off.

Understanding Anger

Anger can come from feeling misunderstood, treated unfairly, or not having control over things. For you, it might be someone breaking a promise, being ignored, or feeling overwhelmed by responsibilities. It's that hot, frustrated energy that can bubble up quickly.

When you're angry, your body reacts fast. Your face feels hot, your fists might clench, and your heart starts pounding. Emotionally, you might feel like yelling, crying, or just wanting to smash something. It's like a storm brewing inside you.

Anger isn't always bad – it can help you stand up for yourself or fix something unfair. But unhealthy anger happens when you let it control you, like lashing out or bottling it up until you explode. Healthy anger means expressing it in a way that solves problems without hurting others or yourself.

What Did You Learn From This Chapter?

You probably started to feel like everything you thought you knew about yourself just went right out the window. Everything you read here felt like kind of an eye-opener, right? This chapter was filled with some new info for you, and just to sum it all up before we move on to the next one, here is what you learned today:

- ✧ You learned that emotions need to be understood
- ✧ You discovered the science behind emotions
- ✧ You learned how emotional brain development happens (and why it hasn't happened to you yet)
- ✧ You learned how to identify and differentiate your emotions – especially the primary and secondary ones
- ✧ How emotions impact you in more ways than you can imagine
- ✧ Some of the most common emotional challenges for you – anger, anxiety, and stress

We may be putting this chapter to a close, but we turn a new leaf, and we open up a new chapter. I have talked plenty about emotions, and now it is time to dedicate an entire chapter to emotional awareness. Don't worry. The more you read, the more you learn! Let's start the next chapter together!

BUILDING EMOTIONAL AWARENESS

"Emotion, which is suffering, ceases to be suffering as soon as we have a clear picture of it."

– Benedict Spinoza

Emotions have a way of influencing our lives in the best and worst ways. However you look at it, we cannot fully enjoy life without emotions. They are an essential part of our being. Being a teenager only amplifies the feelings already within you, which has probably made you feel awkward. The thing is, emotions (and being aware of them) are an important part of who you are – and how you react to situations.

I am sure that many of you can relate to this: There have been many times when you wished you had reacted differently because you could not control your emotions at that moment. I may not have a time machine to return you to those past moments where you can create memories that could have unfolded differently, but I can send you to the future well aware of your emotions and ready to tackle anything. In this chapter, I will help you build emotional self-awareness.

Developing Self-Awareness

Emotions come from inside us, and they impact the way we view ourselves, the people around us, and the world, too. Emotions influence how we live, how we spend our time, whether we are motivated or not, and even the career we choose. In a way, they create guidance and meaning for us.

But when you are not aware of your emotions, things can easily turn for the worse. You could become trapped in a vicious cycle and not be able to break free. This is basically what I call life without emotional awareness.

Developing emotional awareness (or self-awareness) is important if you want to keep making the decisions that are right for you and help you move forward in life. This is how you can maintain your interest, take chances, and continue being curious in life. In order to do all of this, you need to know how to recognize and develop your emotional self-awareness.

The key to all learning in life (no matter what you try to learn) is monitoring yourself. By doing this, you correct your behavior and mistakes, and you try again until you get it right. If you want to increase your self-awareness and be more in tune with your emotions (but not let them control you), you need to first keep a few strategies in mind. I am sharing them with you below so you can see how easy it is to master yourself.

- **Use the emotion wheel** – this is the feeling list (or a wheel) which I introduced earlier that includes a lot of words that describe feelings. These words can be anything you want – from the best to the worst ones. Have this at hand so whenever you feel like you are lost for words, you can immediately find how you feel thanks to this list.

- **Your feelings send you a message** – every single time. The message is usually that you are safe (or not), and it is usually about something that impacts your motivation and/or values. It is all about using this message wisely.

- **Develop resilience** – there are a lot of emotions out there that can make you feel less than what you're truly worth. These can also be very difficult to cope with. It is imperative for you to know a few exercises on how to build this resilience (exercises are just below) to help you cope with these negative emotions better.

- **Mindfulness is important** – Yes, if you want to get the most out of life, of whatever aspect of it, mindfulness is key. It is all about training where your focus and attention go. Once you're able to do this, you can work on it until you perfect it.

- **Don't forget self-compassion** – when you lean into it, you will quickly notice that whenever you feel overwhelmed, it is the act of compassion that can help calm you down. Give yourself the credit you deserve along the way, and accept that, to see things objectively, you will need some time to practice. We are all human, and we all make mistakes from time to time, but that does not mean you have a deep wound that cannot be healed. Trust yourself and the process, and give yourself some time.

✧ **Pause** – as funny as this may sound to a teenager like you, to take full control over your emotions, sometimes you need to pause for a moment. While you do this, observe what you feel and identify the one (or the many) feelings that burst inside of you. Each day, you have the opportunity to work on this because each day, every one of us is faced with different challenges and situations.

✧ **Feel your body** – and listen carefully to what it has to say. It takes a lot of patience and practice to do this. Try to start a conversation with your body. How does it feel when you have these intense emotional episodes? Scan your body and see what it has to say.

✧ **Notice the pattern** – there is always one. In a variety of settings, sometimes you feel things, and they lead to a certain behavior. The thing is, that behavior is usually a pattern (because it's always a specific one). Identify this emotional path because it can interfere with your judgment and lead to a lot of sadness and suffering.

I have a list of a few exercises I would like to share with you in terms of developing self-awareness. These are specifically created to suit your needs, and they can help you turn inward and discover the hidden chambers within yourself – the ones filled with awareness and control.

EXERCISE 4

SELF-REFLECTION JOURNAL

A self-reflection journal is like having a conversation with yourself. It's a way to check in, explore what's going on in your head, and better understand yourself. All you need is a notebook, your thoughts, and a few quiet minutes.

First, think about your day and write down something that stood out – maybe something you're proud of, something that upset you, or just something random that felt important. Let yourself be honest, even if it's messy or doesn't make much sense.

Next, ask yourself questions like: *Why did this moment matter to me? How did it make me feel? What does it tell me about what I want or need?* Try to dig a little deeper, connecting your thoughts to your feelings.

Finally, write down one thing you can take away from this. Maybe you learned something about yourself or realized what you'd do differently next time. Even if you just feel lighter from getting your thoughts out, that's enough.

This journal isn't about being perfect or always having answers - it's about giving yourself space to listen to what's going on inside. The more you practice, the clearer things become.

Date: _____

Something That Stood Out Today: _____

_____

Why is it Important?: _____

_____

_____

Takeaway: _____

_____

_____

———o–◇–o———

Date: _____

Something That Stood Out Today: _____

_____

Why is it Important?: _____

_____

_____

Takeaway: _____

_____

_____

Date: _____

Something That Stood Out Today: _____

_____

Why is it Important?: _____

_____

_____

Takeaway: _____

_____

_____

———o—◇—o———

Date: _____

Something That Stood Out Today: _____

_____

Why is it Important?: _____

_____

_____

Takeaway: _____

_____

_____

Date: _____

Something That Stood Out Today: _____

_____

Why is it Important?: _____

_____

_____

Takeaway: _____

_____

_____

———o–◇–o———

Date: _____

Something That Stood Out Today: _____

_____

Why is it Important?: _____

_____

_____

Takeaway: _____

_____

_____

Date: _____

Something That Stood Out Today: _____

_____

Why is it Important?: _____

_____

_____

Takeaway: _____

_____

_____

EXERCISE 5

WHO AM I? WORKSHEET

The "Who Am I?" worksheet is like a personal scavenger hunt to figure out what makes you *you*. It helps you understand your values, interests, and what's important in your life.

Start by writing down answers to a few simple prompts:

What do I love doing?: _____

_____

_____

What's something I'm really good at?: _____

_____

_____

What makes me feel happy or excited?: _____

_____

_____

Who are the people that matter most to me?: _____

_____

_____

What's something I'd like to improve or work on?: _____

_____

_____

Next, think about how these things connect. For example, if you love helping people and feel happiest when you're around friends, maybe you value connection and kindness. If you enjoy art or sports, it might mean creativity or physical activity is important to you.

Finally, write a short statement about who you are based on your answers, like: *"I'm someone who values creativity, helping others, and spending time with people I care about."* It doesn't have to be perfect - it's just a way to see yourself more clearly.

_____

_____

_____

_____

_____

This worksheet is a great reminder that you're unique, and knowing yourself better helps you figure out where you want to go in life.

EXERCISE 6

EMOTIONAL SELF-AWARENESS QUIZ

This quiz can help you figure out how well you understand your emotions and what you can do to feel more in control. It's not about getting the "right" answers - it's about learning more about yourself.

Just grab a pen and answer these questions honestly:

	Yes	No
1. When I feel upset, can I name the emotion I'm experiencing?	☐	☐

	Yes	No
2. Do I notice how my emotions affect the way I treat others?	☐	☐

	Yes	No
3. Can I tell when I'm starting to feel overwhelmed or stressed?	☐	☐

	Yes	No
4. Do I ever take time to figure out why I'm feeling a certain way?	☐	☐

	Often	Sometimes	Rarely
5. How often do I feel like my emotions control me instead of the other way around?	☐	☐	☐

Once you've answered, think about what your responses tell you. If you struggle to name your emotions or notice their effects, maybe it's a sign you need to slow down and check in with yourself more often. If you feel like your emotions take over a lot, you could try calming techniques like deep breathing or journaling.

This quiz is just a starting point. The more you practice paying attention to your emotions, the better you'll get at understanding and managing them. It's like building a muscle - one step at a time.

EXERCISE 7

REFLECTION ON A RECENT EMOTIONAL EXPERIENCE

This exercise will help you look back on a recent emotional experience to understand it better. It's like replaying a moment in your head to figure out what happened and why it mattered.

First, pick a recent moment when you felt a strong emotion - maybe you were angry, happy, sad, or excited. Write down what happened, just the facts, like you're telling a story: *"I got into an argument with my friend because they cancelled our plans at the last minute."*

What Happened?: _____

_____

_____

Next, ask yourself: *What was I feeling at that moment?* Write down all the emotions you can think of – sometimes, there's more than one. Then, ask yourself: *What triggered that emotion? Was it the situation itself or what I thought about it?*

What Did I Feel?: _____

_____

_____

What Was the Trigger?: _____

_____

_____

Finally, reflect on how you reacted. Did you say or do something you're proud of? Or maybe it's something you'd handle differently next time? Write down one takeaway, like: *"I felt hurt because I value my time with friends. Next time, I want to tell them how I feel instead of keeping quiet."*

Takeaway: _____

_____

_____

_____

This reflection isn't about judging yourself – it's about learning. Each time you do this, you will understand your emotions a little more and figure out better ways to handle them in the future.

Techniques for Gaining Insight into Your Behavior

To make your life more meaningful, you need to use these exercises and think of them as techniques. For example, in every reflection you do, realize that there is a technique there. Ask yourself – is this something that is in line with my values and who I want to be as a person or not? This can help you step back and see the bigger picture.

Recognizing Triggers and Patterns

You experience a lot of emotions during the day. Some of them are bad, some of them are good. Most of them (if not all) relate to specific events that happened. But your response to these events is your starting point.

A trigger (specifically an emotional one) can be anything – from a memory to an experience or an event. This is something that sparks up an emotional reaction. It does not care for your current mood. Emotional triggers are associated with PTSD. To control and overcome yours, you need to know how to identify them first.

Think back on some situations in your life where you felt excluded, ignored, challenged, etc. Or maybe you felt betrayal, rejection, insecurity, loss of independence, helplessness, criticism, disapproval, or simply lost control. These events that have embedded themselves into your mind, soul, and body are the triggers. The way you respond to them (the same way every single time) is the pattern. These two are connected. To recognize and move past them, you need to do three things:

1. **Retreat** – take a step back whenever you feel yourself getting heated, and stop to think about what just happened – and why you acted the way you did.

2. **Go back** – this has happened to you before, hasn't it? Go back to the roots and find the origin – when was the first time you felt that way? Keep in mind – you may need some time to get to the bottom of this.

3. **Curiosity is key** – yes, when I say you need more time, this is what I think. Dedicate some time if the connection is not clear, and try to get as much insight as you can on what triggered you and what made you repeat the patterns you do.

Identify what sets off your emotions. Remember that it is all about finding out what triggers your bursts of emotion. Think hard and dig deep. This is how you can get to the core and thus break the patterns you have been repeating for a very long time.

EXERCISE 8

TRIGGER IDENTIFICATION WORKSHEET

This worksheet can help you identify what triggers your emotions, allowing you to better understand your reactions and feel more in control.

First, think about a time when you felt a strong emotion - maybe you were angry, sad, or anxious. Write down what happened, like: *"I got really mad when someone interrupted me during class."*

What Happened?: _____

_____

_____

Next, ask yourself: *What triggered that emotion?* Was it the situation itself, what someone said or did, or how you interpreted it? For example: *"I felt like they didn't respect what I had to say."*

What Was the Trigger?: _____

_____

_____

Then, dig a little deeper: *Was this about something bigger?* Maybe the trigger reminded you of another time you felt ignored, or maybe you were already stressed, and this made it worse.

Dig Deeper: _____

_____

_____

Finally, contemplate how you reacted and how you might handle it next time. Did your reaction help or make things harder? If you face the same trigger again, what could you do differently? For example, *"Next time, I'll calmly ask for a chance to finish speaking instead of snapping."*

Reflection: _____

_____

_____

By identifying your triggers, you're not just reacting. You're learning to pause, understand, and choose how you respond. It's like uncovering the map of your emotions!

Patterns in Emotional Reactions

As I mentioned earlier, the patterns are the ones you need to look out for whenever you want to deal with emotional triggers. You may have acted the same way for a very long time without noticing it.

EXERCISE 9

EMOTION-TRIGGER LOG

This exercise will help you track your emotions and what triggers them so you can start spotting patterns and understand yourself better. It's like keeping a journal, but it is focused on emotions.

Whenever you notice a strong emotion, write it down. Include:

- ✧ **What happened -** Describe the situation, like: *"I got a bad grade on my test."*

- ✧ **How I felt -** Name the emotion(s) you experienced, like: *"Disappointed, frustrated, and embarrassed."*

- ✧ **What triggered it -** Think about what specifically set off the emotion. Was it the event itself or how you thought about it? For example: *"I felt like I didn't try hard enough, and now my teacher will think I don't care."*

- ✧ **How I reacted -** Write down what you did next, like: *"I avoided my teacher and didn't talk to my friends about it."*

Then, look back at your log at the end of the day or week. Are there certain triggers that keep coming up? Do you notice any patterns in how you react? This reflection helps you figure out what you might want to work on, like handling a situation differently or changing how you think about it.

The more you use your emotion-trigger log, the better you get at understanding what's really going on inside you – and that's a powerful skill to have.

Develop strategies to manage triggers – the triggers can be easily overridden. All you need to do is have a solid plan and a lot of exercises (just like the ones here) that will help you along the way.

What Happened?: _____

_____

How I felt?: _____

_____

What Triggered It?: _____

_____

How I reacted?: _____

_____

——o——◇——o——

What Happened?: _____

_____

How I felt?: _____

_____

What Triggered It?: _____

_____

How I reacted?: _____

_____

What Happened?: _____

_____

How I felt?: _____

_____

What Triggered It?: _____

_____

How I reacted?: _____

_____

———o—◇—o———

What Happened?: _____

_____

How I felt?: _____

_____

What Triggered It?: _____

_____

How I reacted?: _____

_____

What Happened?: _____

_____

How I felt?: _____

_____

What Triggered It?: _____

_____

How I reacted?: _____

_____

————o–◇–o————

What Happened?: _____

_____

How I felt?: _____

_____

What Triggered It?: _____

_____

How I reacted?: _____

_____

What Happened?: _____

_____

How I felt?: _____

_____

What Triggered It?: _____

_____

How I reacted?: _____

_____

——o—◇—o——

What Happened?: _____

_____

How I felt?: _____

_____

What Triggered It?: _____

_____

How I reacted?: _____

_____

What Happened?: _____

_____

How I felt?: _____

_____

What Triggered It?: _____

_____

How I reacted?: _____

_____

—o—◇—o—

What Happened?: _____

_____

How I felt?: _____

_____

What Triggered It?: _____

_____

How I reacted?: _____

_____

EXERCISE 10

TRIGGER MANAGEMENT PLAN

This exercise helps you create a plan for dealing with triggers so you can respond to tough situations in a way that feels calmer and more in control.

First, pick one trigger that keeps coming up – something that often sets off strong emotions. For example: *"When someone criticizes me in front of others."*

Next, write down:

- ❖ **What usually happens** – Describe how you feel and react when this trigger happens, like: *"I feel embarrassed and angry, and I usually shut down or snap back."*

- ❖ **What I want to change** – Think about how you'd prefer to respond. For example: *"I want to stay calm and respond without making it worse."*

Then, make a plan for the next time this trigger shows up:

- ❖ **Pause and breathe** – remind yourself to take a few deep breaths before reacting.

- ❖ **Check my thoughts** – ask yourself, *"Am I making this worse by assuming the worst?"*

- ❖ **Choose my response** – decide what you can say or do to handle the situation better, like: *"I'll calmly say, 'I'd appreciate feedback privately.'"*

Finally, write down how you'll take care of yourself after dealing with the trigger. Maybe it's talking to someone you trust, journaling about it, or doing something that helps you relax.

This plan gives you tools to handle tough situations instead of just reacting to them. The more you practice, the easier it gets to manage your triggers!

Trigger: _____

_____

What Usually Happens: _____

_____

What I Want to Change: _____

_____

Plan for the Next Time: _____

_____

————o—◇—o————

Trigger: _____

_____

What Usually Happens: _____

_____

What I Want to Change: _____

_____

Plan for the Next Time: _____

_____

Trigger: _____

_____

What Usually Happens: _____

_____

What I Want to Change: _____

_____

Plan for the Next Time: _____

_____

———o–◇–o———

Trigger: _____

_____

What Usually Happens: _____

_____

What I Want to Change: _____

_____

Plan for the Next Time: _____

_____

Trigger: _____

_____

What Usually Happens: _____

_____

What I Want to Change: _____

_____

Plan for the Next Time: _____

_____

Emotional Vocabulary

Your emotional vocabulary is what will help you develop better emotional skills. Expanding your emotional vocabulary will leave you with a list of free emotions that you can use, recognize, and learn from each way you feel them. This can feel like a book that offers you brand new sentences every time you open it. Because the more you understand every nuance of every emotion, the deeper understanding you will have of yourself. Creating a rich emotional vocabulary can help you understand yourself, the world around you, and why you feel what you feel.

EXERCISE 11

EMOTION VOCABULARY BUILDING

This exercise is an amazing one if you want to expand your "feelings vocabulary" so you can describe your emotions better. When you can name what you're feeling, it's easier to understand and deal with it.

First, grab a notebook and write down a few basic emotions like happy, sad, angry, scared, or calm. Then, challenge yourself to think of more specific words for each one. For example:

✧ Instead of just "happy," you might write "excited," "grateful," or "proud."

✧ For "sad," you could add "disappointed," "lonely," or "heartbroken."

Next, think about recent situations where you felt something strong. Try to match the emotion you felt to a more specific word. For example: *"When my friend cancelled our plans, I wasn't just mad - I felt let down."*

If you get stuck, you can look up a feelings chart online, take a look at the emotion wheel or think about how you might describe the feeling to someone else.

The more you practice; the more words you'll have to explain your emotions with. Having the right words makes it easier to communicate what you're feeling - and to figure out what you need. It's like building a toolbox for your emotions!

Practice emotional expression – it is not all about how you feel on the inside. It is about what you show on the outside, too. Remember that no matter what, it is always a good rule of thumb to appear calm and collected. Whatever you're feeling, try to articulate it with words.

_____

_____

_____

_____

_____

_____

_____

_____

_____

_____

_____

_____

_____

_____

EXERCISE 12

EXPRESSIVE WRITING ACTIVITY

This activity should be your go-to for letting emotions out on paper. It's not about perfect writing - it's about expressing how you feel without holding back.

Simply grab a notebook or open a document and pick a recent experience that made you feel something strong, like frustration, happiness, or sadness. Then, set a timer for 5–10 minutes and write freely about:

- ⬥ **What happened -** Describe the situation in your own words.
- ⬥ **How I felt -** Write about the emotions you experienced, like: *"I felt hurt and ignored when my friend didn't text me back."*
- ⬥ **Why it mattered -** Explore why this event affected you, like: *"It made me feel like they didn't care about our friendship."*

Don't worry about grammar or making it sound good. Just let your thoughts flow, even if they're messy or random.

When the timer goes off, take a deep breath and read what you wrote (if you want to). Then, ask yourself: *"What did I learn from this? Do I feel lighter after writing it down?"*

This activity helps you process emotions and better understand them. Sometimes, just getting things out of your head and onto paper is enough to make you feel a little more in control.

Language can either make or break something. The expressiveness you feel you need to articulate is excellent, but in order to avoid being overly harsh in a certain situation and avoid hurting yourself or someone around you in the long run – *choose your words carefully.*

_____

_____

_____

_____

_____

_____

_____

_____

_____

_____

_____

_____

_____

What Did You Learn From This Chapter?

This chapter was all about learning how to regulate your emotions. If you want to move forward and create a better version of yourself, then take the most out of this chapter by remembering the following:

- ✧ Develop self-awareness with the help of some incredible techniques
- ✧ What are triggers, and patterns, and how can you recognize and control them
- ✧ The usefulness of an emotional vocabulary

Before we move on to the next chapter, I want to say that I am so proud of you! You have truly come a long way. These exercises I have prepared for you, as well as the fantastic outline are my way of saying that I am here for you – and we can do this together! Now turn the page and let's continue!

COGNITIVE BEHAVIORAL STRATEGIES

"The only limit to our realization of tomorrow will be our doubts of today."

– Franklin D. Roosevelt

I n this chapter, I am focusing my attention on all the strategies that can bring you a step closer to being the most powerful version of yourself. These strategies are a part of CBT, and all of them have proven to be quite effective. They are based on all the connections that happen between your emotions, thoughts, and behaviors.

I have talked plenty about how CBT focuses on giving you the tools to solve all of your issues, but for you, it may have felt a little chaotic. Well, this chapter is filled with exercises and strategies – so buckle up!

Identifying and Challenging Negative Thoughts

Negative thoughts are a part of our lives. The thing is, sometimes we can really get caught up in them and allow them to overflow us. This has probably happened to you many times. Through the exercises you are going to learn today, you will discover multiple ways to identify and challenge your negative thoughts. You may find some of these exercises challenging – but that's the point! Maybe you have assumed that the worst is about to happen for too long. Maybe, just maybe, it is time for you to let yourself go a little bit and focus on yourself, on what's important – on what's good. That is why we will start with one of the most important exercises.

Recognizing Cognitive Distortions

Cognitive distortions are thoughts that may cause you to perceive reality in a much worse way than it actually is. Most of these thoughts are irrational or exaggerated. These are mental fillers that stuff your brain with incorrect assumptions and deductions and create a vicious cycle that can be hard to get out of.

Here is an exercise that can help you tame these thoughts.

EXERCISE 13

COGNITIVE DISTORTION IDENTIFICATION

This exercise helps you catch those tricky thoughts that can mess with how you see things. Sometimes, your brain jumps to conclusions or exaggerates situations, and this helps you spot when that's happening.

Start by thinking about a recent moment when you felt upset, stressed, or anxious. Then, write down the thoughts you had at that moment, such as: *"I'm going to fail this test, and everyone will think I'm stupid."*

_____

_____

_____

Next, ask yourself:

Is this thought realistic? For example, "Is it true that one bad test means I'm a failure? Probably not."

_____

_____

_____

Am I using a cognitive distortion? Check if your thought fits any of these patterns:

- ✧ **All-or-nothing thinking:** Seeing things as only good or bad.
- ✧ **Catastrophizing:** Assuming the worst will happen.
- ✧ **Mind-reading:** Thinking you know what others are thinking.

If you notice a distortion, rewrite the thought in a more balanced way. For example: "Even if I don't do great on this test, I can learn from it and do better next time."

_____

_____

_____

The more you practice, the better you get at catching unhelpful thoughts and replacing them with ones that are more realistic and kinder to yourself. It's like training your brain to see the bigger picture!

Thought Records

I always love it when there is a practical way to make use of everything that happens within you – that is why this strategy of recording your thoughts is one of my favorite ones. It can help you pencil in your thoughts and feelings about a certain situation and even add some evidence for it so you can approach every scenario and every event calmly and logically. Take a look at the exercise below – you'll see what I'm talking about.

EXERCISE 14

THOUGHT RECORD WORKSHEET

This exercise helps you break down your thoughts and emotions so you can understand them better and respond in a healthier way.

Start by writing about a situation that made you feel upset or stressed. For example: *"I argued with my friend because they cancelled our plans at the last minute."*

_____

_____

Then, fill in the following steps:

1. **Emotion:** Write down how you felt in that moment, like: *"Angry and disappointed."*

_____

_____

2. **Thoughts:** Jot down what you were thinking, like: *"They don't care about me."*

_____

_____

3. **Evidence for your thought:** List reasons why your thought might feel true, like: *"They've cancelled plans before."*

_____

_____

4. **Evidence against your thought:** Then, write reasons why your thought might not be true, like: *"They said they had an emergency."*

_____

_____

5. **Balanced thought:** Come up with a more realistic way of seeing things, like: *"Maybe they cancelled because they really couldn't make it, not because they don't care about me."*

_____

_____

Finally, check in with yourself. Ask: *"How do I feel now compared to before?"* Writing things out can often help you feel calmer and more in control. The more you practice, the easier it gets to think through situations instead of just reacting.

_____

_____

_____

_____

_____

_____

_____

_____

_____

_____

_____

_____

_____

_____

_____

_____

_____

_____

_____

_____

_____

_____

Reframing Negative Self-Talk

Oh my, there are so many strategies here that it can be hard to keep track at first, right? Well, don't worry. That is why I have created a section at the end of each chapter – something that will remind you of everything you've learned. And this next one will take you by storm!

If you have indulged in negative self-talk for a while now, it may be possible that you feel the effects of it – you feel worthless and incapable. There is a way to reframe all these statements of negative self-talk that you have inflicted upon yourself so deeply. Take the exercise number 15 as a guideline on how to do that.

EXERCISE 15

REFRAMING STATEMENTS

This exercise helps you turn negative or unhelpful thoughts into more balanced and positive ones. It's like flipping a switch in your mind to see things differently.

Start by writing down a negative thought you've had recently, like: *"I always mess things up."*

_____

_____

Then, go through these steps:

1. **Check the facts:** Ask yourself, *"Is this 100% true? Do I really always mess up?"* Usually, the answer is no.   Yes ☐   No ☐

2. **Look for another perspective:** Think about what you'd say to a friend in the same situation. For example: *"Everyone makes mistakes sometimes, but that doesn't mean they're a failure."*

_____

_____

3. **Reframe the thought:** Rewrite the negative thought in a more realistic and encouraging way, like: *"I made a mistake, but I can learn from it and do better next time."*

_____

_____

Keep practicing with different thoughts until it feels natural to catch and reframe them. Over time, this will help you feel less stuck in negativity and more focused on what you can do to grow and improve.

_____

_____

_____

_____

_____

_____

_____

_____

_____

_____

Goal Setting and Problem-Solving

I can only assume this is something you've probably already seen somewhere. Let me guess – you thought it was a ridiculous idea. Well, it's not. The SMART approach can help you formulate a plan to achieve a certain goal. It works every time – as long as you dedicate yourself to it.

EXERCISE 16

SMART GOALS WORKSHEET

This exercise will assist you in creating goals that are clear and doable. Instead of saying *"I want to be better at school,"* you will learn how to break it down into a plan you can actually follow.

Start by picking one thing you want to work on. Then, use the SMART formula to write your goal:

1. **Specific:** What exactly do you want to do? For example: *"I want to improve my math grade."*

2. **Measurable:** How will you know you've achieved it? Like: *"I'll aim to get at least a B on my next math test."*

3. **Achievable:** Is this realistic for you? If not, make it smaller. Instead of *"Ace every test,"* you might say, *"Study for 30 minutes a day."*

4. **Relevant:** Why does this goal matter to you? For example: *"Doing better in math will help me feel more confident."*

5. **Time-bound:** When will you complete this? Like: *"By the end of the next test week."*

Once you've written your SMART goal, create a small action plan. For example: "I'll review notes every day, ask for help if I'm stuck, and use practice tests to study."

When you follow this process, you can track your progress and feel proud when you hit your goals. It's all about taking small, clear steps toward what you want!

S _____

M _____

A _____

R _____

T _____

Action Plan: _____

_____

S _____

M _____

A _____

R _____

T _____

Action Plan: _____

_____

S _____

M _____

A _____

R _____

T _____

Action Plan: _____

_____

S _____

M _____

A _____

R _____

T _____

Action Plan: _____

_____

S _____

M _____

A _____

R _____

T _____

Action Plan: _____

_____

PROBLEM-SOLVING STEPS

This is an exercise that will help you tackle problems step by step instead of feeling stuck or overwhelmed. It's like building a map to find a solution.

First, think of a problem you've been dealing with – big or small. Then, follow these steps:

1. **Describe the problem:** Write down what's going on, keeping it clear and simple, like: *"I keep forgetting to turn in my homework on time."*

2. **Brainstorm solutions:** List as many ideas as you can, even if they seem silly. For example: *"Set reminders, ask a friend to check in with me, or create a homework checklist."*

3. **Pick the best solution:** Choose the one that seems most realistic and helpful. For example: *"Set reminders on my phone for each assignment."*

4. **Make a plan:** Write down what you'll do step by step. Like: *"After school, I'll set reminders for each assignment and check them off when they're done."*

5. **Try it out:** Put your plan into action and see how it works.

6. **Review:** After a few days, check in with yourself: *"Is this helping? If not, what can I tweak?"*

This process helps you feel more in control and less stressed about problems. It reminds you that there's almost always a way forward, even if you have to try a few different things to find it!

_____

_____

_____

_____

Relaxation Techniques

Any relaxation technique is an excellent way to lower your levels of stress, anger, anxiety – anything that you feel building up inside you. But it is about so much more than that. This is an excellent way to help you cope not only with day-to-day stressors but also with long-term stress.

Deep Breathing Exercises

Has it ever happened to you that you find yourself taking a deep breath and then slowly exhaling in the middle of a certain situation? Trust me, your body knows itself, and when it comes to this breathing technique, it is the best one that can calm you down.

EXERCISE 18

DEEP BREATHING PRACTICE

This exercise helps you calm down whenever you feel stressed, angry, or overwhelmed. It's a simple way to help your body and mind feel relaxed.

Find a quiet spot where you can sit down. Close your eyes or just focus on something in front of you. Then, all you need to do is follow these steps:

1. **Breathe in:** Slowly inhale through your nose for a count of four. Your belly should fill up like a balloon.

2. **Hold:** Then, gently hold your breath for a count of four while your body feels still.

3. **Breathe out:** Finally, exhale slowly through your mouth for a count of six.

Repeat this process for a few minutes and only focus on your breath. If your mind wanders, bring it back to the feeling of the air moving in and out of your body.

Afterward, check in with yourself: *"Do I feel calmer or more focused?"* Deep breathing can easily become your go-to when you need a quick way to reset.

Progressive Muscle Relaxation

Progressive muscle relaxation is something you have to feel yourself. As a teenager, I believe you're already intrigued, so here is the exercise.

EXERCISE 19

MUSCLE RELAXATION

This exercise helps release tension in the body. You focus on relaxing each part of you. This way, you can feel calmer and more in control. For example, all you need to do is find a comfortable place to sit or lie down, close your eyes if you want to, and take a deep breath. Then, you need to do this:

1. **Tense a muscle group:** Start with your feet. Squeeze the muscles in your toes and feet as tightly as you can for about five seconds.

2. **Relax:** Then, let go of the tension and notice how your muscles feel looser. Imagine all the stress leaving that part of your body.

3. **Move up my body:** After that, slowly work your way up, repeating the same process for each muscle group.

Remember to take your time. Notice the difference between tension and relaxation in each area.

When you're done, take a deep breath and let your whole body feel heavy yet calm. This exercise helps you let go of physical stress. It can make your mind feel more peaceful.

Visualization

The power of visualization is a concept that people have been turning to for a long time now. What makes it so good is that you can go as deep and as detailed as you want with it – and the more you do it, the calmer you become.

EXERCISE 20

GUIDED IMAGERY

This exercise is the perfect way to relax. All you need to do is imagine a peaceful place in your mind. All you need to do is follow this example to get it right – sit or lie down somewhere comfortable. Close your eyes and take a few deep breaths. Then, begin to imagine a place where you feel completely safe and happy. It could be a beach, a forest, a cozy room, or anywhere else.

As you picture this place, focus on the details:

- ✧ **What do you see?** Maybe the ocean waves, trees, or soft lights.
- ✧ **What do you hear?** Like birds, water, or a gentle breeze.
- ✧ **What do you smell?** Fresh flowers, salty air, or something like baked cookies.
- ✧ **What do you feel?** Warm sand under your feet, soft grass, or a cozy blanket.

Let yourself stay in this place for a few minutes and enjoy the calm and safety it brings. If your mind starts to wander, gently bring it back to your peaceful scene. When you feel ready, take a deep breath, open your eyes, and carry that calm feeling with you. Try this exercise and reset when you feel stressed or overwhelmed.

Building Resilience Through Positive Thinking

Last but not least, never forget the power of positive thinking and affirmations. These can help you turn your life around! A teenager should have at least one of these exercises in their arsenal – so here is the last exercise for this chapter for you.

EXERCISE 21

POSITIVE AFFIRMATIONS

This exercise can help you build confidence and feel better. All you need to do is focus on positive thoughts. It's like you try to give your mind a pep talk. In this case, start by thinking about something you struggle with or want to feel more positive about. Then, create a simple, somewhat encouraging statement to repeat to yourself. For example:

✧ If you feel like you're not good enough, you should say: *"I'm doing my best, and that's enough."*

✧ If you feel nervous about something, you should say: *"I am strong and capable."*

✧ If you're having a bad day, you should say: *"This moment is tough, but I can handle it."*

Look in the mirror and repeat your affirmation out loud or in your head several times. Focus on the words and how they make you feel. As time passes, the more you practice, the more natural it feels to think positively about yourself. Over time, these affirmations will help you replace negative thoughts with kinder, more supportive ones.

_____

_____

_____

_____

_____

_____

_____

_____

_____

_____

_____

_____

_____

What Did You Learn From This Chapter?

This chapter was filled with interesting techniques and exercises. And I am so happy you got to where you are! Before we move on to the next chapter, let's take a quick look at what you learned from this one:

✧ It is important to challenge your negative thoughts, especially through thought records and cognitive distortions

✧ You reframe the way you talk to yourself and focus on solving issues – one at a time

✧ A few relaxation techniques

✧ How to train your brain to think more positively

Now, let's turn the page and jump into the next chapter together!

5

DIALECTICAL BEHAVIOR THERAPY STRATEGIES

"Feelings are just visitors, let them come and go."

- Mooji

It seems like the perfect quote to start this chapter with. DBT usually focuses on people who feel a lot. These may be people who have been struggling with PTSD or just people who often have deep and intense feelings. But, what you're here for, and what I'm here for, is a way to find out how to move past this stage and into a stage of a lighter sense of being. Noticeably, things have been a little difficult for you lately – but that's why I'm here. To make things a lot lighter for you.

In this chapter, I am going to uncover the most useful and powerful techniques that can help you master DBT and, thus, master yourself.

Mindfulness Techniques

A lot of people want to include a little bit of mindfulness in their lives overall. The thing is, most of them believe that this is a very time-consuming process, and they get discouraged before they even begin. I am happy to tell you that they could not be more wrong! As someone who has been dealing with this topic for a long time, I have created the perfect blueprint that can help you add some mindfulness techniques to your life. Trust me, it is a lot easier than you can imagine.

You're already past that stage where you meet everything with anger, stress, rage, or even impatience. You are here to learn, and I am here to show you how to learn and what you need to learn.

Mindful Breathing

Let's start from the beginning – what's the first thing that comes to mind when you think of mindful breathing? Is it breathing for the mind, or is it just being more aware of the present moment? Mindful breathing is actually a very powerful meditation practice. It focuses on paying attention to the natural flow of your breathing cycle. All you need to do is simply – inhale, exhale, and feel the moment.

EXERCISE 22

MINDFUL BREATHING

This exercise can help you stay in the moment and calm your mind. You need to focus on your breath. It's simple, but it can make a big difference, especially if you feel overwhelmed.

To give you a little bit of a pointer, here is what you should do – find a quiet spot where you can sit down. Close your eyes. Then, follow these steps:

1. Take a slow, deep breath in through your nose. Feel the air fill your lungs.
2. Hold your breath for a second and notice how it feels.
3. Breathe out slowly through your mouth (just like you're blowing out a candle).

As you breathe, focus on how the air feels as it moves in and out - cooler when you breathe in, warmer when you breathe out. If your mind starts to wander, instead of becoming frustrated about it, gently bring your focus back to your breath.

Do this for a few minutes and let your breath guide you. Each time you practice, it gets easier to find a sense of calm and stay present, no matter what's happening around you.

Body Scan

This is a very interesting mindfulness technique that can help you connect with yourself. Considered another powerful meditation practice, it can help you relax your body, mind, and soul within a very short period.

EXERCISE 23

BODY SCAN MEDITATION

This exercise will help you relax and connect with how your body feels. It will make you pay attention to each part of yourself, one area at a time. It's like checking in with yourself from head to toe. Here is what you need to do – find a quiet place to sit or lie down and close your eyes. Take a deep breath in, let it out slowly, and start the scan:

1. Begin at the top of your head, noticing whether it feels tight, heavy, or relaxed. Try to let go of any tension as you exhale.

2. Move to your face – your forehead, eyes, cheeks, and jaw. and check if you're clenching anything and relax those muscles.

3. Next, focus on your neck and shoulders. Let them drop if they feel tight.

4. Work your way down to your arms and hands. Notice any sensations like warmth, coolness, or tension.

5. Then, pay attention to your chest and stomach. Feel the rise and fall of your breath.

6. Finally, continue down to your legs, all the way to your feet and toes, and let go of any tension you notice.

If your mind starts to wander, gently bring your attention back to the part of your body you currently want to focus on. When you're done, take one last deep breath. Once you do this, you will notice how much calmer and more connected you'll feel. This exercise will help you tune in and relax when life feels too much.

Grounding Exercises

The strong emotions you feel come with an overwhelming sense of wanting to calm them down. I get that. You're a teenager, everything feels like it's too much, and sometimes you don't know what to do to calm yourself down. It feels like nothing works, and that makes you even more frustrated. One of the most incredible exercises you can do in the case when you feel like nothing is working is this – a simple grounding exercise. Grounding means bringing your focus back to yourself and your senses – all of them. Just for that purpose, I have prepared the next exercise for you.

EXERCISE 24

5-4-3-2-1 GROUNDING TECHNIQUE

This exercise will help you feel calm and present when you're overwhelmed, anxious, or stuck in your head. It uses all the senses to bring you back to the moment. As an example – take a deep breath, then look around you and do the following:

5 **things you see:** Name five things you can see around you. They can be anything, like a chair, a window, or even the way sunlight hits the wall.

4 **things you feel:** Notice four things you can physically feel, like the texture of your clothes, the floor under your feet, or the cool air on your skin.

3 **things you hear:** Listen for three sounds, like birds outside, your breathing, or faint background noises.

2 **things you smell:** Focus on two scents, like the smell of your shampoo, food nearby, or even just fresh air. If you can't smell anything, try to think about smells you like.

1 **thing you taste:** Pay attention to one taste, like gum, a sip of water, or just the natural taste in your mouth.

Take another deep breath when you finish, noticing how much more grounded and in control you feel. It's a quick and easy way to get through stressful moments.

Emotion Regulation Skills

Skills that can help you navigate your emotions are imperative to possess because they can help you navigate all life's challenges. These can help you control and manage your overall emotional state. Now, of course, sometimes, when you have an emotional response to something, it is normal, but as soon as you notice that regulating your emotions becomes a challenge in many cases, it is time to start working on it. Emotion regulation matters if you want to lead a balanced and happy life.

Identifying and Labeling Emotions

While this is something that is done at the beginning of this book (remember, we already talked about this), I decided to look back and revise this. As you can imagine, this is a very important aspect to focus on (since I mention it more than once). Identifying emotions is the proper way to approach yourself before you address any situation you're in. Take the exercise below as your starting point.

EXERCISE 25

EMOTION LABELING WORKSHEET

This exercise is about understanding and naming what you feel. When you can label your emotions, it's easier to figure out what to do with them. What you should do here is start by thinking about a recent situation that made you feel a strong emotion. Then, write or think about these steps:

1. **What happened?** Describe the situation briefly - who was there, what happened, and how it made you feel.

_____

_____

_____

2. **What did you feel?** Try to name the emotions you experienced. Was it anger, sadness, happiness, frustration, excitement, or something else? If you can't think of the exact word, use phrases like "a mix of..." or "kind of like..." to describe it.

_____

_____

_____

3. **Where did you feel it?** Notice how the emotion showed up in your body. Did you feel butterflies in your stomach, a lump in your throat, or tension in your shoulders?

_____

_____

_____

4. **What made it stronger or weaker?** Think about what made the emotion increase or decrease during the situation.

_____

_____

_____

Writing it down or even just going through the steps in your head helps you make sense of your feelings. The more you practice, the better you get at understanding yourself and what you need at the moment.

_____

_____

Opposite Action

The opposite action is quite an interesting skill. As a teenager (someone who most likely goes against everything they're being told – don't worry, we've all been there), you may find this incredibly intriguing. The focus of this is to act the opposite of the urge to act on the emotions you feel at the moment.

The exercise below can give you more clarity.

EXERCISE 26

OPPOSITE ACTION PLAN

Through this exercise, you can manage intense emotions. All you need to do is the opposite of what the emotion makes you do. It's a way to stay in control when your feelings start to take over. In this case, start by thinking about a situation where you felt an emotion that pushed you to act in a way that didn't really help. Then, follow these steps:

1. **What's the emotion?** Name the emotion you're feeling – like anger, sadness, fear, or frustration.

_____

_____

2. **What does it make you want to do?** Figure out what the emotion is pushing you to do. For example, when you're sad, you might want to isolate yourself. When you're angry, you might feel like yelling.

_____

_____

3. **What's the opposite action?** Choose to do something opposite of what the emotion is telling you. If you feel like isolating yourself, reach out to a friend instead. If you feel like yelling, try to speak calmly or walk away.

_____

_____

4. **What happens?** After trying the opposite action, notice how it changes your mood or the situation.

_____

_____

By practicing opposite actions, you learn that you don't always have to follow your emotions blindly. You can take charge and respond in a way that's more helpful to you.

_____

_____

_____

_____

_____

_____

_____

_____

TIPP Skills

This is another handy skill that can help you regulate yourself in "times of trouble". It is all about learning how to act quickly, on your feet, and effectively regulate your emotions. As you can see, it consists of a few aspects – and I have described all of them in the exercise below.

EXERCISE 27

TIPP SKILLS PRACTICE

This is an exercise that will help you calm down quickly when your emotions feel out of control. TIPP stands for *Temperature, Intense Exercise, Paced Breathing, and Progressive Relaxation* – four steps that can bring you back to a calmer state.

Here's how to practice it:

Temperature: Cool yourself down by holding something cold, like an ice pack or a cold drink, or by splashing cold water on your face. It helps your body and mind reset.

Intense Exercise: Do something physical to burn off energy, like jumping jacks, running in place, or even just shaking your hands and legs. This helps release tension.

Paced Breathing: Slow your breathing by inhaling deeply for four seconds, holding it for four seconds, and then exhaling slowly for six seconds. Repeat this until you feel more grounded.

Progressive Relaxation: Tense and then relax each muscle group in your body, starting from your toes and moving up to your head. This helps you release any leftover physical stress.

You can use these steps all together or just pick the one that works best at the moment. Practicing TIPP helps you handle big emotions and stay in control.

Distress Tolerance

Distress tolerance is closely connected to ACCEPTS skills, as shown below. Distress tolerance means having the skills to accept and perceive the environment as it is and not try to change it or demand it to be different in any way.

ACCEPTS Skills

The ACCEPTS skills outline the perfect strategy you need whenever you want to distract yourself from distress or negative emotions. By doing this, you give them time to settle and lower their intensity.

EXERCISE 28

ACCEPTS WORKSHEET

This exercise helps you distract yourself when your emotions feel too overwhelming. ACCEPTS stands for *Activities, Contributions, Comparisons, Emotions, Pushing Away, Thoughts, and Sensations* – different ways to take your mind off tough feelings.

Here's how to work through it:

Activities: Do something that keeps you busy, like drawing, listening to music, playing a game, or going for a walk.

Contributing: Help someone else, like doing a chore, helping a sibling, or texting a friend to check in on them. Helping others should make you feel better, too.

Comparisons: Remind yourself of other tough times you've gotten through or think about people who've overcome similar challenges.

Emotions: Do something that sparks a different emotion, like watching a funny video, listening to uplifting music, or looking at cute pet pictures.

Pushing Away: Imagine putting the problem in a box and locking it away for now. It's not about ignoring it forever, just giving yourself a break.

Thoughts: Focus on something else entirely, like counting backward from 100 or trying to name all the countries you can think of.

Sensations: Use your senses to distract yourself - holding something cold, lighting a scented candle, or listening to calming sounds.

By practicing ACCEPTS, you remind yourself that you have the tools to manage tough moments. It gives you space to cool down and think more clearly.

Self-Soothing Strategies

Oh, I know – your eager-to-learn teenager eyes have just started to read this over and over again, thinking, "How can I self-soothe myself?" Believe me, there is a perfectly good way to do this, and it all boils down to whether you want to try the exercise below or not. My suggestion – give it a go – you will be surprised.

EXERCISE 29

SELF-SOOTHING ACTIVITIES LIST

As a part of this exercise, you need to create a go-to list of things that make you feel calm and safe when you're overwhelmed or upset. It's all about using your senses to take care of yourself.

Just to give you a little guidance, here's how you should do it:

1. **Sight:** Think of things that are relaxing to look at, like sunsets, calming videos, or fairy lights. Then, write those down.

2. **Sound:** List sounds that calm you, like your favorite music, nature sounds, or even humming softly to yourself.

3. **Touch:** Include comforting things you can feel, like wrapping up in a cozy blanket, holding a stuffed animal, or taking a warm shower.

4. **Taste:** Add foods or drinks that feel comforting, like hot chocolate, tea, or your favorite snack.

5. **Smell:** Think of scents that relax you, like candles, essential oils, or the smell of fresh rain.

Write these all down in a list so that the next time you feel stressed, you will have ideas ready to help you feel better. Practicing self-soothing will remind you that you can take care of yourself in tough moments.

Sight _____

_____

_____

_____

Sound _____

_____

_____

_____

Touch _____

_____

_____

_____

Taste _____

_____

_____

Smell _____

_____

_____

_____

Distracting Techniques

It is all in the name – if you want to keep yourself calm, you need a distraction. It is okay to need a distraction every time you feel overwhelmed or distressed – it's normal! But, with that in mind, you need a good **distraction plan.**

EXERCISE 30

DISTRACTION PLAN

Come up with a plan to distract yourself when your emotions feel too big or overwhelming. It's about giving yourself space to calm down before you deal with what's bothering you.

This is what to do:

1. **Make a list of activities:** Think of things you enjoy, or that keep you busy, like watching a show, playing a game, reading, drawing, or going for a walk.

_____

_____

_____

_____

_____

_____

_____

_____

_____

2. **Choose a focus task:** Pick something that takes your full attention, such as solving a puzzle, organizing your room, or trying a new recipe.

_____

_____

_____

_____

3. **Set a time limit:** Decide how long you'll distract yourself - for example, 20 minutes. After that, check in with how you're feeling.

4. **Have it ready:** Make sure you have easy access to your distraction tools, like books, games, playlists, or art supplies.

Distraction isn't about ignoring your problems forever - it's about giving yourself a break so you can come back to them with a clearer mind. Having a plan means you're ready whenever you need it.

Interpersonal Effectiveness

Lastly, for this chapter, I am about to nudge a topic that is just as important as the topic of you. It is the topic of how you present yourself in front of everyone in the world and how you communicate with people around you. Remember that a balanced life comes from the need to look within when you have to, but also to find the balance outside of you. Interpersonal effectiveness focuses on just that – it gives you the skills and strategies to communicate your needs, maintain excellent relationships with the people around you, and constructively resolve any conflicts or challenges that arise along the way.

EXERCISE 31

DEAR MAN WORKSHEET

This exercise is all about the need to ask for what you need or stand up for yourself in a respectful and confident way. DEAR MAN is an easy-to-remember strategy for communicating effectively.

Here's what you need to do:

1. **Describe:** First, start by clearly describing the situation without adding emotions or blame. For example, "When you cancel plans at the last minute..."

2. **Express:** Then share how you feel about the situation. "I feel hurt and disappointed when that happens."

3. **Assert:** After that, say what you need or want. "I'd like you to let me know earlier if you can't make it."

4. **Reinforce:** Explain why it's worth listening to you. "It'll help us avoid misunderstandings and keep things fair."

5. **Mindful:** Stay focused on the goal and don't get distracted by arguments or emotions.

6. **Appear confident:** Speak in a calm and steady voice, even if you feel nervous inside.

7. **Negotiate:** If needed, be open to compromising or working together to find a solution that works for both of you.

Write out a practice conversation using the DEAR MAN steps, so you feel more prepared. This helps you handle tough situations and get your point across without being aggressive or passive. And honestly, you will immediately feel calmer as soon as you write this down.

_____

_____

_____

_____

_____

_____

_____

_____

_____

_____

_____

_____

_____

_____

_____

_____

_____

_____

What Did You Learn From This Chapter?

Wasn't this a fun chapter? I understand if you need some more time to go through it – you can go as slowly as you need, trying one exercise a day and comparing exercises and techniques until you see what works best for you. But all in all, you can see how DBT helps you create a healthier and calmer version of yourself. Through these exercises, you have gathered a lot of information about yourself (you probably didn't even think about it until now), and before we move along to the next chapter, I'd just like to touch upon what you learned here:

- ✧ There are many mindfulness techniques you can use.
- ✧ Emotion regulation skills and identifying emotions are a big part of who you are and who you want to become.
- ✧ There are many distress tolerance strategies you can choose from – ACCEPTS skills, self-soothing, and even distracting.
- ✧ It is just as important to present yourself well in front of others as it is in front of the mirror.

We covered the ground here, and I believe it is time to move on to the next chapter. There is still a lot more to conquer, so turn the page, and let's go over the next chapter!

BUILDING HEALTHY COPING SKILLS

"Believe you can, and you're halfway there."

– Theodore Roosevelt

There will always be some difficult times in life. As you move forward in life, the things that may have an effect on you may be bigger and bigger. Once you become an adult and are well into your 30s and 40s, you will look back at this time right now and appreciate it. Not just because every new stage of life comes with its own challenges but also because you have found the perfect coping skills to deal with any curveball life throws at you – and it all starts here and now.

Coping skills are a way for you to deal with any kind of stressful situation. It is all about managing your stress. This, in the long run, can help you function better both physically and mentally. There are many ways to make this happen (to deal with an issue). All you need to do is remember the techniques and remember that, in the long run, you are looking for ways to eliminate your stress. This may mean making or altering a plan you've already had. Whatever you do, keep the techniques and exercises from this chapter in mind so you can successfully overcome any situation in life – not just now but overall!

Effective Communication

Whenever you interact with others, you need to know how to listen to them and communicate effectively. These two are the basis of a functional communication channel between yourself and another person. This is something you can benefit from in the future, especially career-wise. But it is also something that can help you deal with any kind of situation or negative feelings and thoughts you may have.

Effective communication also means staying focused and consistent – and offering something valuable to the table, too. When there is communication, there is a focus and a purpose. In itself, the concept allows everyone to get a point across.

Take a look at the techniques and exercises connected to effective communication below.

Assertiveness Training

If you've never come face to face with this phrase before, allow me to explain. Assertiveness training is the right to express everything you want – your thoughts, feelings, and needs to another person, but you need to do it in a respectful way. That being said, instead of being angry, aggressive, or anxious, you need to be calm and articulate yourself in a neutral way. The following exercise can help you do just that.

EXERCISE 32

ASSERTIVE COMMUNICATION PRACTICE

This exercise can help you practice speaking up for yourself clearly, respectfully, and confidently. There is no need to be aggressive or passive-aggressive. Assertive communication can help you express your thoughts and needs while still considering others.

Here's how you can practice it:

1. **Identify a situation:** Simply think of a time when you struggled to speak up - maybe asking for help, setting a boundary, or disagreeing with someone.

_____

_____

2. **Write out what you want to say:** Just make sure your message is clear and direct. Instead of saying, "Whatever, it's fine," try, "I'd like to talk about this because it's important to me."

_____

_____

3. **Use 'I' statements:** Focus on your feelings instead of blaming. Instead of "You never listen to me," say, "I feel unheard when I don't get a chance to share my thoughts."

_____

_____

4. **Practice a strong but calm tone:** Say your statement out loud, and make sure your voice is steady, and your body language is open.

5. **Prepare for responses:** Think about how the other person might react and how you can stay assertive without the need to back down or get defensive.

_____

_____

_____

_____

_____

_____

The more you practice, the easier it gets to stand up for yourself and keep your relationships healthy. Don't worry, I will discuss this again later, in the next chapter, and even have another exercise connected to this made just for you.

Active Listening

Another aspect you need to consider is the part where you actively listen, and you are actively being listened to. As a communication skill, this is the act of going beyond the words that the other person utters at you (or in your presence). To succeed in this case, you need to be alert and present in the moment – just be focused on the entire act of communication.

EXERCISE 33

ACTIVE LISTENING EXERCISE

This exercise will help you practice really listening when someone is talking instead of just waiting for your turn to speak. Active listening makes conversations better and can help you understand people more.

Here's how to do it:

1. **Pick someone to practice with:** A friend, family member, or even a video or podcast works.

2. **Focus fully on them:** Put your phone down, make eye contact, and show that you're paying attention with nods or small responses like "Yeah" or "I see."

3. **Repeat or summarize what you hear:** After they finish, restate what they said in your own words: "So, you're saying that..." or "It sounds like you feel..."

4. **Ask follow-up questions:** Instead of jumping in with your own story, ask something like, "What happened next?" or "How did that make you feel?"

5. **Check your body language:** Always keep an open posture, avoid crossing your arms, and face them to show you're engaged.

Afterward, think about how it felt to listen without interrupting or shifting the focus to yourself. The more you practice, the better you get at making people feel heard and understood. If you feel like you need some assistance with honing your communication skills, I got you covered on that in the next chapter.

Setting Boundaries

Boundaries are designed to protect your mental and personal space. These are the fences we all put up to make ourselves feel safe. Think of them as the limits of the other people's behaviors toward you (how far they can go). These types of boundaries define where you end and where another person begins. With their help, you can get a true sense of who you are and what you want and need in life. They can help you build your self-esteem, your self-control, and your overall well-being.

But what happens when you don't know how to set boundaries? Don't worry. It is not the end of the world – it is simply something you have to work on and tweak a little bit to get what you deserve – peace of mind. I have prepared an exercise that can help you do just that.

EXERCISE 34

BOUNDARY SETTING WORKSHEET

With the help of this exercise, you can figure out your personal boundaries and practice how to set them in a clear and respectful way. Boundaries protect your energy, emotions, and personal space.

These are the best ways how you can make that happen:

1. **Identify your boundaries:** Think about what makes you uncomfortable or stressed in relationships, school, or daily life. Do you need more personal space? More respect for your time? Less negativity from others?

_____

_____

_____

_____

2. **Write a boundary statement:** Here, you need to use clear, direct language. Instead of "I don't like when you do that," say, "I need you to ask before borrowing my stuff."

_____

_____

_____

_____

3. **Practice saying it:** Repeat your boundary out loud, and make sure your tone is calm and firm.

4. **Expect pushback:** Some people might not like your boundaries. In such cases, remind yourself that you have a right to set limits, even if others don't agree.

5. **Decide on consequences:** If someone keeps crossing your boundaries, plan your response. "If you keep texting me late at night, I'll have to mute my notifications."

_____

_____

_____

_____

Write down a few boundaries you want to set and how you will communicate them. Practicing them will help you feel more confident about standing up for yourself in a healthy way. Boundaries are important to have if you want to lead a happy and healthy life. I will talk more about them in the next chapter.

Seeking Support

Sometimes, you just don't know where to begin, or you may feel like you are all alone, trapped in a vicious cycle. You might even feel like you are not doing enough for yourself. This book is here to remind you that no matter how strong or weak you think you are, you don't have to do this alone. When you start to feel like things are getting too much for you (and there will be such moments), you need to remember that you can always reach out to someone else for support. After all, progress is not linear, and even with all the techniques at your disposal, there may still be moments when you find yourself thinking you can't do this. I am always here to remind you that it is okay to feel that way from time to time but that it is also okay to seek out help whenever you feel that way. This is one of those techniques that will amaze you – the power of other people in your life.

Identifying Supportive People

Needless to say, there are always some people who make you feel good, while others make you feel bad. This happens to everyone in life, but in your case, you need to carefully select those people that make you feel amazing. That is why I have created the perfect exercise to help you make that happen.

EXERCISE 35

SUPPORT NETWORK MAP

Through this exercise, you can figure out who you can turn to when you need help, advice, or just someone to listen. When you know your support system, it makes it easier to reach out when you're down.

Take a look at what you need to do:

1. **List your support people:** Write down the names of people you trust - friends, family, teachers, coaches, or even online communities.

_____

_____

_____

_____

_____

_____

2. **Organize by role:** Group them based on how they support you. Who gives good advice? Who cheers you up? Who helps you feel safe?

_____

_____

_____

_____

_____

_____

3. **Identify gaps:** If you notice areas where you don't have enough support, think about ways to build stronger connections.

_____

_____

_____

_____

_____

_____

4. **Make a plan to reach out:** Write down one or two people you can check in with this week, even if it's just a quick message.

_____

_____

_____

_____

_____

_____

_____

5. **Keep it updated:** Your support system might change over time, so revisit it when needed.

6. Once you see your support system written down, it reminds you that you're not alone, even when things feel tough.

Expressing Needs and Asking for Help

Now comes the more challenging bit. You may find your support group, but you need to let them into your life, too. The need to express your feelings, be vulnerable, ask for help – that is all a part of being a human. The thing is, not a lot of people know how to really do this. This is all normal, especially for a teenager. You have all these feelings and thoughts inside you; it constantly feels like your blood is boiling, and sometimes, it may even feel like you can't articulate your message. Thankfully, I have designed an exercise that can help you make that happen in a very short period.

EXERCISE 36

ASKING FOR HELP ROLE-PLAY

Sometimes, asking for help feels awkward or uncomfortable, but practicing it makes it easier. In this exercise, simply imagine a situation where you need support – maybe you feel overwhelmed with school, struggle with a friendship, or deal with stress at home.

First, choose someone you trust to practice with or say your words out loud to yourself. Start with a clear and direct statement, like "I've been feeling really anxious about my grades, and I don't know how to handle it. Can we talk?" or "I need help setting boundaries with a friend, but I'm not sure how to do it."

If you practice with someone, pay attention to their response. Do they seem supportive? Do they understand? If you practice alone, imagine different ways the conversation could go and how you might respond.

Afterward, try to reflect on how it felt to ask for help. Did you feel nervous? Relieved? The more you practice, the more confident you become when you truly need to reach out when you need support.

_____

_____

_____

Self-Care Practices

No matter what you do, nothing in the world can help you – not my techniques or exercises, anything – if you don't properly take care of yourself. I know that this may seem strange to read, but taking care of yourself is just as important as learning how to communicate your needs to someone else in a healthy way. Self-care has always been important. This is how you make sure your needs are met.

Good self-care will keep any imbalance, stress, and burnout at bay. Some of the best practices that I mention below will help you reconnect with yourself, relax, and have some fun. These are the things you should enjoy the most.

Importance of Sleep, Nutrition, and Exercise

Need I say more? These three aspects are the main ones when it comes to taking care of your physical self. There is a connection between the mind and the body, and you can nurture it through proper nutrition, exercise, and sleep. I know this may initially seem like too much. Take a look at the exercise below and take it as your starting point on your journey.

EXERCISE 37

SELF-CARE ASSESSMENT

If you want to take care of yourself, this isn't just about relaxing – it's about making sure you meet your physical, emotional, and mental needs. This exercise can help you figure out where you do well and where you might need to focus more on self-care.

Go through the categories below and rate how often you do each one: **Often, Sometimes, or Rarely.**

	Often	Sometimes	Rarely
1. **Physical Self-Care:** Am I getting enough sleep? Eating foods that give me energy? Moving my body in ways that feel good?	☐	☐	☐
2. **Emotional Self-Care:** Do I let myself feel and process emotions instead of ignoring them? Do I have healthy ways to cope with stress?	☐	☐	☐
3. **Mental Self-Care:** Do I challenge negative thoughts? Do I give myself breaks when I need them? Do I spend time doing things that help me grow?	☐	☐	☐
4. **Social Self-Care:** Do I spend time with people who make me feel good? Set boundaries when I need to? Do I reach out for support when I'm struggling?	☐	☐	☐
5. **Fun & Relaxation:** Do I make time for hobbies, creativity, or things that bring me joy?	☐	☐	☐

After you finish, look at the areas where you answered **Rarely** and pick one small step you can take to improve. Self-care isn't about being perfect - it's about making sure you take care of yourself in ways that actually help.

Hobbies and Activities for Stress Relief

After you take care of the physical, there comes the mental aspect of your self-care process. What you decide to do with your mind results in whether you stay mentally fit or not. So, choose the former, and start investing yourself in activities and hobbies that keep your mind sharp. Trust me, this will go miles in improving your overall well-being.

EXERCISE 38

STRESS-RELIEF ACTIVITY PLAN

When you're stressed, it helps to have a plan, so you don't get overwhelmed. This exercise can help you create a go-to list of activities that actually help you feel better. First, think about what kind of stress you have – school pressure, friendship drama, feeling exhausted, or just too many emotions at once. Then, choose activities that match what you need.

- ✧ **If you need to calm down:** Take deep breaths, listen to music, take a warm shower, or do a body scan.
- ✧ **If you need to release energy:** Go for a walk, stretch, dance, or squeeze a stress ball.
- ✧ **If you need a distraction:** Watch a funny show, play a game, read, or do a hobby.
- ✧ **If you need support:** Talk to a friend, journal, or write down what you'd say to someone if you could.

Write down at least five activities that help you overcome each kind of stressor you can think of, so when stress hits, you don't have to think too hard - just pick one and do it.

_____

_____

_____

_____

Developing a Coping Toolbox

Everyone has different ways of dealing with stress – even you. These are the things you probably developed at a very early stage when you weren't quite aware of yourself as much as you are right now. That is okay. These are all skills that can be honed and improved as time passes. Sometimes, they are supportive, sometimes, you just realize that you can do better – and find new ones.

No matter what the case, it is important to have a toolbox of coping skills that can help you each time you feel upset or emotionally activated. Think of it as literally a box – one you can open every time you need help with something. Every time you feel like your tolerance level is low, or you feel anger, sadness, and just too much of everything, you can turn to this toolbox. Simply open it and take what you need.

But how do we build this toolbox? The following exercise explains just that.

EXERCISE 39

COPING TOOLBOX CHECKLIST

To have a coping toolbox means you have go-to strategies ready when you feel overwhelmed, stressed, or upset. This checklist helps you figure out what works best for you so you can build your own personal toolkit.

✓ Calming Techniques

Deep breathing exercises

Listening to music that relaxes you

Taking a warm shower or bath

Doing a body scan or progressive muscle relaxation

Using grounding techniques (like 5-4-3-2-1)

_____

_____

_____

✓ Emotional Release

Journaling your thoughts and feelings

Talking to someone you trust

Cry if you need to

Draw, paint, or create something

Write a letter (even if you don't send it)

_____

_____

_____

_____

✓ Physical Activities

Taking a walk outside

Stretching or yoga

Dancing to music

Squeezing a stress ball or fidget toy

Doing any movement that feels good

_____

_____

_____

_____

_____

✓ Distractions

Watching a favorite movie or show

Reading a book or comic

Playing a game

Doing a hobby (crafts, puzzles, baking, etc.)

Organizing or cleaning a small space

_____

_____

_____

_____

✓ Comfort Items

A soft blanket or stuffed animal

A scented candle or essential oils

A playlist of songs that make you feel safe

A photo or memory that reminds you you're loved

_____

_____

_____

_____

_____

_____

A note to yourself with encouraging words

Check off the ones that already work for you and add any new ideas you want to try. When you feel overwhelmed, you can look at the list and pick something that helps.

What Did You Learn in This Chapter?

Another chapter successfully finished – I am so proud of you! You have come such a long way in this challenge, and it feels like you are conquering your thoughts, feelings, and emotions one step at a time! I cannot imagine how strong you feel right now. We covered a lot of ground in this chapter, let's do a little summation of what you learned:

✧ It is important to build healthy coping skills for long-term success in life

✧ Learn how to communicate your needs with others

✧ It is always okay to ask for help when you feel like you need it

✧ Self-care as a pillar of your overall well-being

✧ Having a coping toolbox handy can be quite beneficial

Now, it is time to move on to the next chapter – one filled with many new and exciting things for you. I have carefully prepared each exercise so far, and this continues in the following pages – so turn the page around, and let's focus on our journey together!

BUILDING HEALTHY RELATIONSHIPS

*"Don't walk in front of me – I may not follow. Don't walk behind me –
I may not lead. Just walk beside me and be my friend."*

– Albert Camus

A beautiful quote, isn't it? But sometimes, it feels like the only thing you can reply to this is – easier said than done. In those exact cases, you need to be more patient and daring – in a good way. The foundation of every relationship you will have in your life is based on your relationship with yourself. Yes, I know, this entire chapter will be food for thought. But also, in this chapter, you will learn how to build healthy relationships – both with yourself and with the people around you.

It seems like this is a two-way street, so this is your queue to invest your side of the effort.

Communication Skills

Let's start from the very beginning. Communication skills are the things you apply whenever you receive any kind of information. You may not have noticed this until now, but you already have a certain set of communication skills developed. You use them every time you interact with someone. The thing is, there is a difference between having communication skills and honing them to perfection. As I mentioned in the last chapter, here we are going to (again) focus on making your communication skills exceptionally sharp. And yes, we are going to do this together.

I have covered the communications skills (and subskills) that you need to work on, so you will have no trouble expressing yourself and giving feedback to anyone, ever.

Active Listening

The first one is active listening. As you can imagine, this is being mindful when you listen to someone else. It means you pay close attention to what they have to say, ask them things that are not clear to you, and give them proper feedback.

Active listening is a very important technique you should practice. When someone notices you have it, it builds both respect and understanding. This is a skill that will help you build yourself up and climb the societal ladder with ease.

It is not difficult to engage in active listening. Some of the most popular techniques include paying attention to the facial expressions of the person you're speaking to, their body language, and their tone. Another popular technique includes shutting out all technology while you're talking to someone (or rather listening to them); this way, you remove all distractions and give them your full attention.

If you're still unsure how to approach this skill, don't worry – you can always refer back to exercise 33 in the last chapter to practice this skill.

Assertive Communication

The second one is assertive communication. Basically, this is learning how to clearly and respectfully state what you need. When you are assertive when doing so, you show other people where you stand, and you show them that you know where they stand too. To succeed in assertive communication, you need to focus on your feelings, avoid being judgemental, and just be honest when you say what you need or want. I know this seems like a practice that can take up a lot of time – and it will. But as time passes, you will notice that assertive communication is one of the pillars when it comes to strengthening your relationships. You promote growth, reduce conflict, and easily overcome any difficult situations.

Differentiating Between Passive, Aggressive, and Assertive Communication

You just learned what assertive communication means. But if you're here, that means you probably don't use this. So, what kind of a communicator are you? There are two other cases where you might stand on this one (of course, not being fully aware of them). While assertiveness is considered to be the middle ground when it comes to communication, you are probably at one or the other end of the spectrum at the moment. What does this mean?

It means you are either passive or aggressive in communication. Let's explain so you know the difference. Passive communication is when you feel stressed, depressed, and tense for a long period, and you start to feel resentment. Passivity leads to you being constantly quiet for a long time and then suddenly lashing out.

On the other side, aggressive communication is when you're actively (and constantly) dissatisfied with everything that surrounds you. In this case, you force your needs onto someone else, you cross all boundaries and disrespect others (even bully them), and you weaken all the relationships you have.

At the end of the day, it is all about knowing how to communicate your needs, wants, and rights while being respectful and understanding of the other side's needs and wants. There are many ways to practice assertiveness and excel at it, but the following exercise is probably one of my personal favorites. Once you go through it, you will realize that it is the perfect fit for you.

EXERCISE 40
ASSERTIVENESS ROLE-PLAY

Being assertive means to stand up for yourself and still respect others. This exercise will help you practice speaking up in a clear, confident way. With this exercise, you will avoid being aggressive or passive. Find a friend or family member, or even practice in front of a mirror. Pick a situation where you need to be assertive - maybe when you ask a teacher for extra help, set a boundary with a friend, or say no to something you're uncomfortable with.

Follow these steps:

1. **Use "I" statements.** Instead of blaming or accusing, focus on your feelings and needs. Example: "I feel frustrated when I don't get a chance to speak. I'd like to share my thoughts too."

2. **Keep your tone calm and steady.** Speak clearly, make eye contact, and stand with confidence.

3. **Be direct but respectful.** Say what you need without apologizing unnecessarily or backing down. Example: "I can't help with that today, but I hope it goes well."

After you practice, ask yourself: Did I stay calm? Did I get my point across? How did it feel to speak up? The more you practice, the easier it becomes to be assertive in real-life situations.

Nonverbal Communication

The third one of the communication skills has actually nothing to do with communication. But also, it has everything to do with it. In many cases, when we speak (or when other people speak) and are fully invested in the topic, the body follows. Nonverbal communication means conveying a message without the use of words. Here, a speaker may use their hands to make a gesture, use their face as they make eye contact, or even use their entire body to express something.

It has probably happened to you many times – you met someone who is excellent at nonverbal communication, and you either felt happy that you could completely understand them, or you felt a little bit intimidated by their skill. Whatever the case may be, you can easily learn how to communicate without using your words – and I am here to teach you just that. Let's cover the most important aspects of it.

You can get a lot of information just by looking at someone's posture and movement. Think about it, you have probably already noticed this. When someone is mad or defensive, they cross their hands. When someone wants to explain something, and they're really invested in it, they do a lot of gestures and so on. Body language can show you when someone has strong feelings and attitudes about something (be that positive or negative). All you need to do is observe.

Facial expressions are probably responsible for the largest portion of nonverbal communication. You can say so much by making a simple face. For example, think of how many things have been communicated only by a smile or a frown. It's amazing, right? Sometimes, when you see the look on someone's face, you immediately know what they want to say or what they think. Because the face is the first thing we see, even before someone speaks to us, it is the first form of communication before you actually utter any words.

When you focus on improving your nonverbal communication skills, you focus on adding importance to your conversations. A big portion of the communication that happens among people is nonverbal, so you need to be fluent in that too. This exercise I've created for you focuses on that.

EXERCISE 41

NONVERBAL COMMUNICATION PRACTICE

Communication isn't just about words - your body language, facial expressions, and tone of voice can say just as much (or more) than what you actually say. This exercise helps you become more aware of how you communicate without words and how to read nonverbal cues from others.

Step 1: Observe Yourself

Stand in front of a mirror or record yourself while saying a simple sentence like, "I'm fine." Try saying it in different ways:

- ✦ With a smile and relaxed posture
- ✦ With crossed arms and a frown
- ✦ While you avoid eye contact and mumbling

Notice how each version sends a completely different message, even though the words don't change. Ask yourself: What emotions come across in my expressions and body language? Do they match my words?

Step 2: Practice with a Friend

Ask a friend or family member to talk briefly with you about anything. Focus on using positive nonverbal cues, like:

- ✦ Making eye contact
- ✦ Nodding or using small reactions to show you're engaged
- ✦ Keeping an open posture (not crossing your arms or looking away)

Then, switch roles and try the opposite. Cross your arms, avoid eye contact, or fidget. See how it changes the way the conversation feels.

Step 3: Reflect

Think about a time when you misread someone's body language or when yours didn't match what you were saying. How can being more aware of nonverbal communication help you express yourself better and understand others more clearly? Nonverbal cues are powerful, and being mindful of them can make a big difference in how you connect with people.

Building Empathy

It is time to move on to the next skill, which is kind of an important one. Before I begin, I must say this – there is a little bit of empathy in every one of us. While some people know how to express it better, and others may not, empathy is always there – entwined in the core of our being.

In your instance, empathy can be a true game-changer when it comes to building the best version of yourself. This is how you can cultivate connection and openness. This is how you can help yourself and the people around you feel less alone. Through building empathy, you can improve your commitment to creating a better life for yourself, your overall well-being, mindfulness, and willingness to do better.

You may have mistaken empathy for compassion or sympathy, but these are not the same things. They seem like they are, but empathy is something a lot deeper. When we talk about empathy, we talk about our feelings with people – not just for them. For example, when you are empathetic toward someone, you don't just guess how they feel. You feel the same feelings they have, and you are there for them.

Practicing Empathy

This sounds a little bit tricky, but no worries – I am here to guide you every step of the way. Think of building empathy as building a muscle. The longer you work on it, the better it gets. You can do many exercises to make this happen – and of course, I have included the best ones here. The only thing you need to be mindful of before you begin is that you need to be patient with yourself. There is no need to put some stress on yourself through your journey. All you need to be is calm and trustworthy in the process.

It is all about being curious about other people's experiences. These can tell you a lot. They can also help you deepen your understanding of them and their journey. So, when you want to practice empathy, start by giving them your full attention. Pay attention to the nonverbal communication as well, and ask them questions that will help you clarify their situation. Try to avoid making assumptions, and with every word, step out of your comfort zone and into a kinder, more mindful one.

I believe the best way to learn empathy is to take on a few roles. The role-playing exercises I created for this book are an amazing starting point. They can help you see your own perspective more clearly and the perspective of the person or people standing opposite you. Here is the next exercise.

PRESCRIPTIVE-TALKING ROLE-PLAY

Seeing things from someone else's point of view can help you understand their feelings, strengthen relationships, and avoid unnecessary conflict. This exercise will help you practice how to step into someone else's shoes and consider their perspective before you react.

Step 1: Pick a Scenario

Choose a situation where two people might see things differently. Here are some ideas:

✧ A friend cancels plans at the last minute, and you feel annoyed.

✧ A teacher gives you extra homework, and you think it's unfair.

✧ A sibling takes something of yours without asking, and you feel disrespected.

Step 2: Play Both Roles

First, take your own perspective. Say out loud how you feel and why. Be honest about your frustration, disappointment, or confusion.

Next, switch roles. Pretend you are the other person. Why might they have acted the way they did? What might they be feeling? For example:

✧ **Friend's perspective:** "I know I cancelled, but I had a really stressful day and needed time alone."

✧ **Teacher's perspective:** "I assigned extra homework because I want my students to be fully prepared for the test."

✧ **Sibling's perspective:** "I didn't think borrowing it would be a big deal, and I meant to put it back."

Step 3: Reflect and Adjust Your Response

Now that you've considered both sides, think about how this changes your reaction. Do you still feel as upset? How would you handle the situation differently now?

Try responding in a way that acknowledges both your feelings and theirs. For example:

- ✧ "I get that you needed a break, but I was looking forward to seeing you. Next time, just let me know earlier."
- ✧ "I still don't love having extra homework, but I understand why you assigned it."
- ✧ "I'd appreciate it if you ask before borrowing my stuff. That way, we can avoid any misunderstandings."

Step 4: Apply It in Real Life

The next time you feel frustrated with someone, pause for a moment and ask yourself: *What might be going on from their perspective?* It doesn't mean you have to agree with them, but understanding their side can help you respond more patiently and confidently.

Reflective listening

Reflective listening means both hearing and understanding what the other person is trying to say to you, but in the meantime letting them know that they are heard and understood by you. This takes active listening (which we already talked about) and giving them feedback too. Here, your attention needs to only focus on the person you're talking to at the moment – no one and nothing else. Here is an exercise that can help you do that.

EXERCISE 43

REFLECTIVE LISTENING PRACTICE

Listening isn't just about hearing words – it's about making the other person feel understood. Reflective listening helps you stay engaged in conversations, show empathy, and avoid misunderstandings. This exercise will guide you through practicing reflective listening so you can improve your communication skills.

Step 1: Find a Partner

Ask a friend, family member, or classmate to have a conversation with you. Let them choose a topic – something they care about, whether it's a recent experience, a problem, or something exciting happening in their life. Your goal is to listen actively and reflect on their words.

Step 2: Listen Without Interrupting

As they speak, focus on:

- ✧ Making eye contact
- ✧ Nodding or using small verbal cues like "I see" or "That makes sense"
- ✧ Avoiding distractions (no phone-checking or thinking about what you'll say next)

Resist the urge to give advice, correct them, or share your own story. Just listen.

Step 3: Reflect What You Heard

Once they finish speaking, summarize what they said in your own words to check if you understood correctly. Use phrases like:

- ✧ "So, what I'm hearing is…"
- ✧ "It sounds like you're feeling…"
- ✧ "You're saying that…"

For example, if they say, "I'm so stressed about my exam. I feel like no matter how much I study, I'll still mess up," you could reflect:

- ✧ "It sounds like you're really worried about the exam and feel like studying isn't helping as much as you'd like."

If they agree, great! If not, ask, "Did I get that right?" and let them clarify.

Step 4: Validate Their Feelings

Even if you don't fully understand or agree, acknowledge their emotions. You might say:

- ✧ "That sounds really frustrating."
- ✧ "I can see why you'd feel that way."
- ✧ "That makes sense."

Validation doesn't mean you have to fix their problem—it just shows that their feelings are real and important.

Step 5: Switch Roles and Reflect

Now, let your partner practice reflective listening while you talk about something on your mind. Notice how it feels when someone truly listens to you.

Step 6: Apply It in Real Life

Try using reflective listening in daily conversations. Whether a friend is venting, a teacher is giving instructions, or a family member is sharing something important, take a moment to listen, reflect, and validate. It can make a huge difference in how people connect with you.

Empathy in Conflict Resolution

Empathy can go a long way, especially when you want to resolve a conflict with someone. It can help you understand the other side's perspective and feelings. In terms of conflict, it can act as a bridge both parties need to cross to get to a mutual understanding (or meet halfway, whatever works for you). Suppose you utilize empathy whenever you try to resolve a certain issue. In that case, you will have a unique opportunity to understand the other person's emotions and point of view and find a common ground where you can both agree on something. By doing this, you will be able to diffuse any tension and reach an understanding. Allow me to further explain how you can do this.

It is all about the ability to humanize the person standing across from you. When tensions arise and a situation gets heated, it is easy to forget that you are speaking to another human being. Emotions get the best of you, and you may act out – quite impulsively. In this case, whenever you feel like you need to calm yourself down and get to the bottom of the conflict, it is important to stop and remind yourself that the other person is human too. They have their own thoughts and feelings, and they want to express them too. Step into their shoes for a moment and see what it is like from the other side. Use empathy in such cases so you can get the best results.

When it comes to techniques for empathetic communication, we have covered most of them during the course of this book. The best ones that I can mention here include active listening and validation of the other person's point of view. Also, bring them a sense of safety by showing them you will understand them rather than lash out at them. Furthermore, you can identify the points where miscommunication may happen and try to bridge that gap. By doing all of this, you will create a sense of safety and start to engage in a constructive conversation. It is indeed easier to lash out at someone, but this will by far have the better result.

EMPATHY IN CONFLICT RESOLUTION SCENARIOS

Conflict happens. It's part of life. But how you handle it can make a huge difference in your relationships. This exercise will help you practice using empathy to resolve conflicts in a way that strengthens connections rather than damages them.

Step 1: Understanding Empathy in Conflict

Empathy means putting yourself in someone else's shoes and trying to see things from their perspective. In a conflict, this doesn't mean agreeing with everything the other person says – it just means acknowledging their feelings and making them feel heard.

When conflict arises, people often focus on proving they're right instead of understanding the other person's emotions. But if you listen with empathy, you're more likely to find a solution that works for both of you.

Step 2: Choose a Scenario

Pick one of these situations (or think of your own) and imagine how you would normally react:

◇ A friend snaps at you for no reason, and you feel hurt.

◇ A classmate takes credit for something you did in a group project.

◇ Your parent or guardian keeps telling you to do something you don't think is fair.

◇ A sibling borrows your stuff without asking and doesn't return it.

_____

_____

_____

_____

Now, instead of reacting with anger or frustration, you will work through the situation with empathy.

Step 3: Pause and Identify Emotions

Before responding, take a deep breath and ask yourself:

- ✧ What emotions am I feeling? (Hurt? Frustration? Annoyance?)
- ✧ What might they be feeling? (Stressed? Overwhelmed? Misunderstood?)
- ✧ Is there something deeper going on for them?

For example, if a friend snaps at you, your first reaction might be to snap back. But if you stop and think, you might realize they've had a rough day, and their response isn't actually about you.

_____

_____

_____

_____

_____

Step 4: Respond with Empathy

Now, rewrite how you would handle the situation using empathy. Instead of saying, "Why are you being so rude?" you might say, "Hey, you seem upset. Did something happen?"

Here are a few empathy-based responses you can use in conflicts:

- ✧ **Acknowledging feelings:** "I get why you're frustrated."
- ✧ **Asking open-ended questions:** "Can you help me understand why this upset you?"
- ✧ **Validating their perspective:** "I see why that would bother you."
- ✧ **Offering a compromise:** "What if we tried this instead?"

Take your chosen scenario and write out both an instinctive reaction (without empathy) and an empathetic response. Compare the two. Which one is more likely to lead to a resolution?

_____

_____

_____

_____

Step 5: Reflect and Apply

Think about a recent conflict in your life. Could empathy have changed the outcome? How will you handle a future conflict differently now that you've practiced responding with understanding?

Next time you're in a tough situation, pause and use this strategy. You might be surprised at how much smoother things go when people feel heard and understood.

Managing Relationship Challenges

By this stage in your life, you probably already have your own idea of what your relationships with other people should look like. Whether you think of a relationship with yourself, a partner, your family, your friends, or your teachers, there is a clear idea of what that should look like. The thing is, not everybody thinks the same way you do. When you're young, this idea usually comes from what surrounds you and what you see – the relationship between your family, movies you watch, series, and even books you read – oh, and the media, too! But, these are not always realistic ideas of what relationships overall should look like. That is mostly the reason why young people like yourself get in conflict in the first place (yes, not everything is your fault).

To manage a challenge in a relationship takes effort – and it takes two. However, no matter what the case is, start from yourself, work on yourself, and you will immediately see how things will get better. There are two main things you can focus on, and I've covered both of them – let's see them together.

Handling Peer Pressure

There is always a desire to fit in – society, with classmates, with any type of group. But, when you want to enter a new group, there is always something called peer pressure hanging over your head. Handling peer pressure is not always challenging, especially when you are among people who share the same thoughts, opinions, and values as you do. But if that isn't the case, the peer pressure is strong.

Do you know how you can recognize peer pressure? I call this trusting your gut. You are most likely put in a situation you don't really like (deep down), and you need to do something that you wouldn't normally do or something you know is wrong. All of this has one goal – to become accepted into a certain group.

You probably came up with some ideas on your own while you were reading this, but just in case you didn't, here are a few techniques you can use to resist any negative influence. First things first, remember that you don't have to please anyone and that you are enough. Then, try to avoid situations and people who make you feel uncomfortable. If someone is pushing your boundaries, stand firm on your feet and decline. Focus on spending time with people who make you feel supported, loved, and understood. It may be difficult to understand, but not everyone will like you – and that's okay. And if all else fails, you can always turn to someone for support or help.

Having a little confidence in yourself can go a long way. It can teach you how to act better in such situations. You will not succumb to the pressure you're faced with and will come out the other side a winner. All you need to do is remember that you are good enough just as you are and that you are doing everything you can to become better with each passing day.

EXERCISE 45

PEER PRESSURE RESISTANCE SCENARIOS

Peer pressure can be tough. Sometimes, it's obvious – like someone daring you to do something risky. Other times, it's more subtle, like feeling you have to dress a certain way or agree with something just to fit in. This exercise will help you practice standing up for yourself and making choices that align with what *you* truly want.

Step 1: Recognizing Peer Pressure

Before you can resist peer pressure, you have to recognize it. Think about situations where you might feel pressured to do something you're not comfortable with. It could be:

- ◇ A friend pushing you to try something you don't want to (drinking, smoking, skipping class).
- ◇ Classmates making fun of someone and expecting you to join in.
- ◇ A group convincing you to spend money on something you don't need.
- ◇ Friends pushing you to post something online that doesn't feel right.

Peer pressure can be direct (someone telling you what to do) or indirect (feeling like you have to do something to fit in). Take a moment to think about a time when you felt pressured. What did it feel like? How did you respond?

_____

_____

_____

_____

_____

_____

_____

_____

Step 2: Choose a Scenario

Pick one of the scenarios below (or come up with your own) and imagine you're in that situation:

- ✧ **Scenario 1:** Your friends are sneaking out at night and expect you to join them. When you hesitate, they tease you for being "too scared."

- ✧ **Scenario 2:** A classmate offers you a vape and says, "Come on, it's not a big deal. Everyone's doing it."

- ✧ **Scenario 3:** Your friends are making fun of someone online and want you to comment something mean to fit in.

- ✧ **Scenario 4:** You're at a party where people are drinking. Someone hands you a drink and says, "Just one sip won't hurt."

- ✧ **Scenario 5:** A friend is pressuring you to let them copy your homework. When you refuse, they act annoyed and say, "I thought we were friends."

_____

_____

_____

_____

Step 3: Identify Your Feelings and Values

Before responding, pause and ask yourself:

- ✧ How do I feel about this? (Nervous? Annoyed? Stressed?)
- ✧ What are my values in this situation? (Honesty? Safety? Self-respect?)
- ✧ Will doing this make me feel good about myself later?

Knowing your values makes it easier to stand your ground. If something doesn't align with what *you* want, it's okay to say no.

_____

_____

_____

_____

_____

_____

_____

_____

Step 4: Practice Saying No

Now, rewrite how you would respond to your chosen scenario in a way that's firm but respectful. You don't have to make a big scene – you just need to make it clear that you're not interested.

Here are some ways to say no:

- ✧ **Be direct:** "No thanks, I'm not into that."
- ✧ **Use humor:** "Yeah, I don't feel like getting grounded today."
- ✧ **Suggest an alternative:** "Let's do something else instead."

- ✧ **Blame something else:** "My parents would get mad at me if they found out."
- ✧ **Walk away:** If they won't take no for an answer, remove yourself from the situation.

Now, write out your response for the scenario you picked. How do you feel about your response? Would you be able to say it in real life?

Step 5: Reflect and Apply

Think about how peer pressure affects your life. Have there been times when you said yes to something you didn't want to? How did it feel afterward?

Now that you've practiced, challenge yourself to notice peer pressure when it happens and use these strategies to stand up for yourself. Remember – real friends respect your choices, even if they're different from theirs.

Healthy Boundaries

The other thing you can always focus on to get the best results in terms of managing relationship challenges is to set healthy boundaries. Now, even though we already discussed them in the last chapter, I feel like it is worth it to mention them again. These can help you define what appropriate behavior means to you – especially in a healthy relationship. This is called healthy because it is based on keeping both parties involved safe. It is also a crucial step if you want to create a foundation for a long-lasting and positive relationship – with anyone.

As I mentioned, these boundaries differ from person to person and are usually governed by culture, social context, and personality. They are interpersonal limits that help us function better as individuals and as members of society.

When you set boundaries for yourself, it means you are aware of yourself. It means that you have expectations set in place which can help you determine whether you are comfortable or not in a certain situation. But also, as the importance of setting boundaries is always present, so is the ability to communicate clearly. As you mature and grow up, you will see that these two are actually intertwined – one cannot go without the other.

It is easy to set and maintain boundaries if you know how to approach this topic right. It all comes down to being assertive. Assertiveness means you need to know how to openly and respectfully share what it is you want, need, and feel. Think of your priorities as a form of self-care. Just be clear in what it is you want to articulate, try not to raise your voice, and accept that, sometimes, there may be a little discomfort on both ends (when you state what you want) – and all of that is a normal part of the process.

Finally, as much as you'd like other people to respect your boundaries, you need to respect theirs as well. This is something that can help you overcome any challenge you have in life, especially when communicating with another person. Just take a look at the exercise below, and things will get a lot clearer for you.

EXERCISE 46

BOUNDARY-SETTING PRACTICE

Setting boundaries means knowing what makes you feel comfortable and standing up for yourself when someone crosses the line. Boundaries help you protect your time, energy, emotions, and personal space. This exercise will help you practice recognizing when boundaries are needed and how to enforce them in a way that is clear and confident.

Step 1: Understanding Boundaries

There are different types of boundaries:

- ❖ **Physical boundaries** – Deciding who can touch you, how close people can get, and when you need personal space.

- ❖ **Emotional boundaries** – Protecting your feelings and not taking on other people's emotions as your own.

- ❖ **Time boundaries** – Managing your time so you don't feel overcommitted or pressured.

- ❖ **Digital boundaries** – Deciding who can contact you, what personal information you share, and how much time you spend online.

Think about a time when someone made you feel uncomfortable by ignoring one of your boundaries. What happened? How did you react? If you need some help with this, I suggest you reflect on the boundary-setting worksheet from the previous chapter. This can be an excellent starting point for you.

Step 2: Recognizing When a Boundary is Needed

Boundaries are needed when:

- ❖ Someone pressures you to do something you don't want to do.
- ❖ A friend or family member disrespects your feelings.
- ❖ People constantly ask for your time or energy, leaving you exhausted.
- ❖ Someone invades your privacy, like reading your messages or touching your belongings without permission.
- ❖ A person crosses a personal or emotional limit that makes you uncomfortable.

Choose one situation from above (or one from your own life) and write down how it made you feel.

_____

_____

_____

_____

Step 3: Practicing Boundary Statements

The best way to set a boundary is to be **clear, calm, and direct**. Boundaries are not about being rude or controlling—they're about respecting yourself.

Here's a simple formula:

"I feel [emotion] when [behavior] happens. I need [boundary]."

For example:

- ✧ "I feel overwhelmed when I get too many messages late at night. I need people to text me earlier in the day."
- ✧ "I feel uncomfortable when people touch my stuff without asking. I need you to ask before using my things."
- ✧ "I feel stressed when my time isn't respected. I need to leave by 9 PM, so I can't stay later."

Now, write your own boundary statement for the situation you picked in Step 2. How does it feel to say it?

_____

_____

_____

_____

_____

_____

_____

Step 4: Handling Pushback

Sometimes, people don't like hearing "no." They might:

- ✧ Guilt-trip you ("Come on, don't be like that!")
- ✧ Ignore your boundary ("You're being too sensitive.")
- ✧ Keep pushing ("Just this one time?")

If someone doesn't respect your boundary, you can:

- ✧ **Repeat your boundary**: "I already said I can't stay late. Please respect that."
- ✧ **Offer an alternative**: "I can't hang out tonight, but let's meet up tomorrow."
- ✧ **Walk away**: If they refuse to respect you, you don't have to stay in the conversation.

Write down ways you could respond if someone pushes against your boundary.

_____

_____

_____

_____

_____

_____

Step 5: Apply It in Real Life

Think about one area in your life where you need stronger boundaries. How will you start enforcing them? Who do you need to communicate with?

Practice saying your boundary statement out loud. If setting boundaries feels uncomfortable, remember: You are allowed to protect your space, energy, and emotions. The people who respect you will respect your boundaries.

What Did You Learn From This Chapter?

Congratulations on completing the longest chapter of this book! Before we move on to the final chapter, let's just make a small recap of everything you've learned here.

- ✦ Communication skills, especially active listening, assertiveness, and nonverbal communication, are incredibly important in creating a better and stronger version of yourself.
- ✦ Empathy has a big role in the process.
- ✦ Learn how to practice empathy and use it whenever you come in contact with someone.
- ✦ Every relationship in life comes with its own set of challenges – but now you have the tools to overcome anything that comes your way.
- ✦ You can easily become who you want to be as long as you set healthy boundaries.

Your magnificent mind is filled with plenty of useful information – but it still feels like something is missing. Well, it is time for me to say this for the last time – turn the page, and let's discover the last bit of what you need to step into the most powerful version of yourself!

LONG-TERM EMOTIONAL REGULATION STRATEGIES

"We don't know where we're going, we don't know what's going to happen, but no one can take away from you what you put in your own mind."

– Edith Eger

We've talked about the good things, and we've talked about the bad things. We've covered how to identify and regulate your emotions and deal with negative thoughts. But now, you may start to wonder – how long can you keep this up? Is this really working on yourself, or are these just techniques that will help you patch things up for just a little while?

It's okay to have these questions. These are a part of growing up. And honestly, you don't know what's going to happen tomorrow, but you do want to see that you can cope with whatever comes your way. That is why I am dedicating this chapter to long-term emotional regulation strategies. While you now know how to deal with any kind of situation, you also need a little bit of support so you can easily handle anything and everything in the future.

Developing Consistent Habits

As you go through life, you will notice the power of consistency – especially the part where you show up for yourself, day after day. I have divided this chapter into two sections you need to focus on – and this is the first one. Developing constant habits is a very easy thing to do – it only takes a few weeks to become consistent in anything. But, deep down, when it comes to your core, remember that you can choose to be whoever you want every day. This is where your consistency should come from. If you want to become the best version of yourself, it is all about focusing on the right habits. And what are these "right habits"? Well, they are all the things I mentioned in all the previous chapters – the techniques, the exercises – everything!

So you see? This kind of goes full circle – one cannot go without the other.

Daily Emotional Check-Ins

The emotional check-in is the time in your day when you need to stop for a minute and assess how you feel. This is a very important thing to do because it can help you become more honest about yourself. It can bring you calmness (knowing that you can identify your feelings), it can help you talk about them more openly, and it can help you cope with them better. Also, doing this is a proactive problem-solving tool, it can help you build self-awareness skills and help you create a connection between your thoughts and feelings.

There is a lot of importance in checking in with yourself on a regular basis. As humans, we are constantly preoccupied with many things, and sometimes, it can be very easy to stray away from our path. In these situations (and yes, they are very likely to happen), you need to be gentle with yourself rather than harsh. You need to give yourself a break but remind yourself that you have a goal, you have something quite attainable, and you are going for it every day.

I found the best way to check in with yourself is through the worksheets I designed for the next exercises. They are probably the best techniques, and as you can see, they can also be helpful tools. I'm presenting these techniques to you in the form of worksheets. Now, for your keen teenager eye, it will seem like they are extremely similar (and you're right about it, sort of). The worksheets are quite similar, though as soon as you delve a little deeper into them, you will notice that they are focused on different things. Take a look for yourself and see.

EXERCISE 47

DAILY EMOTIONAL CHECK-IN WORKSHEET

Checking in with your emotions every day helps you better understand yourself, recognize patterns, and build emotional awareness. Instead of letting emotions control you, this practice gives you the power to notice how you feel and respond in a healthy way. This worksheet will guide you through a simple emotional check-in that you can do daily.

Step 1: Pause and Notice

Take a deep breath. Close your eyes for a moment and check in with yourself. How do you feel right now? Don't rush – just notice. Are you calm? Stressed? Excited? Tired? Write down the first words that come to mind.

Today, I feel: _____

_____

Step 2: Identify the Cause

Think about what might be influencing your emotions today. It could be something that happened at school, a conversation with a friend, upcoming responsibilities, or even how much sleep you got last night. Try to name the main reason behind how you're feeling.

I think I feel this way because: _____

_____

Step 3: Rate Your Emotions

On a scale of **1-10**, where **1** is "not intense at all" and **10** is "overwhelming," rate how strong your emotions are.

My emotional intensity is: _____ /10

If your number is **7 or higher**, it might help to use a coping skill (like deep breathing, journaling, or talking to someone). If it's **3 or lower**, you might be in a good place to focus on goals and productivity.

Step 4: Check Your Body

Emotions don't just exist in your mind – they show up in your body too. Where do you feel your emotions physically? Do you have tension in your shoulders? A tight chest? A headache? Maybe your stomach feels weird, or you feel extra energetic.

Right now, I notice in my body: _____

_____

Step 5: Respond to Your Emotions

Now that you've identified how you feel and why, think about what you need. Do you need to calm down, cheer up, take a break, or talk to someone? What action can you take right now that would be helpful?

One thing I can do to take care of myself today is: _____

_____

Step 6: Set an Intention

End your check-in by setting a small intention for the rest of the day. It can be something like:

- ✧ "I will take deep breaths when I feel overwhelmed."
- ✧ "I will focus on things I can control."
- ✧ "I will remind myself that my feelings are valid."

My intention for today is: _____

_____

Final Reflection

Doing this check-in every day helps you stay connected to your emotions and respond in a healthy way. Try it for a week and see how it affects your mood, stress levels, and decision-making. If you notice patterns in your emotions, you can start making changes that help you feel better.

Today, I feel: _____

I think I feel this way because: _____

_____

My emotional intensity is: _____ / 10

Right now, I notice in my body: _____

_____

One thing I can do to take care of myself today is: _____

_____

My intention for today is: _____

_____

———o–◇–o———

Today, I feel: _____

I think I feel this way because: _____

_____

My emotional intensity is: _____ / 10

Right now, I notice in my body: _____

_____

One thing I can do to take care of myself today is: _____

_____

My intention for today is: _____

_____

Today, I feel: _____

I think I feel this way because: _____

_____

My emotional intensity is: _____ / 10

Right now, I notice in my body: _____

_____

One thing I can do to take care of myself today is: _____

_____

My intention for today is: _____

_____

————o–◇–o————

Today, I feel: _____

I think I feel this way because: _____

_____

My emotional intensity is: _____ / 10

Right now, I notice in my body: _____

_____

One thing I can do to take care of myself today is: _____

_____

My intention for today is: _____

_____

Today, I feel: _____

I think I feel this way because: _____

_____

My emotional intensity is: _____ / 10

Right now, I notice in my body: _____

_____

One thing I can do to take care of myself today is: _____

_____

My intention for today is: _____

_____

———o–◇–o———

Today, I feel: _____

I think I feel this way because: _____

_____

My emotional intensity is: _____ / 10

Right now, I notice in my body: _____

_____

One thing I can do to take care of myself today is: _____

_____

My intention for today is: _____

_____

EXERCISE 48

DAILY MOOD TRACKER

Keeping track of your mood each day helps you notice patterns, understand what affects your emotions, and make better choices for your well-being. This exercise will guide you through tracking your mood and identifying factors that influence how you feel. The more you pay attention to your emotions, the easier it becomes to manage them in a healthy way.

Step 1: Record Your Mood

Think about how you've felt today. Try to sum it up in one or two words. You don't need to overthink it—just write down what feels right.

Today, I feel: _____

Step 2: Rate Your Mood

On a scale of **1-10**, where **1** is the lowest (really bad) and **10** is the highest (really great), rate your overall mood for today.

My mood rating for today is: _____ / 10

Step 3: Identify the Main Emotion

Write down the main emotion that stood out today. You might have felt many emotions, but choose the one that was strongest.

✧ Happy	✧ Angry	✧ Overwhelmed
✧ Excited	✧ Frustrated	✧ Anxious
✧ Calm	✧ Sad	✧ Bored
✧ Confident	✧ Lonely	

My strongest emotion today was: _____

Step 4: What Affected Your Mood?

Think about what influenced how you felt today. Did something specific happen? Maybe a conversation, an event, or even just how well you slept? Choose or write down the biggest factors that impact your mood.

- ✦ **School:** Tests, homework, classes, teachers
- ✦ **Friends:** Conversations, conflicts, fun moments
- ✦ **Family:** Support, tension, time together
- ✦ **Sleep:** Well-rested or tired
- ✦ **Food & Drink:** Healthy eating, too much sugar, caffeine
- ✦ **Social Media:** Positive or negative experiences online
- ✦ **Weather:** Rainy, sunny, cold, warm
- ✦ **Physical Activity:** Exercise, lack of movement
- ✦ **Personal Thoughts:** Overthinking, self-doubt, confidence

The biggest factors affecting my mood today were: _____

_____

_____

Step 5: How Did You React to Your Mood?

Now, think about how you responded to your emotions. Did you cope in a healthy way? If you were stressed, did you do something that helped? If you were happy, did you share it with others? If you reacted in a way you'd like to change, what could you do differently next time?

Today, I responded to my emotions by: _____

_____

_____

Step 6: What's One Thing You Can Do Tomorrow?

No matter what kind of day you have, you can always make small changes to improve your mood for tomorrow. You may want to get more sleep, take deep breaths when stressed, or spend time with someone who makes you feel good.

One thing I will do tomorrow to take care of my mood is: _____

_____

_____

Final Reflection

Tracking your mood every day helps you see patterns over time. Are there days of the week when you feel better or worse? Do certain activities improve your mood? If you do this for a week or more, you might start to notice connections between your emotions and your daily choices. The more you understand your mood, the more control you have over how you respond to it.

Today, I feel: _____

My mood rating for today is: _____ / 10

My strongest emotion today was: _____

The biggest factors affecting my mood today were: _____

_____

_____

Today, I responded to my emotions by: _____

_____

_____

One thing I will do tomorrow to take care of my mood is: _____

_____

Today, I feel: _____

My mood rating for today is: _____ / 10

My strongest emotion today was: _____

The biggest factors affecting my mood today were: _____

_____

_____

Today, I responded to my emotions by: _____

_____

One thing I will do tomorrow to take care of my mood is: _____

_____

————o–◇–o————

Today, I feel: _____

My mood rating for today is: _____ / 10

My strongest emotion today was: _____

The biggest factors affecting my mood today were: _____

_____

_____

Today, I responded to my emotions by: _____

_____

One thing I will do tomorrow to take care of my mood is: _____

_____

Today, I feel: _____

My mood rating for today is: _____ / 10

My strongest emotion today was: _____

The biggest factors affecting my mood today were: _____

_____

_____

Today, I responded to my emotions by: _____

_____

One thing I will do tomorrow to take care of my mood is: _____

_____

———o–◇–o———

Today, I feel: _____

My mood rating for today is: _____ / 10

My strongest emotion today was: _____

The biggest factors affecting my mood today were: _____

_____

_____

Today, I responded to my emotions by: _____

_____

One thing I will do tomorrow to take care of my mood is: _____

_____

Today, I feel: _____

My mood rating for today is: _____ / 10

My strongest emotion today was: _____

The biggest factors affecting my mood today were: _____

_____

_____

Today, I responded to my emotions by: _____

_____

One thing I will do tomorrow to take care of my mood is: _____

_____

STRESS LEVEL LOG

Tracking your stress levels helps you understand what triggers your stress, how it affects you, and what you can do to manage it better. Stress isn't always bad – sometimes it pushes you to get things done – but it can take a toll on your mind and body when it builds up. This log will help you check in with yourself and make small changes to reduce stress before it overwhelms you.

Step 1: Rate Your Stress Level

Think about your overall stress level today. On a scale of **1-10**, where **1** is completely relaxed, and **10** is extremely overwhelmed, choose a number that best represents how stressed you felt.

My stress level today was: _____ / 10

Step 2: Identify Your Stress Triggers

What caused your stress today? Stress can come from many sources, and sometimes you may not even realize what's overwhelming you. Take a moment to think about what might have contributed to your stress.

- ✧ **School:** Homework, tests, deadlines, difficult subjects
- ✧ **Friends:** Arguments, feeling left out, peer pressure
- ✧ **Family:** Expectations, conflicts, responsibilities
- ✧ **Social Media:** Comparison, negativity, overwhelming news
- ✧ **Health:** Lack of sleep, poor diet, feeling sick, not enough exercise
- ✧ **Future Worries:** College, career, and life decisions
- ✧ **Other:** Unexpected events, feeling unmotivated, too much on your plate

The biggest stressors for me today were: _____

_____

_____

Step 3: How Did Your Stress Show Up?

Stress doesn't just stay in your mind; it also affects your body and behavior. Think about how your stress showed up today. Did you notice any of these signs?

Physical Signs:

- ✧ Headache or stomach ache
- ✧ Tired but unable to relax
- ✧ Fast heartbeat or shallow breathing
- ✧ Muscle tension or clenched jaw
- ✧ Restlessness or fidgeting

Emotional Signs:

- ✧ Feeling frustrated or irritable
- ✧ Anxiety or constant worrying
- ✧ Lack of motivation
- ✧ Feeling overwhelmed or helpless
- ✧ Mood swings or wanting to isolate yourself

Today, my stress affected me in these ways: _____

_____

_____

Step 4: How Did You React to Your Stress?

When you felt stressed today, how did you handle it? Did you use a healthy coping strategy, or did you react in a way that made things harder? Think about what you did when stress hit.

- ✧ **Healthy Responses:** Deep breaths, exercise, journal, listen to music, take breaks, talk to someone
- ✧ **Unhelpful Responses:** Shut down, avoid responsibilities, lash out, procrastinate, overeat, doom-scrolling on social media

I responded to my stress today by: _____

_____

_____

Step 5: What Can You Do Differently Next Time?

Stress will always be a part of life, but how you handle it can make a big difference. Next time you feel stressed, think about one thing you can do differently. For example, take a deep breath before reacting, ask for help, or step away from the situation to clear your mind.

Next time I feel stressed, I will try to: _____

_____

_____

Final Reflection

Keeping a stress log helps you see patterns in what stresses you out and how you respond. If you track your stress for a week or more, you might notice certain things that trigger it or ways to manage it better. Stress isn't always avoidable, but with practice, you can learn to handle it in a way that protects your mental and physical health.

My stress level today was: _____ / 10

The biggest stressors for me today were: _____

_____

_____

Today, my stress affected me in these ways: _____

_____

_____

I responded to my stress today by: _____

_____

_____

Next time I feel stressed, I will try to: _____

_____

_____

———o–◇–o———

My stress level today was: _____ / 10

The biggest stressors for me today were: _____

_____

_____

Today, my stress affected me in these ways: _____

_____

_____

I responded to my stress today by: _____

_____

_____

Next time I feel stressed, I will try to: _____

_____

_____

—o—◇—o—

My stress level today was: _____ / 10

The biggest stressors for me today were: _____

_____

_____

Today, my stress affected me in these ways: _____

_____

_____

I responded to my stress today by: _____

_____

_____

Next time I feel stressed, I will try to: _____

_____

_____

———o–◇–o———

My stress level today was: _____ / 10

The biggest stressors for me today were: _____

_____

_____

Today, my stress affected me in these ways: _____

_____

_____

I responded to my stress today by: _____

_____

_____

Next time I feel stressed, I will try to: _____

_____

_____

———o—◇—o———

My stress level today was: _____ / 10

The biggest stressors for me today were: _____

_____

_____

Today, my stress affected me in these ways: _____

_____

_____

I responded to my stress today by: _____

_____

_____

Next time I feel stressed, I will try to: _____

_____

_____

—o—◇—o—

My stress level today was: _____ / 10

The biggest stressors for me today were: _____

_____

_____

Today, my stress affected me in these ways: _____

_____

_____

I responded to my stress today by: _____

_____

_____

Next time I feel stressed, I will try to: _____

_____

_____

————o–◇–o————

It is important to integrate these check-ins into your routine as they will give you a better insight into yourself. As time passes, you will notice many more patterns that you have (and you have broken) just because you decided to use these exercises.

Creating a Balanced Life

When life comes at you hard, you may find yourself facing challenges you never knew you'd be facing before. The responsibilities can easily pile up, leaving you unable to figure out where to begin if you want to start creating a healthier lifestyle. Well, as funny as it sounds, it is all about balance. Of course, not just balance by itself – but one achieved with the right strategies, exercises, techniques, and mindset.

Balance your life, and you will balance your emotions. It is as simple as it sounds. This will increase your productivity, it will improve your overall well-being, and it will help you nurture yourself at one point and focus on doing something at another point.

Of course, I will once again mention the self-care routines as they are an inevitable part of your life. Through them, you give yourself the break you need, you listen to your body, mind, and soul, and answer their calls every time. That will inspire you to create harmony – both within and outside of you.

Adapting to Life Changes

I dedicated the second part to adapting to the changes in life. At times, you may find yourself challenged – where it seems easier to lash out and burst in the moment rather than take a step back and assess the situation. Well, I'm here to tell you that the latter is the right choice – every time. I'm not saying it's easy, but it is imperative if you want to continue moving ahead in life.

Coping with Major Life Events

The only thing you need to do in this instance is to acknowledge that change is happening. Now, most people either lash out at the moment or retreat and just ignore that a major life event is happening. Either way, you know this is a wrong approach. Coping with major life events takes time and effort and here is how you can do that.

First things first, acknowledge what is happening, and write down everything positive you can about it. You may not find it at first, but that is why you take a step back and objectively look at the situation. Quiet your mind and prepare yourself for the change. Be kind to yourself through the process, and if you feel like it, turn to someone for support. Talk it out on time.

As you can look at the last exercise for this chapter (and this book), you can see that it all comes down to coping with change. This change will vary from one period to the next – all you need to do is adapt it to your current situation and make the most out of it.

EXERCISE 50

COPING WITH CHANGE

Change can be exciting, scary, or overwhelming – sometimes all at once. Whether it's switching schools, making new friends, dealing with family changes, or adjusting to unexpected life events, change can shake up your emotions and make you feel uncertain. This exercise will help you understand how you react to change, recognize your emotions, and find ways to cope with change in a healthy way.

Step 1: Identify a Recent Change

Think about a recent change in your life – big or small. It could be something personal, social, academic, or even something within your family. Change doesn't always have to be negative; sometimes, even positive changes can bring stress.

Describe a recent change in your life: _____

_____

_____

Now, reflect on how this change has affected you. Ask yourself:

- ✧ Was this change expected or unexpected?
- ✧ Did I have any control over it?
- ✧ How did I feel when it first happened?
- ✧ How do I feel about it now?

This change made me feel: _____

_____

_____

Step 2: Recognizing Your Reactions to Change

When change happens, you might experience a mix of emotions – excitement, fear, frustration, sadness, or even relief. Your thoughts and behaviors may shift as well. Take a moment to reflect on how you reacted.

Which of these reactions do you relate to?

Emotional Reactions:

✧ Feeling anxious or worried

✧ Feeling excited but nervous

✧ Feeling overwhelmed or stressed

✧ Feeling sad or disappointed

✧ Feeling frustrated or helpless

Behavioral Reactions:

✧ Avoiding the situation or ignoring it

✧ Trying to control everything

✧ Talking to someone about it

✧ Finding ways to adjust to the new situation

✧ Dwelling on the past or wishing things would go back to the way they were

My reaction to this change was: _____

_____

_____

Are there any reactions you'd like to change next time you experience something new?

Step 3: What Helps You Cope With Change?

Not all change is easy, but there are ways to handle it so that it doesn't feel so overwhelming. What strategies have helped you in the past when you've gone through significant changes?

Healthy Coping Strategies:

- ✦ Talking to a trusted friend or family member
- ✦ Writing down your thoughts and feelings
- ✦ Breaking things into smaller steps to feel less overwhelmed
- ✦ Focusing on what you can control instead of what you can't
- ✦ Practicing mindfulness, deep breathing, or relaxation techniques
- ✦ Reminding yourself that change can lead to growth

Unhelpful Coping Strategies:

- ✦ Avoiding the situation or pretending it's not happening
- ✦ Isolating yourself from friends or family
- ✦ Letting negative thoughts take over
- ✦ Ignoring your emotions instead of acknowledging them
- ✦ Lashing out or taking frustrations out on others

One healthy coping strategy I will try moving forward is: _____

_____

_____

Step 4: Finding the Silver Lining

Even difficult changes can lead to personal growth, new opportunities, or important life lessons. Think about the change you wrote about earlier – can you find anything positive that has come from it?

Ask yourself:

- ✦ What have I learned from this experience?
- ✦ Has this change helped me grow in any way?
- ✦ Have I discovered new strengths or skills because of it?
- ✦ Is there anything good that has come from this situation?

One thing I have learned from this change is: _____

_____

_____

Final Reflection: Your Personal Growth Plan

Change will always be a part of life, but you have the power to decide how you respond to it. Take a deep breath and remind yourself that you are strong, adaptable, and capable of handling challenges.

Next time I face a big change, I will: _____

_____

_____

By understanding your reactions, recognizing your feelings, and practicing healthy coping strategies, you can build resilience and confidence for the next time you face whatever comes your way.

Building Future Resilience

Last but not least, before I wrap this chapter up, I am here to remind you that everything is about resilience. This is something that you build over time, not in a week or two. It takes a lot of courage, focus, investing your time in it, and adapting to changes through the process. Resilience means being strong enough to withstand and cope with life's challenges.

This is the first thing you need to do. Constantly remind yourself that you have a set of values and skills you have learned from this book that can help you overcome everything. This is a growth mindset, where you know you can always learn something new from every experience you have. That is how you rebound from any situation. And, of course, stay calm through the process.

The one technique I would like to mention here (in addition to everything else I have mentioned in this book) is establishing what you want to achieve. Recognize your strengths and work on your weaknesses. Manage your time effectively and do your best to excel.

There is a certain importance in lifelong learning. By doing this, you commit to a forever-growing mindset. The advantages that come from that are plenty. You get to see and enjoy yourself growing with each passing day. You get to advance in your career, increase your confidence, and work on yourself every day. And in the middle of everything, you will see that you have created a versatile life that you enjoy so, so much!

What Did You Learn From This Chapter?

Well, as this chapter comes to a close, the end of your journey is near. You have grasped the concept of what it means to focus and work on yourself your entire life, and now you have all the tools you need to make that happen for you. But just before we say our final goodbyes, let's recap what you learned in this chapter:

- ✧ There are some habits you need to make consistent – those are the ones that lift you up in life
- ✧ The power of a balanced life helps you create a happy life
- ✧ Change is inevitable. It's how you react to it that is important
- ✧ Resilience of the future is the right way to go – it will set you up on a path of lifelong learning

I am so happy that you have finally come to this chapter. Turn the page, and let's give ourselves the proper sendoff!

CONCLUSION

Y ou've made it to the end of this workbook. That alone is something to be proud of!

Through the 50 exercises I've created, you learned how to recognize your emotions. You also learned how to challenge negative thoughts and develop healthier coping strategies. With my help, you explored how Cognitive Behavioral Therapy (CBT) can help you change your negative thought patterns. Oh, and also - how Dialectical Behavior Therapy (DBT) can help you regulate your emotions, manage stress, and build stronger relationships. But most importantly, you stumbled upon something even more valuable here. That is a deep understanding of yourself.

And for that, I'll repeat it – I am so much proud of you!

Just think back to when you started this workbook. At the time, your emotions probably felt like too much to handle. All the stress, self-doubt, or anxiety took over in ways that made your life harder than it should have been in the first place. I get that.

But now, you have a whole set of tools to help you handle those moments. You understand how your thoughts influence your feelings and behaviors. Also, you have the skills to challenge and reframe unhelpful thoughts. Together, we practiced CBT techniques. Because of that, you now have the ability to shift your perspective every time things get out of control. Now, you don't believe every negative thought but question it, challenge it, and replace it with something more balanced and realistic.

Also, you learned about the power of DBT strategies, too! You saw firsthand how these skills can help you manage your emotions. They don't control you anymore. From distress tolerance techniques like the TIPP method and ACCEPTS to emotion regulation exercises – you discovered practical ways to calm yourself when emotions try to get the best of you. Along with my help, you practiced mindfulness as well. Now you know how to stay present and not get lost in worries about the past or future.

Let me remind you of another thing you did – you developed interpersonal effectiveness skills. These will allow you to communicate your needs, set boundaries, and build healthier relationships in the future.

But your journey wasn't just about understanding CBT and DBT. It was about learning how to apply these strategies in real life. Through the exercises, you discovered how to Identify and manage stress before it becomes too much to handle. You can now challenge self-criticism and build a more positive inner dialogue. You can happily say that you can also recognize emotional triggers and respond calmly rather than with an outburst. Moreover, you have a set of healthy coping skills (that can actually help avoid all the different kinds of unhealthy behavior).

You even managed to strengthen your relationships. Now, you express yourself clearly and listen with empathy. Last but not least, you learned some emotional regulation strategies that will support your mental well-being.

Now, the question is – what comes next?

The end of this workbook doesn't mean the end of your growth. The skills you learned here are tools you can use throughout your whole life. You can turn to them when you need support, clarity, or emotional balance. The more you practice these strategies, the more natural they'll become to you. I know that some days will still be tough, but now you have a solid foundation to help you handle anything with confidence.

I'd like to address another thing – one of the biggest shifts you made is in your emotional awareness. You learned that emotions aren't something you need to fear or avoid. On the contrary, you need to think of them as signals, messages from your mind and body that help you understand what's going on. Now you know how to recognize and accept your emotions. Now, you have the power to respond in ways that align with your goals and values.

I have also helped you build healthy coping skills. You don't need to rely on quick fixes anymore. I mean, you saw it yourself – they can make you feel worse than before. You know that true self-care isn't just bubble baths and relaxation (even though this can be nice every once in a while). It is all about the right choices. They will support your well-being. By that, I mean how to set boundaries, practice gratitude, and challenge negative self-talk.

Finally (and most importantly), you took control of your emotional health. Suddenly, you don't feel stuck in old patterns anymore. This is all because now you have the knowledge and skills to navigate through life with resilience.

You can build stronger relationships. You know how to communicate effectively and set healthy boundaries. You're sure that no matter what life throws at you, you have strategies to manage it.

So, as you close this workbook, always remind yourself that you did all the work and learned the skills. I know that now, you can do anything! Practice and grow – do it constantly. And remember that every step forward (no matter how small) is a step toward a healthier, more balanced you. This isn't the end of your journey – it's only the beginning.

THANK YOU

Thank you so much for purchasing my book.

The marketplace is filled with dozens and dozens of other similar books, but you took a chance and chose this one. I hope it was well worth it.

So again, THANK YOU for getting this book and for making it all the way to the end.

Before you go, I wanted to ask you for one small favor.

Could you please consider posting a review for my book on the platform? Posting a review is the best and easiest way to support the work of independent authors like me.

Your feedback will help me to keep writing the kind of books that will help you get the results you want. It would mean a lot to me to hear from you.

Leave a Review on Amazon US →

Leave a Review on Amazon UK →

ABOUT THE AUTHOR

Emily Carter is an author who loves helping teens with their biggest turning point in life, adulting. She grew up in New York and is happily married to her high school sweetheart. She also has two of her own children.

In her free time, Emily is an avid volunteer at a local food bank and enjoys hiking, traveling, and reading books on personal development. With over a decade of experience in the education and parenting field she has seen the difference that good parenting and the right tips can make in a teenager's life. She is now an aspiring writer through which she shares her insights and advice on raising happy, healthy, and resilient children, teens, and young adults.

Emily's own struggles with navigating adulthood and overcoming obstacles inspired her to write. She noticed a gap in education regarding teaching essential life skills to teens and young adults. She decided to write comprehensive guides covering everything from money and time management to job searching and communication skills. Emily hopes her book will empower teens and young adults to live their best lives and reach their full potential.

To find more of her books, visit her Amazon Author page at:

https://www.amazon.com/author/emily-carter

REFERENCES

Self-Regulation Workbook for Teens

Ackerman, C. (2017). *21 Mindfulness Exercises & Activities For Adults (+ PDF)*. Positive Psychology. Available at: https://positivepsychology.com/mindfulness-exercises-techniques-activities/#mindfulness-interventions-techniques-worksheets

Ackerman, C. (2017). *Cognitive Distortions: 22 Examples & Worksheets (& PDF)*. Positive Psychology. Available at: https://positivepsychology.com/cognitive-distortions/#common-cognitive-distortions

Apex Recovery. (2023). *Relapse Prevention: Coping Skills And Warning Signs*. Available at: https://apex.rehab/relapse-prevention-coping-skills-warning-signs/

Ayushka. (2023). *The Art Of Non-Judgment: Cultivating Compassion And Empathy*. Medium. Available at: https://medium.com/@ayusingh2506/the-art-of-non-judgment-cultivating-compassion-and-empathy-158f038c6f2a

Behavioral Therapy? Healthline. Available at: https://www.healthline.com/health/abc-model#benefits-and-examples

Better Help. (2024). *Behaviors, Emotions, And Feelings: How They Work Together*. Available at: https://www.betterhelp.com/advice/behavior/behaviors-emotions-and-feelings-how-they-work-together/

Bonfil, A. & Wagage, S. (2020) A Course in CBT Techniques: A Free Online CBT Workbook. Available at: https://cogbtherapy.com/introduction-to-cbt

Calm. (2024). *Reframing Negative Thoughts: How To Challenge Negative Thinking*. Available at: https://www.calm.com/blog/reframing-negative-thoughts

Carroll, D. (2019). *The Relationship Between Thoughts, Feelings, And Behaviors*. Debbie Woodall Carroll. Available at: https://debbiewoodallcarroll.com/the-relationship-between-thoughts-feelings-and-behaviors/

Classroom Mental Health. (2024) Helping Students Connect The Dots: Thoughts, Feelings, & Behaviors. Available at: https://classroommentalhealth.org/in-class/thoughts/

Cleveland Clinic. (2024) *Stress: Coping With Life's Stressors*. Available at: https://my.clevelandclinic.org/health/articles/6392-stress-coping-with-lifes-stressors

Counselling Life Coaching. (2024). *Understanding The Cognitive Triad In Cognitive Behavioral Therapy (CBT)*. Available at: https://counselling-lifecoaching.com/understanding-the-cognitive-triad-in-cognitive-behavioral-therapy-cbt/

Darcy, A. (2023). *Balanced Thinking – What Is It, And How Can You Benefit?* Harley Therapy Mental Health Blog. Available at: https://www.harleytherapy.co.uk/counselling/balanced-thinking-benefits.htm

Davis, T. (2021). *Ultimate Positive Thinking Exercises (+ 3 Great Techniques).* Positive Psychology. Available at: https://positivepsychology.com/positive-thinking-exercises/#techniques

Delaware Psychological Services. (2021). *10 Ways To Practice Positive Self-Talk.* Available at: https://www.delawarepsychologicalservices.com/post/10-ways-to-practice-positive-self-talk

Get Self Help. (2024) *Positive Coping Statements.* Available at: https://www.getselfhelp.co.uk/positive-coping-statements/

Great Expectations. (2024) *Quotes About Problem-Solving.* Available at: https://www.greatexpectations.org/resources/life-principles/problem-solving/quotes-about-problem-solving/

Grouport. (2024) Empowering CBT Techniques Quotes: Words Of Wisdom For Personal Growth And Cognitive Mastery. Grouport Therapy. Available at: https://www.grouporttherapy.com/blog/cbt-quotes

Health Direct. (2022). *Self Talk.* Available at: https://www.healthdirect.gov.au/self-talk

Hope + Wellness. (2024). *How To Make A Coping Skills Toolbox.* Available at: https://www.hope-wellness.com/blog/how-to-make-a-coping-skills-toolbox

IIENSTITU. (2023). *Mastering Problem Solving: Daily Exercises To Elevate Your Skills.* LinkedIn. Available at: https://www.linkedin.com/pulse/mastering-problem-solving-daily-exercises-elevate-your-skills/

Indeed. (2022). *What Is Assertiveness Training? Definition, Benefits, And Steps.* Available at: https://www.indeed.com/career-advice/career-development/what-is-assertiveness-training

Kara. (2019). *How To Develop And Implement Healthy Coping Skills Into Your Daily Routine.* Hartzell Counseling. Available at: https://hartzellcounseling.com/how-to-develop-and-implement-healthy-coping-skills-into-your-daily-routine/

Kitazawa, E. (2022). *Behavioral Patterns In Psychology: Learn To Accept Yourself.* Shortform. Available at: https://www.shortform.com/blog/behavioral-patterns-psychology/

Loving Roots Project. (2019). *Using Positive Affirmations To Create A Good Mindset.* Available at: https://www.lovingrootsproject.com/allblogposts/using-positive-affirmations-to-create-a-good-mindset

Maini, N. (2023). *5 Simple Steps To Effective Problem Solving.* Synergogy. Available at: https://synergogy.com/5-simple-steps-to-effective-problem-solving/

Mind Tools. (2024) *Smart Goals.* Available at: https://www.mindtools.com/a4wo118/smart-goals

Mindful. (2024) *Getting Started With Mindfulness.* Available at: https://www.mindful.org/meditation/mindfulness-getting-started/

Mitchell, K. (2017). *15 Positive Thinking Exercises & Activities To Transform Your Life.* Thoughts Catalog. Available at: https://thoughtcatalog.com/kathy-mitchell/2017/03/15-positive-thinking-exercises-activities-to-transform-your-life/

My Self Help Habit. (2020). *Ten Tips For Maintaining Progress Towards Your Goals*. Available at: https://www.myselfhelphabit.co.uk/2020/01/24/ten-tips-for-maintaining-progress-towards-your-goals/

Newport Academy. (2022). *CBT For Teens: How Cognitive Behavioral Therapy Works*. Newport Academy. Available at: https://www.newportacademy.com/resources/mental-health/cbt-treatment/

Newport Academy. (2022). *The 5 Types Of Coping Skills For Teens, Plus 10 Healthy Coping Strategies*. Available at: https://www.newportacademy.com/resources/empowering-teens/coping-skills-teens/

NHS. (2024) Reframing Unhelpful Thoughts. Available at: https://www.nhs.uk/every-mind-matters/mental-wellbeing-tips/self-help-cbt-techniques/reframing-unhelpful-thoughts/

Nunez, K. (2020). *What Is The ABC Model In Cognitive*

Pelzer, K. (2023*). Looking Ahead – 100 Quotes On Strength And Resilience To Help Get Us Through Tough Times*. Parade. Available at: https://parade.com/1012592/kelseypelzer/quotes-for-tough-times/

Pietrangelo, A. (2020). *Is Impulsive Behavior A Disorder?* Healthline. Available at: https://www.healthline.com/health/mental-health/impulsive-behavior#causes

Positive Mind Works. (2023). *The Importance Of Assertive Communication*. Available at: https://www.positivemindworks.co/the-importance-of-assertive-communication/

Problem Solving (2024) How Do You Implement Your Solution? LinkedIn. Available at: https://www.linkedin.com/advice/0/how-do-you-implement-your-solution-skills-problem-solving

Raypole, C. (2020). *How To Identify And Manage Your Emotional Triggers*. Healthline. Available at: https://www.healthline.com/health/mental-health/emotional-triggers#finding-yours

Raypole, C. (2022). *How To Do A Body Scan Meditation (And Why You Should)*. Healthline. Available at: https://www.healthline.com/health/body-scan-meditation#how-to-do-it

Rice, A. (2021). *How To Challenge Negative Self-Talk*. Psych Central. Available at: https://psychcentral.com/lib/challenging-negative-self-talk

Shawn, B. (2009) *61 Self-Control Quotes That Can Change Your Life*. Happy Publishing. Available at: https://www.happypublishing.com/blog/self-control-quotes/

Sutton, J. (2021). *How To Perform Assertiveness Training: 6 Exercises*. Positive Psychology. Available at: https://positivepsychology.com/assertiveness-training/#assertiveness

Vallejo, M. (2022). *Automatic Negative Thoughts (Ants): How To Identify And Fix Them*. Mental Health Center Kids. Available at: https://mentalhealthcenterkids.com/blogs/articles/automatic-negative-thoughts

Vogel, K. (2022). *The Basic Principles Of Cognitive Behavioral Therapy*. PsychCentral. Available at: https://psychcentral.com/pro/the-basic-principles-of-cognitive-behavior-therapy#basic-principles

WebMD. (2023). *What Is Box Breathing?* Available at: https://www.webmd.com/balance/what-is-box-breathing

Whitworth, E. (2023). *8 Radical Acceptance Exercises To Help You Be Fully Present*. Shortform. Available at: https://www.shortform.com/blog/radical-acceptance-exercises/

DBT WorkBook for Teens

Barila, A. (2020) *How To: Effectively Set Boundaries*. Therapy With AB. Available: https://www.therapywithab.com/blog/2020/10/12/how-to-effectively-set-boundaries

Bariso, J. (2019) *28 Emotional Intelligence Quotes That Can Help Make Emotions Work For You, Instead Of Against You*. Inc. Available: https://www.inc.com/justin-bariso/28-emotional-intelligence-quotes-that-can-help-make-emotions-work-for-you-instead-of-against-you.html

Butler, A. (2024) *How To Access Your Intuitive Knowing, Or "Wise Mind"*. Available: https://www.sagetherapy.com/post/how-to-access-your-intuitive-knowing-or-wise-mind

Center Stone. (2024) *Healthy Vs. Unhealthy Coping Mechanisms*. Available: https://centerstone.org/our-resources/health-wellness/substance-use-disorder-healthy-vs-unhealthy-coping-mechanisms/

Charlie Health. (2023) *Check The Facts DBT*. Available: https://www.charliehealth.com/post/check-the-facts-dbt

Counceling Center. (2024) *DBT Skill Radical Acceptance: For Mental Health Healing*. Available: https://counselingcentergroup.com/dbt-skill-radical-acceptance/

Cuncic, A. (2024) *How To Embrace Radical Acceptance*. Very Well Mind. Available: https://www.verywellmind.com/what-is-radical-acceptance-5120614#toc-how-to-practice-radical-acceptance

Da Costa, J. (2023) *Self-Soothe DBT Skills: Sensory Strategies For Distress Tolerance*. Center For DBT. Available: https://centerforcbt.org/2023/11/06/self-soothe-dbt-skills/

DBT Tools. (2024) *Emotional Regulation Skills*. Available: https://dbt.tools/emotional_regulation/index.php

DBTSelfHelp.com. (2024) *How Skills: One-Mindfully, Non-Judgmentally, Effectively*. Available: https://dbtselfhelp.com/how-skills-one-mindfully-non-judgmentally-effectively/

DBTSelfHelp.com. (2024) *Objectives Effectiveness: Dear Man*. Available: https://dbtselfhelp.com/objectives-effectiveness-dear-man/

DBTSelfHelp.com. (2024) Pros And Cons. Available: https://dbtselfhelp.com/pros-and-cons/

DBTSelfHelp.com. (2024) *Relationship Effectiveness: Give*. Available: https://dbtselfhelp.com/relationship-effectiveness-give/#google_vignette

DBTSelfHelp.com. (2024) *Self-Respect Effectiveness: Fast*. Available: https://dbtselfhelp.com/self-respect-effectiveness-fast/

DBTSelfHelp.com. (2024) *What Skills: Observe, Describe, Participate*. Available: https://dbtselfhelp.com/what-skills-observe-describe-participate/

Dialectical Behavior Therapy. (2024) *DBT Distress Tolerance: Exercises, Videos, And Worksheets*. Available: https://dialecticalbehaviortherapy.com/distress-tolerance/

Grouport Therapy. (2024) *Inspiring Quotes To Live By: Embracing DBT Skills For Personal Growth And Transformation*. Available: https://www.grouporttherapy.com/blog/dialectical-behavior-therapy-quotes

Iraheta, N. (2023) *Four DBT Problem-Solving Techniques*. Health And Healing Therapy. Available: https://www.healthandhealingtherapy.com/dbt-problem-solving-techniques/

Klynn, B. (2021) *Emotional Regulation: Skills, Exercises, And Strategies*. Better Up. Available: https://www.betterup.com/blog/emotional-regulation-skills

Lagace, M. (2024) *91 Mind Quotes To Make You Wiser*. Wisdom Quotes. Available: https://wisdomquotes.com/mind-quotes/

Mindful. (2020) *What Is Mindfulness?* Available: https://www.mindful.org/what-is-mindfulness/

Modern Recovery Services. (2023) *Boundary Setting: Definition, Benefits, And Techniques*. Available: https://modernrecoveryservices.com/wellness/coping/skills/social/boundary-setting/

My Cleveland Clinic. (2022) *Dialectical Behavior Therapy (DBT)*. Available: https://my.clevelandclinic.org/health/treatments/22838-dialectical-behavior-therapy-dbt

Psychiatric Associates. (2024) *How Interpersonal Effectiveness Improves Your Relationships*. Available: https://psychassociates.net/how-interpersonal-effectiveness-improves-your-relationships/

Resource Group. (2024) *The Wise Mind Technique In DBT*. Available: https://resourcegrp.org/blog/what-is-the-wise-mind-technique-in-dbt/

Sunrise. (2017) *DBT Interpersonal Effectiveness Skills: The Guide To Healthy Relationships*. Available: https://sunrisertc.com/interpersonal-effectiveness/

Sunrise. (2017). *DBT Distress Tolerance Skills: Your 6-Skill Guide To Navigate Emotional Crises*. Available: https://sunrisertc.com/distress-tolerance-skills/

Zencare. (2024) *Distract, Relax, And Cope: Distress Tolerance Skills*. Available: https://blog.zencare.co/distract-relax-and-cope-distress-tolerance-skills/

Coping Skills WorkBook for Teens

Asicrecovery. (2024, March 18). DBT Principles — The Complete Guide - ASIC Recovery. ASIC Recovery. Available at: https://www.asicrecoveryservices.com/post/dbt-principles-the-complete-guide/

Bariso, J. (30 September 2019). 28 Emotional Intelligence Quotes That Can Help Make Emotions Work for You, Instead of Against You. Inc. Available at: https://www.inc.com/justin-bariso/28-emotional-intelligence-quotes-that-can-help-make-emotions-work-for-you-instead-of-against-you.html

Better Health. Every Mind Matters. (2025). nhs.uk. Available at: https://www.nhs.uk/every-mind-matters/mental-wellbeing-tips/self-help-cbt-techniques/thought-record/

Beyond The Shop Door. (10 September 2020). 35 Powerful Quotes on the Importance of Emotional Intelligence!. Beyond The Shop Door. Available at: https://beyondtheshopdoor.com/2020/09/10/35-powerful-quotes-on-the-importance-of-emotional-intelligence/

Bogers, N. (13 February 2024). The Science Behind Your Emotions. Noldus. Available at: https://www.noldus.com/blog/science-of-emotions

Brooten-Brooks, M. (16 July 2024). How to Set Healthy Boundaries With Anyone. Very Well Health. Available at: https://www.verywellhealth.com/setting-boundaries-5208802

Buckner, L. (29 January 2025). What Is Effective Communication? (With Benefits and Tips). Indeed. Available at: https://www.indeed.com/career-advice/career-development/effective-communication

California Prime Recovery. (2025). 10 Motivational Quotes for Well-Being and Resilience. California Prime Recovery. Available at: https://californiaprimerecovery.com/10-motivational-quotes-well-being-and-resilience/

Centerstone. (2025). 6 Tips to Adjusting to Change: How to Adapt and Overcome. Centerstone. Available at: https://centerstone.org/adjusting-to-change-adapt-and-overcome/

Cherry, K. (30 January 2025). 9 Types of Nonverbal Communication. Very Well Mind. Available at: https://www.verywellmind.com/types-of-nonverbal-communication-2795397

Connections Child and Family Center. (02 October 2023). TIPP Skill: Turning the Temperature Down on Emotional Intensity. Connections Family Center. Available at: https://connectionsfamilycenter.com/tipp-skill-turning-the-temperature-down-on-emotional-intensity/

Edis, N. (2023, February 2). 30 best quotes about Emotional Intelligence. ThinkPsych. Available at: https://thinkpsych.com/blogs/posts/30-best-quotes-about-emotional-intelligence?srsltid=AfmBOorCRS2SXNZGI7yU9ru43j-OhutWOdsljAw4P-CrjBzU49NeNw-c

Golden, B., PhD. (2023, October 9). Emotional awareness is essential for our emotional and social well-being. Psychology Today. Available at: https://www.psychologytoday.com/intl/blog/overcoming-destructive-anger/202310/10-ways-to-increase-your-emotional-awareness

Grinspoon, P. (04 May 2022). How To Recognize And Tame Your Cognitive Distortions. Harvard Health Publishing. Available at: https://www.health.harvard.edu/blog/how-to-recognize-and-tame-your-cognitive-distortions-202205042738

Grouport. (2025). Empowering CBT Techniques Quotes: Words of Wisdom for Personal Growth and Cognitive Mastery | Grouport Journal. Grouport. Available at: https://www.grouporttherapy.com/blog/cbt-quotes

Grouport. (2025). *Empowering DBT Skills Quotes: Words of Wisdom for Personal Growth and Emotional Resilience | Grouport Journal.* Grouport. Available at: https://www.grouporttherapy.com/blog/dbt-quotes

Hofmann, S. G., Asnaani, A., Vonk, I. J. J., Sawyer, A. T., & Fang, A. (2012). The Efficacy of Cognitive Behavioral Therapy: A Review of Meta-analyses. *Cognitive Therapy and Research*, 36(5), 427–440. https://doi.org/10.1007/s10608-012-9476-1

Karla McLaren. (2024, May 17). Your emotional vocabulary list | Karla McLaren | Karla McLaren. Available at: https://karlamclaren.com/emotional-vocabulary-page/

Klynn, B. (28 November 2024). Emotional Regulation: Skills, Exercises, And Strategies. Better Up. Available at: https://www.betterup.com/blog/emotional-regulation-skills

Martin, S. (30 January 2017). 16 Quotes To Inspire Healthy Relationships. Psych Central. Available at: https://psychcentral.com/blog/imperfect/2017/01/16-quotes-to-inspire-healthy-relationships#Quotes-to-Inspire-Healthy-Relationships

Mayo Clinic. (24 January 2024). Relaxation Techniques: Try These Steps To Lower Stress. Mayo Clinic. Available at: https://www.mayoclinic.org/healthy-lifestyle/stress-management/in-depth/relaxation-technique/art-20045368

Meinke, H. (30 December 2019). Understanding the Stages of Emotional Development in Children. Rasmussen University. Available at: https://www.rasmussen.edu/degrees/education/blog/stages-of-emotional-development/

Miller, C. (06 October 2021). Primary And Secondary Emotions. Optimum Joy. Available at: https://optimumjoy.com/blog/primary-and-secondary-emotions-clair-miller/

Moore, M. (2022, September 21). What's the Difference Between CBT & DBT? Psych Central. Available at: https://psychcentral.com/lib/whats-the-difference-between-cbt-and-dbt

Morgan, S. (07 August 2023). The Power of Empathy in Conflict Resolution. LinkedIn. Available at: https://www.linkedin.com/pulse/power-empathy-conflict-resolution-sarah-morgan/

Morin, A. (03 novemvber 2023). Healthy Coping Skills for Uncomfortable Emotions. Very Well Mind. Available at: https://www.verywellmind.com/forty-healthy-coping-skills-4586742

Nash, J. (05 January 2018). How to Set Healthy Boundaries & Build Positive Relationships. Positive Psychology. Available at: https://positivepsychology.com/great-self-care-setting-healthy-boundaries/

NHS. (2022, November 10). Overview - Cognitive behavioural therapy (CBT). nhs.uk. Available at: https://www.nhs.uk/mental-health/talking-therapies-medicine-treatments/talking-therapies-and-counselling/cognitive-behavioural-therapy-cbt/overview/

Northup, G. (02 August 2023). 10 Communication Skills For Your Life And Career Success. Indeed. Available at: https://www.indeed.com/career-advice/resumes-cover-letters/communication-skills

Pal, P., Hauck, C., Goldstein, E., Bobinet, K., Bradley, C. (14 October 2024). 5 Simple Mindfulness Practices for Daily Life. Mindful. Available at: https://www.mindful.org/take-a-mindful-moment-5-simple-practices-for-daily-life/

Pietrangelo, A. (12 December 2019). 9 CBT Techniques for Better Mental Health. Healthline. Available at: https://www.healthline.com/health/cbt-techniques

Quino, M. (22 February 2024). Creating Harmony: 9 Tips for a Balanced Lifestyle. D&V Philippines. Available at: https://www.dvphilippines.com/blog/tips-for-a-balanced-lifestyle

Raypole, C. (13 November 2020). How to Identify and Manage Your Emotional Triggers. Healthline. Available at: https://www.healthline.com/health/mental-health/emotional-triggers

Schimelpfening, N. (2023, November 2). Dialectical Behavior Therapy (DBT): definition, techniques, and benefits. Verywell Mind. Available at: https://www.verywellmind.com/dialectical-behavior-therapy-1067402

Scott, E. (06 March 2024). 5 Types of Self-Care for Every Area of Your Life. Very Well Mind. Available at: https://www.verywellmind.com/self-care-strategies-overall-stress-reduction-3144729

Scott, E. (26 September 2023). How to Use Assertive Communication. Very Well Mind. Available at: https://www.verywellmind.com/learn-assertive-communication-in-five-simple-steps-3144969#toc-assertive-vs-aggressive-vs-passive-communication

Tura, N., MA. (2024, December 5). How to Develop Insight Into Your Own Life (with Pictures). wikiHow. Available at: https://www.wikihow.com/Develop-Insight-Into-Your-Own-Life

University of Rochester Medical Center. (2025). URMC. Encyclopedia. Undersranding the Teen Brain. Available at: https://www.urmc.rochester.edu/encyclopedia/content?ContentID=3051&ContentTypeID=1

Vijayapriya, C., & Tamarana, R. (2023). Effectiveness of dialectical behavior therapy as a transdiagnostic treatment for improving cognitive functions: a systematic review. *Research in Psychotherapy: Psychopathology, Process and Outcome*, 26(2). https://doi.org/10.4081/ripppo.2023.662

Made in the USA
Monee, IL
20 May 2025

17799038R10280